Profiles in Success

Compliments of

BERNHARDT
WEALTH MANAGEMENT

7601 Lewinsville Road, Suite 210
McLean, VA 22102
(703) 356-4380
www.BernhardtWealth.com

Profiles in Success

Inspiration from Executive Leaders

Volume 13

GORDON J. BERNHARDT, CFP®, AIF®

Copyright © 2018 Gordon J. Bernhardt, CFP®, AIF®

ISBN: 979-8-9861435-2-1

All rights reserved. No part of this publication may be reproduced, distributed, or transmitted in any form or by any means without the prior written permission of the copyright holder, except in the case of brief quotations embodied in critical reviews and certain noncommercial uses permitted by copyright law. For permission requests or information on bulk purchases, contact the copyright holder.

First edition

Gordon Bernhardt conducts interviews of business leaders primarily in the Washington D.C. area who come recommended by their peers. The profiles included in this volume are a result of these interviews. As a result of these additional insights Mr. Bernhardt has published these profiles. Gordon Bernhardt is the President and CEO of Bernhardt Wealth Management, a registered investment adviser with the Securities and Exchange Commission. Registration is mandatory for all persons meeting the definition of investment adviser and does not imply a certain level of skill or training. The business leaders may or may not be clients of Bernhardt Wealth Management. These interviews are independent of investment advisory services and do not imply any endorsement of Gordon Bernhardt or Bernhardt Wealth Management by the business leaders.

This book exists because of all the inspirational individuals who so graciously shared their stories with me. I am thankful for the opportunity to get to know each and every one of you. I feel like a better person thanks to what I learned from you and your story.

To my team at Bernhardt Wealth Management—Tim Koehl, Solon Vlasto, Bonnie Armstrong, Chay Willette, Cameron Farbotko, Reed Hurt, Olivia Lee and Zachary Larmour. I would never have been able to do this without your efforts and support throughout the process. Thank you for all you do for each other and for our clients.

I am deeply grateful to Clyde Northrop, Master Chair at Vistage International, and to Peter Schwartz, Master Chair of Vistage Worldwide, for your help and encouragement on this project. Thank you.

And lastly, this book would not have been possible without the guidance and creative support of Karen Embry.

Table of Contents

Foreword ix
Introduction xiii

PROFILES
Imran Aftab 3
Shueyb Ali 13
Anwar Allen 21
Chris Assenmacher 29
Beth Perl Berman 37
Kevin Beverly 45
Richard Bodson 57
Dr. Daniel Carlin, MD 67
Piper Phillips Caswell 77
Brian Chavis 87
Fred Diamond 97
Bruce Ehlert 107
Bobby Feisee 115
Erika Flora 125
Tom Frana 135
Francisco Gali 145
Amy Jaller Gleklen 155
Scott Goss 165
Noe Landini 175
Jack Maier II 185
Michael May 195
Gregory K. McDonough 209
Michael N. Mercurio 219
Clyde Northrop 229
Dawn Peters 239
Kathleen M. Poorbaugh 249
Sherri Renée Romm 259
Lee Self 269
Mark J. Silverman 279
James L. Speros 291
Gerry Stephens 307
Kimberly H. Stewart 317
Dawn Sweeney 325
Randy Taussig 335
Paul Thieberger 345
Jenni Utz 355
Charles Vollmer 365
Mark Watson 377
Jeffrey Weinstock 387
Mary G.R. Whitley 397

About the Author 409
From Gifford to Hickman 411

Foreword

In 2016, it was reported that there were 29.5 million businesses in the United States, encompassing all sizes. In 2013, Bloomberg ran an article reporting that eight out of 10 of these businesses fail within 18 months or less. That article listed these top four reasons for failure:

1. Not really in touch with customers through deep dialogue
2. No real differentiation in the market
3. Failure to communicate value propositions in clear, concise, and compelling fashion
4. Leadership breakdown at the top

A couple of years ago, I had the good fortune to finally meet Gordon Bernhardt after reading Profiles in Success and hearing his name mentioned by various business associates and clients. I was pleased when Gordon invited me to be interviewed for his fine work, and even more honored to write this foreword for Volume 13.

Reading the profiles of some of the most inspiring and successful business leaders in the District, Maryland, and Virginia area, I am struck by how the folks Gordon profiles are the solution to the problems listed above. Gordon is an excellent example, too.

To be interviewed by Gordon is an experience of having a deep dialogue, over an extended period of time, to tell your story. Profiles in Success has deservedly become THE publication in the market to focus on the person behind the company. The value could not be more clear, concise, and compelling, while Gordon, himself, also personifies caring, values-based leadership.

After nearly 45 years in business—the last twenty of those working with Vistage, an international group that sets up private advisory peer groups for CEO's, executives, and business owners—I realize that the other most important similarity among the folks in this community of success is the drive, the grit, the sheer will to succeed, as well as the confidence to believe in themselves. When I first meet a CEO/business owner, they have almost always cleared that 18-month elimination period, and are interested in truly growing both personally and professionally. Since I believe a company can only grow as fast as the leader is willing to grow, I am always looking for growth oriented people to invite into my Vistage peer groups. In reading the profiles featured in Gordon's books, I find that growth orientation—not just for the business, but for the individual leader as a person. This, after all, is the real inspiration that makes reading about these individuals so compelling.

Thank you, Gordon, for your positive modeling of a driven, deeply connected, personal-growth oriented leader. Now let's read about some other dynamic leaders and be inspired!

– Clyde Northrop
Master Chair
Vistage International
www.vistage.com

*Clyde Northrop is a seasoned business executive with nearly 45 years of leadership experience. Clyde is also a well-known and highly respected Executive Coach, developing, mentoring, and guiding CEOs and other C-level executives to be more successful. At Vistage, the world's largest executive coaching organization, Clyde provides leadership training and guidance to help professionals open doors to new successes and new heights. At Vistage for twenty years, Clyde has worked with approximately 1,200 business leaders in over 10,000 hours of one-on-one coaching.*

BERNHARDT
WEALTH MANAGEMENT

Introduction

*"Every generation laughs at the old fashions,
but follows religiously the new."*
— HENRY DAVID THOREAU, WALDEN

The younger generations always seem to lack the qualities or hardships of their elders. Haven't you heard a version of someone older than you who walked 10 miles to and from school–uphill both ways? Undoubtedly, you've read articles admonishing millennials for the threat their values present to society. Believed to be raised with an inflated sense of personal uniqueness, "snowflakes" are said to lack resilience and are too easily offended. But aren't they also known as the most tech savvy generation that highly values diversity and meaningful work that could make the world a better place for everyone?

In truth, each generation has shaped society and the dynamics of business with their generally shared characteristics. So how do executives balance the unique talents and expectations of each generation within one work environment? A little insight into the different perspectives, motivations and work styles among generations can help us better understand and leverage the strengths of an entire team and avoid forcing guidelines that limit possibilities.

Mostly gone now, the Greatest Generation acquired their nickname for winning World War II. They were known for their sense of responsibility and patriotism, a strong work ethic and humble dignity. The Silent Generation followed but were less-often discussed; quietly sandwiched between the Greatest and the Boomers. Now in their 70s or older, some are still working in the C-suite or serving on Boards. They embraced the strong work ethic of their parents and the belief the getting ahead required long, hard hours at the office. I've interviewed leaders from this generation for Profiles and am fortunate to have many more as clients, from whom I've personally learned valuable lessons.

No one can deny the significant influence of the large Baby Boom generation. Coming of age in the 60s and 70s, boomers were more likely to question establishment, demand equal rights and seek personal gratification sooner than later. Ideologies often stood in stark contrast to those of their parents. However, they also believed anything was possible, were team-oriented and sought to make a difference. And despite rebellion, most retained or repurposed the lessons of previous generations, including a hard work-ethic.

Kevin Beverly learned the life-long importance of hard work on his first day of work when only 10 years old. After his father left home, Kevin's older brother took him under his wing and taught him to be the first one there (school or a job) and work the hardest. "And if someone gives you something to do, you do it on their time, not yours. If someone's asking you to get something done, you do it as quickly and efficiently as possible."

During the Vietnam War Tom Frana followed in his father's patriotic steps and decided to serve. Rather than waiting to be drafted he wanted to make his own decision about where in the military he'd go. So in choosing to join the Marine Corps, the experience laid the foundation for his own brand of leadership. "I learned, first of all, how important it is to look out for the welfare of your people at all times," Tom explains.

The team-oriented Jim Speros followed his passion for football; seeking a work-life different than that of his parents while retaining the tenets of grit and hard-work he learned from them. He underscores the

INTRODUCTION

truth that people make people. "My success has always come from associating myself with good people," he says. "I've tried to emulate and learn from them, and I've tried to support them by building strong teams."

A much smaller group, Generation X entered the workplace with a different work ethic and culture than previously seen. Having witnessed the burnout or layoffs of their hardworking parents, this generation has placed a premium on family time. While still ambitious and hardworking, they also strongly value work/life balance. With an entrepreneurial spirit and distain for rigid work requirements, Gen Xers introduced businesses to the world of flex schedules, virtual home-offices and payment for work completed rather than for hours worked. They also thrive on diversity, challenge, responsibility and creative input.

The millennials have delivered a string of 20-something philanthropic millionaires/billionaires and work spaces that look more like playgrounds than the offices of highly successful enterprises. Their love of minimalism and Tiny Homes spurs hope for a lasting desire to live within their means. With so much attention on Generation Y, did you happen to notice that the youngest members of the service-oriented Gen Z, aka Net-Gen, will soon be heading to college?

No matter what our peer-like characteristics or influences from other generations, successful leaders ultimately recognize that the determination to keep learning, keep trying and keep achieving must come from within themselves. Dawn Sweeny and Scott Goss both describe a time when this happened to each of them. "It was a defining moment because it was so clear to me what I needed to do, because it made me so happy to do it. It wasn't about recognition or presentation. I just wanted to help," said Dawn. Scott explained, "I can't say what spurred that moment of waking up, but I know that it didn't come from my parents, or the doctors, or any of the external voices trying to get through to me. It was a decision I, and only I, could make for myself."

Thinking back on a recent Profiles in Success awards event, I credit the unique attributes of each person for helping to make it a fun and successful time. They are some of the same attributes we use in our wealth management efforts for our clients. Together we have generated a list of fundamental behaviors that describe how we put our focus on Character, Chemistry, Caring and Competence into action each day. It is called The Bernhardt Way.

Do you find the distinctive characteristics of other age groups compliment your business experience or challenge it? I hope you discover something in these pages that continue to move you and your team towards greater achievements.

– **Gordon J. Bernhardt, CPA, PFS, CFP®, AIF®**
Founder, President and CEO
Bernhardt Wealth Management, Inc.
www.BernhardtWealth.com

Since establishing his firm in 1994, Gordon Bernhardt has been focused on providing high-quality service and independent financial advice in order to help his clients make smart decisions about their money. He specializes in addressing the unique needs of successful professionals, entrepreneurs and retirees, as well as women in transition throughout the Washington, DC area. Over the years, Gordon has been sought out by numerous media outlets including MSN Money, CNN Money, Kiplinger and The New York Times for his insight into subjects related to personal finance.

Profiles

BERNHARDT
WEALTH MANAGEMENT

Imran Aftab

Creating Opportunities

At the age of sixteen, Imran Aftab was preparing himself to drop out of a well-regarded Jesuit school in Karachi. Although he worked as a tutor to supplement his family's income, his father had struggled to find work for seven long years. The political situation in Pakistan was unstable, jobs were scarce, and it looked as though Imran's school fees were becoming too hefty to manage.

Imran and his father went to meet with the Bishop to explain their situation. There, Bishop Lobo presented them with a blank white sheet of paper, and asked Mr. Aftab to write down whatever amount he could afford. "My dad had tears in his eyes," recalls Imran. "The Bishop said he could go home and instead wanted to deal with me directly. He agreed to let me study for free—an incredibly life-defining moment, considering it was one of the best schools in Pakistan. It was a kindness that came with no strings attached, but made all the difference. I could have been in the streets. Instead, I was able to take my SATs and get a scholarship, all thanks to that little act of kindness."

Today, Imran's commitment to achievement is driven by his desire to create opportunity for others to succeed, both here in the United States and back in his native Pakistan. He brings his scientific, engineering, business, and finance expertise to bear as the CEO of 10Pearls, a software development firm he founded in 2004. The business employs over 300 people in four offices—about 80 percent in Karachi, with the rest in Toronto, Dubai, and Herndon, Virginia.

With the help of his brother in Pakistan, Imran launched 10Pearls with a mere $2,000 while still working full-time at AOL. In his capacity as Head of Global Sourcing there, he had spent years travelling to India, the Philippines, South Africa, and Brazil, witnessing first-hand the effect of well-paying work on poor communities. "When people have an opportunity to earn money, all they want to do is spend it on their kids," Imran says. "People in America don't understand that, especially in the rest of the world, society is much more interconnected. There are joined family systems, and one dollar—or a single created opportunity—can go a long way."

Imran often observed that such job creation would be beneficial in Pakistan, and that the country was ripe for the blended-shore business model. After all, Pakistan is the third largest English speaking country in the world, with a strong technology education system and favorable IP laws. On top of all that, competition for the best talent is scarce. "India is super saturated," explains Imran. "Unless you have a substantial amount of money you want to spend, good luck hiring Tier 1 people. Why would I work for 10Pearls when I can go work for Google India? Bangalore has more start-ups than Washington, DC!"

Still, the job at AOL was comfortable, and these thoughts were initially theoretical. The idea of starting his own software business that sourced talent in Pakistan didn't really begin to take shape until a chance encounter forced Imran to articulate his purpose aloud. While flying with other AOL executives, a colleague asked a question about his background. "One of the executives said to me, 'Imran, are you from Pakistan? You seem normal. What's wrong with the others?' Oh boy! That started a 90-minute conversation which really refined and clarified for me the purpose of my existence," he recounts. Having achieved a great deal of success, Imran found that he felt called to give back. Just as the Bishop at the Jesuit school had given him a leg up, Imran set about creating opportunity for those still in Karachi.

Armed with inspiration, he didn't overthink his plan. He'd been inspired by a short video, called "Business Backwards," detailing a new strategy in which you work first and then make detailed plans later. So Imran sent his brother, Zeeshan Aftab, $2,000 in Karachi and asked him to join the venture and help execute on the vision. Their first employee served as a developer, designer, and QA while they got off the ground. Working in a small empty bedroom by the kitchen, this first employee always got hungry when Mrs. Aftab, Imran's mother, started cooking. Imran and his brother made a decision: free lunch would be provided for every 10Pearls employee in Pakistan. Twelve years later, they've never missed a meal.

Today, the 300 employees at 10Pearls work with clients large and small to help businesses compete in the digital age. From developing mobile applications, to redefining and automating business processes, to focusing on service and human-centered design, to assisting with secure cloud technology, the company is brought in on all things digital, and boasts end-to-end capabilities. Imran's blended team leverages the high availability of excellent, yet affordable technical talent in Pakistan, in conjunction with world-class expert contributors stateside who work shoulder-to-shoulder with clients. And because the work they do has a larger purpose, it's never work for the sake of work. "You need to understand how to use technology for the sake of business, instead of vice versa," he explains. "You don't want to pursue capabilities just because someone else is, and a 'me too' play does not get you anywhere. We're excited because we're thinkers—we love problem solving, and there's a level of satisfaction you get when you come up with the right solution for someone. That's the intrinsic motivation."

True to that ethos, 10Pearls is working with one major client, AARP, to develop digital products for caregivers. Because Western nations are dealing with an aging population, caregiving responsibilities, especially among young people, are becoming increasingly common. A full quarter of caregivers are millennials, and that market is crying out for modernization. "These people demand mobile technology and digital tools," says Imran. "Why should they be on hold with a healthcare provider, when they could just be texting them at their leisure? Why could they not go to an online marketplace to find out the best nutrition provider, or a replacement caregiver when they're on vacation? How can they schedule a ride for mom and make sure she got there safely? How can they emotionally connect with another caregiver? In the past, all these interesting sorts of interactions have been done in person, on the phone, and in emails. Now, thanks to the digital revolution, there's all this great advancement. We're living in a world that's going to be virtual as well as physical, and we're going to see some amazing new opportunities as a result." Thanks to this vision and work ethic, AARP named 10Pearls their Supplier of the Year for 2016, a competitive award that honors companies that use technology to change lives for the better.

Imran's expansive ambitions are not despite his humble beginnings, but rather because of them. His childhood in Karachi was a kind of "rags to riches to rags" story, but even the "riches" were relatively modest. Before he entered Grade 2, Imran's father, an accountant by education, landed a good job working for the airlines in Singapore. For two years, the family's financial woes receded. Savings accumulated, and Imran enjoyed life in Singapore. "Grade 2 to Grade 4 were some of the best times of my life," Imran recalls. "But overnight, everything just flipped, and political strife destabilized the region." Imran, his parents, and his five siblings returned to Karachi, where they survived on the family's savings for a time. But money became tighter and tighter. Imran took on his tutoring work, while Mrs. Aftab made every dollar stretch. "We had a period where we would say, we won't eat meat these days. And mom would make paddies from these kidney beans that taste like meat. She was an amazing cook," Imran remembers. "We were managing, and we took out loans to get by. Everyone in the family knew they needed to contribute in some way."

Although Imran's father felt that the kids could quit school and go to work full time, his mother was insistent that they have the opportunity to get an education. "My mom said we would starve before they took us kids out of school," says Imran. "She never had access to the education and opportunity that could have changed her life dramatically, and she wanted a better life for us. She had an amazing spirit about her, and her commitment to education created the opportunity we needed to lay the foundation for success later on."

When he wasn't working, Imran played cricket and football, read fantasy novels, and devoted himself to his studies. He hoped to excel in school and ultimately land a scholarship to study in the U.S. The Jesuit school was filled with competitive kids from wealthy families, and most of them aspired to do just that. But while many of the kids could count on financial support from their parents, Imran knew he would have to land a scholarship if he wanted to go at all. At age 17, he filled out the applications, submitted glowing letters of recommendation, and received some acceptances, but not enough scholarship money. He would still be expected to contribute $7,000 to his tuition, and he didn't have a penny.

It was a crucial fork in the road for Imran. He considered attending the local university, and even passed the exam to attend one of the top computer science colleges. But instead, he made a gamble and decided to take a job teaching high school chemistry, offered by the very same Bishop who had changed his life several years earlier. For a year, Imran was an 18-year-old high school chemistry teacher by day, and a tutor by night. He saved every penny, and the following year, he re-applied to school and received an acceptance letter and full scholarship to Bard College in upstate New York. He had applied for and been accepted into their Distinguished Scientist program, awarded to only ten students each year. Imran had to cover $4,000 in expenses, but with the money he'd saved—plus $1,000 from his father, and a campus job—he was able to start his life in the U.S. as a student at a small, liberal arts school.

Imran immediately made his mark at Bard. "I was a superstar there," he remembers. "They called me a wizard. I was able to take math and physics classes as well. More importantly, I was able to take several courses in humanities that helped tremendously. Bard was in the middle of nowhere, so there really wasn't anything to do but study." The rarified college campus was a perfect learning environment, but upon graduation, he found that there were no jobs. Imran decided to apply for a Chemistry PhD program instead. He was accepted into three prominent programs, and ultimately went with UNC Chapel Hill. "Purdue is top notch, but they made the mistake of flying me out in the middle of winter," Imran laughs. "Chapel Hill was smart enough to fly me out in the middle of March Madness!"

But after some time in North Carolina, Imran began to have doubts about pursuing a career in chemistry. The lab work had become boring, and he didn't feel like his work was directly applicable to the real world. Most of all, Imran wanted to ensure that, when he came out of school, he'd be able to do more to help his family back home in Karachi. So he began looking at courses at UNC's Kenan-Flagler Business School, and decided to try his hand at corporate finance. Right away, something clicked. After years of study in math and the hard sciences, finance courses were a breeze. Despite having completed two years of coursework and a Master's degree, Imran decided to leave his PhD program with what's known as an "ABD"—all but dissertation. In

1996, Imran gambled on himself again and got a job stuffing envelopes on Wall Street, biding his time for a big break.

In 1997, Imran landed an interview with Chase Manhattan Bank for a job with the chemicals industry group doing syndicated finance. The interview went well, in part because Imran had much in common with the interviewer. "The guy interviewing me had a PhD in Chemistry. What's the likelihood of that?" exclaims Imran. "It seemed as if it was all scripted, right? He saw himself in me, and he could see the next steps I was trying to take in relating sciences and finances." With that, he landed the job and worked for Chase until 1999.

Imran's Muslim faith has played an important role in the development of his career, and that was not the first or last life-changing event in which he sees a divine providence. His next move was motivated by a desire to be closer to family in Virginia, and although he was reluctant to leave banking at the time, in retrospect he feels fortunate that he did. He took a job with MicroStrategy, where he began his career in technology. The company was hiring young people, training them in a kind of tech boot camp, and using them as consultants. For five years, Imran developed his familiarity with the tech world and continued to expand his skill set.

Then, in 2003, AOL came knocking. It was shortly after their acquisition by Time Warner, and they were looking for data experts to work with them on an operational overhaul. Imran had spent some time in the business world by that point, but AOL exposed him to a whole new level of leadership and infrastructure. "AOL gave me exposure to deal making," Imran says. "Because it was such a big company, it gave me the opportunity to explore a wide range of functions. I learned how to manage relationships and the political aspects of things. I was able to manage people and manage budgets. I was also brought into the outsourcing group, where they had a risk-reward model. I learned about outsourcing and how to incentivize lenders better. I travelled internationally to all these place, and I made amazing connections along the way."

AOL solidified and expanded the skill set Imran needed to make the jump to executive of his own firm. Armed with his experiences in the sciences, in the financial world, in a business environment, and in the tech sector, Imran's solo venture was poised from the outset to achieve the success and potential it is well on its way to fully realizing. But Imran is quick to share the credit with those around him, including his brother, Zeeshan Aftab, who has been an instrumental right-hand man and partner. Imran also carries with him his father's humility and his mother's willpower. And his wife, Salma Naseer, is both a rock that grounds him and a compass that guides him.

Imran felt a kindship with Salma right away. Like him, she started out in America with practically nothing, and like him, she is self-made. Her father brought the family from India when she was 17, but he died of a stroke before he could finish his exams at Veterinary school. The couple married in 2000. In 2004, a few days before the birth of their first son, Salma's sister and brother-in-law died in an accident. Facing so much tragedy was difficult, but Salma channeled her emotional pain into her spiritual life, and constantly reminds Imran to value what is truly important. "She has a very different outlook on life," Imran states admiringly. "Material things don't affect her at all. She's always focused on the spiritual side of life, which is very important to me because it's easy to get lost in this material world. She insures that we focus on the bigger purpose of helping people for the sake of helping and creating opportunity; not because we want to get our names out there."

To that end, the Aftabs have launched a 10Pearls charity initiative, the Empower Foundation. The foundation focuses on the needs of children and women, both in Virginia and in Karachi. Among Imran's goals is the expansion of the foundation, along with growing the business.

Imran's goal of creating opportunity for those in need is one he hopes new generations of entrepreneurs will take on as well. In advising young people entering the working world today, he encourages young people to focus on the change they want to be in their lives and their societies. "Before you pick a career, figure out what problem you want to solve," he says. "Rather than constantly working to make more money for yourself, work backwards and figure out what you need. Then figure out how you can use your skills to expand opportunity for those around you. It's a different mindset, and one that allows you to chart the course of your life with care and intention. Otherwise you're constantly chasing that next promotion or maintaining the status quo. Sixty years later, you retire, and what was it all for? When you orient yourself around making a difference, there's always more to do."

With an eye to the future, Imran is confident in the direction 10Pearls is headed, thanks in large part to his lifelong commitment to positive global change. "I don't know if you'd call it fearless, but I'm not afraid," he says. "I'm not afraid of losing at all. My wife and I always remember that we came into this world with nothing. We came to this country with nothing, and we're going to go with nothing, so why not take risks and be bold? We're not saying be reckless, but why not keep thinking and imagining? Why not keeping working and creating opportunity for the benefit of the environment, society, and the children of tomorrow?"

BERNHARDT
WEALTH MANAGEMENT

Shueyb Ali

No Gray Area

"The way I look at it, you have two options," the principal told fourteen-year-old Shueyb Ali and his father. "When you start at this school, you'll witness a lot. There are shootings and drugs, and people will try to bring you down through negative influences. You can either succumb to those, or you can join ROTC."

He went on to tell Shueyb that the ROTC kids were top notch, and always went on to futures in the military or in college. "It's your choice, Option A or Option B," he said. "But there's no gray area."

Raised by a single mother, Shueyb had grown up a rebellious, headstrong kid with no respect for authority. He did what he wanted to do, when and how he wanted to do it, without compromise. Once he reached his teenage years, he grew so rebellious that he was sent from North Carolina to Macon, Georgia, to live with his father. Up to that point, the two had spent a week or two together each year, but little more.

For his first two weeks living under his father's roof, Shueyb was allowed to come and go as he pleased. "My father was feeling me out, learning my patterns and habits to get a sense of what was upsetting my mother so much," he recalls today. "Then one day, out of the blue, he asked me to rake the yard. I told him I would do it when I came back from playing basketball, and he told me that wasn't the answer he was looking for. I told him to talk to me about it when I got back."

His father didn't protest, but instead asked him to come inside to sit down for a minute before he left. Seated in the living room, Shueyb was shocked when his father pulled out a gun. "You're not going to disrespect my name," he said. "You're going to listen to me, and you're going to listen to this." Calmly, he set the 357 on the table.

Shueyb had suspected he was living in a new world, and now, he was sure of it. The weight of reality sunk in, and from that moment on, things were different. He showed respect to his father by raking the yard, and he showed respect for himself by joining ROTC. "The program reinforced many of the important lessons my parents had always tried to impart—respect for authority, discipline, integrity, and a strong sense of values," he says. "When I first put on that uniform, I felt like a different person, and it was the bridge that allowed me to become that person."

Several decades later, Shueyb had achieved the unimaginable, landing a VP position at a company he loved. He planned to stay until he retired, but in time, he found himself at a crossroads when he became aware that a senior leader was mismanaging the company. He then discovered that the individual was also being dishonest, creating a climate that was completely antithetical to the strong values he had cultivated in his teenage years.

Shueyb had decided long ago that when it came to his values and standards, there was no gray area. He immediately gave his two weeks' notice with no backup plan and no outside network to fall back on. "I had to go out and essentially redefine myself," he says. "The economy was bad at that time, and jobs were scarce. My clients had always asked when I was going to go out on my own, so I figured why not? Why not try it now?"

With that, in 2010, Shueyb launched World Services LLC, an IT consulting firm serving both government and commercial clients. Based in Alexandria, Virginia, the company provides system engineering, software development, digitization and scanning, project management services, with a primary focus on federal, state, and local government clients. Today, their largest client is the U.S. Department of Housing and Urban Development, where they work directly with the Chief Information Officer to modernize the agency's IT infrastructure, implement processes, and update their IT operations and maintenance.

The fledgling government contractor survived sequestration, but struggled to get its footing despite its designation as a Service Disabled Veteran Owned Small Business. It wasn't until it also secured an 8(a) designation that it started seeing real success—a source of disappointment for Shueyb. "It was disappointing to realize that the federal government doesn't value the Service-Disabled Veteran designation as much as it values some other vehicles on the market," he says.

Nevertheless, World Services pressed forward, cultivating a stellar reputation and a track record of strong past performance. Before long, it was growing at ten percent a year, and by 2013, their annual growth rate had reached an impressive fifty percent. The company now has 35 seasoned, top-notch employees and revenue of $12 million, with a strong pipeline of exceptional opportunities and plans to double in the next year as they begin landing work with the Food and Drug Administration (FDA).

Had Shueyb been willing to compromise his values, World Services could have seized on opportunities that would have made it a hundred-person company already, but thanks to his high school years, gray areas were never going to be part of the equation. Trust, honesty, and integrity are the foundational tenets of the World Services culture, and he maintains a steady checks-and-balances dialogue with his COO that thoroughly examines the merits and ethics of every decision. "We would never run up numbers to win a contract, and we refuse to work with someone who's dishonest in how they represent themselves to the federal government," he affirms. "Our values are extremely important to us."

This sense of integrity was first modeled for Shueyb by his mother, who separated from his father shortly after Shueyb was born. She raised him and his two older sisters in Kalamazoo, Michigan, where she worked as a county commissioner making a modest salary. Living in Georgia, his father was a musician playing at the local church and teaching in elementary schools.

Growing up in a rough neighborhood, Shueyb was a troubled kid who bucked authority from an early age. But he remembers his mother trying to set a positive tone, showing the children how to set up lemonade stands and help the elderly next-door neighbors shovel snow in the winters. Because parents entrusted their children to his mother's care, their house was a hub for the neighborhood kids, and there was always a game of kickball going on in the backyard. She also loved to cook when she wasn't working, and would introduce kids to foods they had never been exposed to before. "She always made sure our home was a stable, peaceful, loving environment, no matter what was going on outside," he remembers. "She taught us about community and the importance of being involved in what's around you. Never complacent, she showed us we had a voice and a way to change things."

When Shueyb was eight years old, his mother moved the family to Chapel Hill, where she enrolled in law school. She had grown up there and still had family in the area willing to help, so she knew it would be a much better environment to raise her children. Still, Shueyb continued to struggle in school because classroom teaching at that time wasn't geared toward visual learners like him. "I had issues keeping up, but I knew I wasn't stupid," he recounts. "They put me in a remedial class, which I hated. My mom did all she could to encourage me, but she had so many other things going on at that time, so she delegated some of that to my older sister. She didn't know that I was a visual learner and just needed a different teaching style, so I continued to struggle."

Shueyb met two very good friends, and he began getting into sports in earnest when they started playing basketball and football together. His cousins in the area were also all very athletic, which opened his eyes to his own talent. He also started to understand for the first time that he was missing out on a father figure—someone who had been invested in developing and molding his abilities. "I never had that, so instead, I was a streetball player," he says. "That's all I knew, and it was hard to adapt that style into organized sports."

Fortunately, Shueyb's football coach recognized his talent and encouraged him to pursue the sport. His family couldn't afford the camps and programs the coach recommended, but he was able to attend Carolina Basketball Camp through a program that admitted economically disadvantaged kids for free. "Michael Jordan was there at the time, and I remember how cool it was to meet some of those players," he remembers.

When Shueyb moved in with his father in Macon at the age of fourteen and enrolled in ROTC, his innate athleticism landed him spots on both the football and basketball teams in his freshman year. His biology teacher also helped him understand that there was something different in the way he learned, pointing out that he was an intelligent student who grasped the material when it was presented visually. She refused to allow the school to put Shueyb in remedial classes, instead committing to tutor him personally. It was an important turning point for him, and he began to truly excel.

Shueyb balanced all these positive changes with a part-time job first at a pizza shop, and then at a photo store in the mall nearby. "I liked that there was process and order to the way you develop film in a darkroom," he remarks. As college neared, he began applying to colleges and was accepted to several schools, but he knew it would be hard to cover the costs on his mother's salary. He instead opted to enlist in the military when he graduated from high school in 1988, which meant he'd be eligible to take college classes after his first year of service. He commenced his military career at McGuire Air Force Base in New Jersey, and once he was eligible, he began taking night classes whenever he could.

Shueyb soon left New Jersey for Clark Air Base in the Philippines, where a nearby volcano erupted soon after his arrival. The ash cloud spewed up into the atmosphere and covered the sun, plunging them into 48 hours of darkness punctuated by earthquakes and a typhoon. "I honestly thought I was going to die," he remembers. "Afterward, I was part of the Mission Essential team that stayed back to help clean up as we closed down the base to hand it over to the Philippine government."

After ten months in the Philippines, Shueyb was sent to Germany, where he was invited to play tackle football on the Interfellow Europe team. He never thought of himself as a leader, so he was shocked when, in 1992, he won the military's distinguished John Levitow Award. The recognition is given to enlisted individuals that demonstrate strong leadership skills, achieve high-level academic success in the leadership school, and receive a high vote by their peers. "It was a defining moment for me because I never knew that other people saw me that way," he remarks. "That moment helped shape me into who I am now because It made me want to learn more about leadership and see how far I could take it. I started to nurture it, reading more leadership books and taking more management classes."

From then on, Shueyb began to realize that people either wanted to work with him or work for him. After Germany, he was stationed in Korea, and then New Mexico, before his final post at Bolling Air Force Base in DC. It was 1998 by that time, and as the IT boom heated up, he had grown adept at data retrieval, database maintenance, and programming. He saw that consultants with his same proficiencies where making triple his salary, so he decided it was time to make a change.

When he decided to leave the Air Force in 1998 after ten years of active duty, Shueyb took a job at Advanced Technology Systems, an IT firm, as a database analyst. "I saw my peers doing average work, but that just wasn't who I was," he recalls. He completed his undergraduate degree in Computer Studies and continued to learn from an ATS database administrator who would work late into the evenings, with Shueyb studying over his shoulder. "He showed me how to manipulate data in ways I didn't even think were possible," Shueyb remembers. "It really opened my eyes to the vastness of IT."

Shueyb's work ethic and commitment to exceeding expectations quickly caught the attention of management, and he rose through the ranks to Technical Lead and then to Project Manager before landing a Director position at another company in 2003. Over the next two years, he began leading larger teams, managing problems with innate ease and adeptly navigating complex challenges until a client offered him a VP position. "I thought that would be challenging and outside my comfort zone, because I'd have to help set everything up," Shueyb says. Though he never imagined he'd be an entrepreneur starting his own company, the experience was excellent training for the launch of World Services soon thereafter.

In a testament to his mother, who always believed strongly in the power of education, and to his own evolution, Shueyb decided to go back to school several years ago and was accepted to Harvard to get his Masters in Management. "I haven't always been the best student, so to get into a school of that caliber and see that I could excel, was a shocking accomplishment," he remarks. "You have to have a certain level of confidence in this industry because it's so competitive, and getting into Harvard showed me there was absolutely nothing I can't do. And on hard days, I think about my mother, who was relentless and never let anything get in her way. I still wonder how she raised and supported three kids while making it through law school." Shueyb continues to hold his own academically and is slated to complete the program in 2018.

Through it all, Shueyb has been supported and loved by his wife Ambre, the young woman he met through mutual friends in 2001 who is now a loving mother to their ten-year-old son and six-year-old daughter. "She has been completely amazing," Shueyb says. "Her faith in me and my ability have never wavered, and she's believed in me even when I haven't believed in myself. I am so grateful I found her."

In advising young people entering the working world today, Shueyb emphasizes the importance of face-to-face communication in a world that is increasingly digital. "If you see a problem in the workplace, you should be able to vocalize it constructively to executive management," he says. "More importantly, you should come with solutions in mind." He also underscores the importance of finding the right mentor—something he didn't find until recently. "I always wanted a mentor, but it took me a long time to find someone I was comfortable with," he says. "It always felt like there was a catch and they wanted something out of it. But when I met my mentor, Ahmed Ali, I instantly felt comfortable. He was selfless and did things for me that nobody had ever done, in all my years in business. That was very powerful."

In a sense, Shueyb undertakes the hard work of leadership precisely because it's a form of mentorship. A compassionate, strong leader, he knows that you can't always be a hard charging crusader who doesn't take no for an answer. "Sometimes people need you to be relatable," he says. "They need to know that you, as a leader, care about them on more than just a professional level. When people share my vision and want to create the type of environment and culture that I do, they become an extended member of my family, and there's nothing I won't do for them. I do what I do because I believe I can make a difference in the lives of individuals, molding them toward the goals they have for themselves. I know how gray and confusing the world can seem when you don't have that leadership to look to in your life. For others, I want something better."

Anwar Allen

Path and Purpose

Through the chaos and violence of World War II, bright spots of human spirit and endurance shone through—Americans whose purpose led them to battlefields across the Atlantic to fight for the future of global freedom. Some might even say it was those bright spots that ultimately led the Allies to victory through those dark days. Anwar Allen's grandfather was one of those bright spots.

In 1941, when America entered the war, it was a nation still marred by segregation, with less than 4,000 African Americans serving in the military. But when duty called, they answered. Anwar's grandfather served as part of the Red Ball Express, a trucking unit that helped supply the front lines. Though African Americans were largely barred from combat units at first, their contributions were vital to the victory that would change the course of human history, and by 1945, over 1.2 million were serving. "It's so meaningful to me that, at a time when African Americans weren't openly accepted in society, my grandfather went over to fight for freedoms that he didn't get to take full advantage of," Anwar says today. "He fought for the values we take for granted today."

When the war ended, Anwar's grandfather followed his path and purpose home to Washington, DC, where, through the support of his wife and her family, he started his own trash collection company. Though he only had a third-grade education, the business excelled, flourishing for forty years. Through that time, he trained and mentored his son-in-law, Anwar's father, passing the company into his capable hands just before his death. And to his grandson, Anwar, he passed on three things: the dog tags he wore during those transformative years of war, the entrepreneurial spirit that led him to create success when opportunity was hard to come by, and the strong sense of purpose that has always guided him.

Now the founder and CEO of Revecent, a cutting-edge sales consulting firm dedicated to assessing, recruiting and optimizing sales teams for their clients, Anwar has followed his own path and purpose to open doors for others. "I think God has a purpose for all of us, and a path for us to reach that purpose," he says. "Mine is helping people and companies reach their full potential. It's exciting to be a part of emerging companies that are looking to take their businesses to the next level."

Launched in 2007, Revecent began as Pipeline Management Consulting, a sales outsourcing company oriented around the development of sales pipelines. It evolved as clients required additional help in recruiting and optimizing their sales force, adding more offerings and solutions to their portfolio of services until 2015, when Anwar saw that outsourcing wasn't his true purpose. "Outsourcing was great, but it's more of an ad-hoc, temporary solution," he explains. "I wanted to leverage my expertise to help companies build successful sales teams internally, addressing the needs of the organization for its growth trajectory and long-term plans." With that, the company rebranded as Revecent.

Today, Revecent uses its proven methodology and system for building high-performance sales teams to help organizations develop their sales forces. With an experienced team highly specialized in their unique sales area specialties, they focus on people, process and technology. "We bring in the right talent to execute the sales plan that we help develop, while providing the interim management needed to hold the team accountable to meeting their goals," Anwar says.

Committed to the idea of revving up revenue, Revecent helps clients take their businesses to new heights. It can provide customized sales services based on the client's unique needs, but sets itself apart in the industry by bringing a complete solution to the table. "Typically you have recruiting and consulting companies, and then you have training organizations that are separate," he explains. "Revecent brings these services together in a streamlined solution, allowing small and emerging growth companies to leverage our expertise across a variety of sales disciplines to realize their goals."

Shepherding potential from the spark of an idea all the way through to a fully-realized concept, Revecent focuses on business to business sales in the tech and professional services industries, dealing primarily with enterprise products and solutions. Most of its client organizations were founded by entrepreneurs with engineering or technical backgrounds—people who have developed a great product but lack the sales and marketing expertise they need to bring it to market. Anwar loves helping candidates reach that next step in their careers through the recruiting side of the business. "Our goal is to create the infrastructure for sales success, which in turn helps all parties reach their potential," he affirms.

Helping people reach their potential is an integral part of his own path and purpose—something he has pursued since the earliest days of his childhood, thanks to the positive influences of his parents and grandparents. Anwar's father and grandfather are pastors, and growing up in the church, his faith has always been a cornerstone of his character. "My faith has very much had an influence over who I am today," he says.

Anwar was born in Washington, DC, and moved to Northern Virginia at the age of three. He loved being outside, always riding bikes and playing sports with other kids in the neighborhood. They had free reign during the day and only had to be home by dark—a lifestyle that can only be imagined by most of today's children. With his grandparents and extended family all living in the area, Anwar spent a lot of time with family. "As the only boy with three sisters, I got a lot of attention, and everyone had high expectations for me," he remembers. "Growing up in that environment, family has always been very important to me."

Anwar's mother, a nurturing and supportive woman, worked in human resources for Fairfax County. His father, a consummate leader both professionally and spiritually, operated the family waste management company he had inherited. Being the only boy, Anwar felt a strong sense of independence and responsibility growing up, and enjoyed going to work with his father and watching him run the business. "Even from an early age, I knew I wouldn't work for someone else long-term," he says. "All my friends' parents worked for other people, and I thought it was cool that my dad and grandfather worked for themselves. I saw their entrepreneurial spirits and knew I wanted to run my own business someday."

As a kid, Anwar loved going to Redskins games with his dad. In fifth grade, he made the life-changing decision to start playing football—the sport that would dominate his days all the way through high school graduation. Without brothers at home to compete with, his large reserves of untapped drive finally had an outlet, and as his athleticism developed, he found that he loved the challenges—both physical and mental—that come with winning. "Those challenges shaped my sense of discipline and accountability," he says. "I learned how to collaborate and work with others, even if I didn't agree with everyone on the team. Winning is about finding that common ground to reach your shared goal."

This commitment to overall team success was balanced with the need to compete internally for rank within the team—a dynamic Anwar embraced with great success. He always set his sights on being number one, and though that goal created an internal sense of pressure, it cultivated a lifelong drive to fight, win, and achieve his goals—one that is just as impactful in the business world today as it was on the field all those years ago. "I'm still friends with those teammates today because we share this great camaraderie," he says. "We don't talk that often, but when we get together, we don't skip a beat."

While Anwar disliked his first job, a short-lived stint as a cashier at Burger King at the age of sixteen, he soon landed his first sales job working for a window and siding company out of a condo basement. There, he made cold calls all night offering free in-home estimates. "Those were the kind of calls people would get in the middle of dinner and hate," he laughs. "But I found it was actually fun to talk to different people. When I got rejected, it didn't bother me, I just moved on to the next call. It taught me how to prospect, and most importantly, how to handle rejection—an important aspect of sales. If one call didn't work out, I'd think, 'maybe the next one.' I could get rejected 99 times, but if I had that one win, the night was still a success."

Anwar's passion for the work was also fueled by his competitive spirit, which was stoked by the whiteboard on the wall that tracked the success of the ten young people working side-by-side in the call center. Whenever an appointment was made, a bell was rung, lighting a friendly fire under the other callers to pick up the pace. "I loved the race to see who was going to make the most money each night, and it allowed me to control my own income for the first time," Anwar remarks. "I saw that in sales, you aren't limited to making a fixed dollar amount per hour. There's the possibility to make more, and you control your own destiny by working hard. That's when I realized that sales was what I wanted to do." Anwar did remarkably well for himself, often raking in $20 an hour.

Upon graduating from high school, he enrolled at Radford University, where he chose to major in business. In his junior year, he transferred to the George Mason University School of Business. His life then took another unexpected turn when he went in to interview for his first real software sales job. He happened to run into his brother-in-law's father as he was walking into the interview, only to discover that he worked for the very same company. Thanks to a good word from him, Anwar landed the job, ultimately opting to switch to a part-time student so he could focus on making the most of it.

At Allen Systems Group, Anwar worked in federal sales, where the cold calling skills he had cultivated in high school quickly propelled him to remarkable success. "I was selling a more sophisticated and technical product, and though I had natural sales ability, his mentorship really polished me into a pro," Anwar affirms. "He taught me how to qualify opportunities, develop relationships, and master the fundamentals." Anwar also underwent formal sales training programs, which were helpful but did not always impart lasting improvements. For him, the most transformative learning came through the daily work of implementing improvements through integrating them into his process. "I saw what didn't work in sales force training," he says. "That's why now, with Revecent, we focus on the overall sales system and reinforcement."

During that time, in 2004, Anwar and his high school sweetheart, Betsy, welcomed their first child into the world. He then accepted a sales and business development positon at Winward Consulting Group, an IT services company, in 2005. There, Anwar worked to open the door to large accounts and partnered with software companies to resell their products, and was very successful at landing appointments with hard-to-reach decisions makers. "Through that work, I realized that a lot of companies struggle with business development, lead generation, and getting in the door with new accounts," he recalls. "They're great at managing and growing existing accounts, but they didn't know how to unlock new opportunities through proper cold calling and prospecting techniques. I realized I could package up those skills as a service, so I decided to start my business."

It was a big lifestyle change to go from earning a sizeable income to reinvesting everything into launching a new business. Anwar was blessed to have a wife that supported his vision. "She's been so supportive at every step of the way," he reflects. "Whenever she saw that something was important to me and to our family, she would help make it happen, never doubting me. We had to make a lot of sacrifices for me to run my own company, and it hasn't always been easy. I'm so grateful that she's stuck with me and my vision, when most people would have told me to give up and pursue a safer option."

Anwar and Betsy now have three children, and thanks to their commitment and hard work, the professional risks have paid off. For instance, his approach and success recently landed him in Mindshare's Class of 2017, a network of like-minded entrepreneurs and business owners who share their experiences and insights to lift each other up. "I've done a lot of learning along the way, and I don't have a board of directors or mentors, so Mindshare is incredibly helpful," he remarks. "It's a way of giving back, and you get a lot in return." Anwar also supports Facets, a Fairfax County nonprofit fighting to combat homelessness.

In advising young people entering the working world today, Anwar urges them to connect with their purpose in choosing their path through life. "Be passionate and professional, and take the time to figure out what's most meaningful to you," he says. "Once you know, pursue it with all you have. Purpose is the line that connects my family from one generation to the next, linking me to the perseverance of my grandfather and the leadership legacy of my father. Purpose is what compels me to be a responsible, accountable person that others can look up to and depend on. And purpose is the path that connects each person to a happy, successful life, even when they feel lost. When you walk with purpose, you're bound to find your way forward."

Chris Assenmacher

It's About the Team

Imagine being hired by a private investment group to consult on an acquisition that was in a difficult situation, only to have the group ask you to jump out of the frying pan and into the fire: to leave your consulting job and take the helm of the troubled company—to transform a troubled asset into a high-performing company.

That's exactly the decision that faced Chris Assenmacher about six years ago. The result? The company, Carter Control Systems Inc. (CCS), has since gone from being essentially a one-client enterprise with rapidly declining sales to a thriving firm with a diversified and growing customer base, and an expanded product and services offering. "I was brought in at a difficult time, when the private equity firm was trying to decide what to do. Things were not going well," Chris reports. "Ultimately, we decided that it was worth repositioning and moving into new products, markets, and services, and fortunately we've been pretty successful doing that over the past five years." Chris attributes much of the credit for the successful outcome to the people he works with at CCS. "I will be forever indebted to the people who helped the company through the difficult times. There are some long-term employees that have been with the company for ten and twenty-plus years, but everybody just sort of pitched in and rolled up their sleeves. Some people did three different jobs, and that effort got us through a tough period."

It is not surprising that Chris credits the people at CCS with making the company's dramatic turnaround happen; building and leading teams has been a dominant theme throughout his career. "I think I have a very collaborative approach to leadership," he says. "I'm very team-oriented in anything I do, and I think it's important to get everyone on the same page. I welcome input from everybody; I know that I don't know everything and I'm never going to know everything." As Chris mentions the names of people at CCS who, he says, went above and beyond all reasonable expectations because of their determination to help the company succeed—people from the management to the engineers to the shop—it is obvious that he thoroughly understands the indispensable process of assembling a team around a vision and then empowering them to make the vision a reality. "I'm incredibly amazed at everybody that got us through that period," he says.

That sense of vision and focus came into play for Chris at a fairly young age, when in the sixth grade he set a goal of earning admission into a rigorous private preparatory school not far from his home in suburban Philadelphia. "Honestly, looking back, I don't remember exactly why I wanted to go there, but I knew that it was really important to me. Committing myself to that was an early defining moment in my life." One of the more significant outcomes of that commitment was Chris's opportunity to take a public speaking class, taught by a man who would become an early mentor, Tony Figliola. "I was a pretty shy kid, growing up, and I decided to take the class. I think it helped me come out of my shell, and the skills that I learned in that class have carried through my entire life. I use them in business every day. Looking back, I think that was an interesting decision that ended up being a fairly formative one for me." Chris subsequently became involved with the school's forensics team, sponsored by Figliola, which gave him the opportunity to compete in public speaking and oratory events all over the country. "We would go to tournaments at places like Harvard and Emory, and you had to keep your grades up and get approvals from teachers to do these things, so it was a unique opportunity." Chris credits this experience with helping him really become comfortable in his own skin. "We were expected to lead and to mentor underclassmen; we knew we represented the school, and so I think all of that came together for me during high school."

As time rolled around for college, Chris applied to a number of outstanding universities. "I applied to a few in the DC area, because at the time I had some interest in politics," he says. He also knew that he would need a combination of scholarships and work-study in order to finance his higher education. "My parents helped, but a good portion of it was scholarships and working." Chris was no stranger to work, however, because even as a kid at home, there was a clear expectation that if he wanted something, he would have to work for it. "My mom and my stepfather's approach was always, 'If you want it, you have to go work for it and figure it out.' That was the expectation; if we wanted a car, we had to pay for it and pay for the insurance. Working through high school, working through college, that's just always the way it was for me and my brothers." Chris ultimately enrolled at the University of Delaware with a double major in business and philosophy. "I got into the honors program, which allowed me to create my own curriculum. I wanted to be a philosophy major, but there just isn't a whole lot out there for philosophy majors. So, the business side seemed obvious to me as a practical choice." Going from a small high school with a fairly tight-knit student body to a larger university where he knew literally no one when he got there was a challenging transition for Chris, but one that he managed fairly well. By this time, he explains, he had enough confidence in himself to speak up in class and otherwise negotiate the complexities of campus life. "It was a pretty standard college experience; you go out and have fun the weekends, spend a lot of your time studying during the week. And of course, like almost every kid that goes to college, this was the first time in my life when I didn't have anyone to cook for me, to do my laundry, and so forth. But I think most kids go through that."

After graduation from Delaware, Chris opted to backpack around Europe. "I took off and made my way around. I had never been to Europe at that point. It was a lot of fun, and the experience also made me comfortable being by myself. It was a terrific experience." Chris was there during the summer when the reunification of Germany was taking place, which was especially exciting as a second-generation German-American.

Upon returning to the United States, Chris encountered the unpleasant surprise that getting his first professional job wasn't going to be as simple as he had imagined. "I thought it was going to be as easy as sending out my résumé and getting the job of my dreams. But in the early '90s, the labor market wasn't very good, so it took me awhile to find a job." Chris's stepmother actually connected him with a mediation/arbitration organization, and he ended up working for the firm for a period of time. "I had originally thought I wanted to go to law school, so it was an interesting opportunity and those were useful tools to have, even though I didn't ultimately go to law school." While working at the firm, Chris started taking graduate courses at Temple University toward a graduate degree in economics. "It was exhausting; I was going to school almost full time and working full time. My friends were going to the beach and having fun, and I was taking classes. I remember struggling with that and asking myself, 'Why am I doing this?'" He had a goal of getting into consulting work and believed the graduate degree would be the best preparation. Still, it was a tough few years, he says.

Chris's first job following graduate school was with a DC-area CPA and consulting firm with offices across the country that was looking to grow its consulting business. "They basically said, 'We're trying to figure this out and we'll help you as best we can.' There were two of us, creating this practice around strategy and IT, which was becoming very big at the time." Chris and his colleagues managed to build the consulting practice into a significant profit center for the firm, "and I sort of had to figure a lot of it out on my own, which was another defining moment for me, understanding that I could do this and make it work without a whole lot of structure around me." During this period, Chris met his wife, Michele, and enjoyed the atmosphere in Washington, DC during the Clinton years. "It was the first time I really hired people and created a team. We did some really interesting things, and it was definitely a learning experience."

Not that everything was rosy, however. Chris recalls the night, during this period, when he first lost sleep due to job-related stress. "I remember the first time I was actually lying awake in the middle of the night and thinking, 'We have got to find another project! What am I going to do?'" On the other hand, his experiences in this first job also occasioned another of his defining moments, when an early client came to him and expressed heartfelt gratitude for the services Chris had been able to provide. "I was a young guy, in my twenties, and I still remember this executive thanking me for helping him and his company work through this issue they were having. It made an impression on me, and I think that moment really committed me to taking a certain approach to business and to doing things a certain way."

After about five years at the firm, Chris moved to San Francisco to start an Internet company. "I had this idea around web-based technology for employee benefits that the CPA firm supported, and we went out and found another backer who helped fund the idea. The Bay Area was the center of where all the technology-driven activity was happening at the time. So we started a company out there. We had two investors who gave us a limited amount of capital, and we couldn't waste it. Unlike a lot of startups, we focused on getting cash flow–positive quickly. But, we were spending all of our money on the IT side and not enough on marketing. It was an interesting experience, and I learned a lot, even though it really didn't go as well as I had hoped for me personally." Chris reports that he spent some time "butting heads" with the board of the company, "because I thought I knew better than they did," providing him with what he calls his first "board experience." After about a year and a half with the technology start up, Chris took a job with a Bay Area publicly traded consulting firm in order to help them develop a new practice. "That taught me a lot about how I don't want to do certain things." Still, Chris managed to help the firm build its consulting practice from basically nothing to some $60 million in sales. "I worked with some great people, and it was a fun and successful experience, in terms of the dollars and cents, but the whole publicly traded environment, with its focus on the quarterly revenue goals—I just didn't really get that."

About four years later, Chris and Michele moved back to Washington, DC, following an opportunity for Michele. At that time, he started his own consulting practice, which he was pursuing at the time the private equity group approached him for assistance and advice with Carter Control Systems.

"They bought the company from the guy who founded it about ten years ago, and it had some serious issues, in that its primary customer, the US Postal Service, had pretty much stopped buying their type of product." CCS designs and manufactures automated material handling systems and industrial automation solutions. Though it was highly profitable at the time it was acquired, the ongoing changes in technology and communication soon began to seriously impact the Postal Service, leading to declining orders and a revenue drop for CCS. "At the time the company was acquired by the private equity group, the Postal

Service had previously been spending hundreds of millions of dollars on equipment and systems, much of it focused on first-class mail," Chris says. But, with the continuing rise of the Internet and technology, the industry landscape shifted significantly. "Revenue declined slowly over a two- or three-year period, and then more dramatically." The general economic downturn in 2008–2009 also affected the business.

"I had done a lot of work with private equity and venture capital firms around analyzing opportunities and figuring out strategies for where to go," Chris says. "And, I think my location [near CCS's Frederick, Maryland, headquarters] seemed like an advantage." So, when Chris came back to them after about three weeks with his recommendations, the equity group asked him to lead the CCS team through its turnaround.

"We needed to reposition into commercial markets, and we had a product that we could fit to other applications. Intelligent automation for material handling systems was not very common at the time, but the people at CCS, because of their work with USPS, really understood how to design systems that allow you to track things wherever they are. They built some software that is really the brains behind what happens in the warehouse, which is critical to the operation of e-commerce companies, or any other distribution or manufacturing facility. Not many people had this type of depth at the time, and this was when e-commerce was really starting to pick up. We were able to figure out how all that needs to work together. There was a real opportunity there, and we had some initial success in e-commerce." Next, CCS expanded into the more traditional distribution markets. "This would be any retail or wholesale company that sells a wide variety of products, where you're working with much larger orders and product sizes—at the pallet and case level. We just started slowly expanding our capabilities and experience so that we could cover a much wider range of markets." From there, CCS expanded into robotics, which got them into the manufacturing space, including automotive work and medical device assembly. "It has been one step at a time over the years," Chris says, "to get us to the point where we are now able to provide a full array of services and products."

As a result of Chris's strategic leadership and his team's hard work, CCS has more than doubled sales from the year he took over. "I think we're well positioned right now. And we're at the point where growing organically is going to be harder, so we're now having strategy discussions around where we need to go from here." The company's principal enterprise focuses on three areas: post and parcel handling, distribution (which encompasses e-commerce, retail, and wholesale customers), and manufacturing.

Chris's team-focused approach comes through in the advice he gives to young people entering business. "Don't be afraid to step up and be a leader," he says. "In my experience, real leaders in the business world are lacking, and I think a lot of times it's because people are simply hesitant to step up. Also, don't be afraid to make mistakes. That's what life is, and you need to learn from them and figure out how to turn a negative into a positive. And then, I would say that you need to have the right attitude. You need to be accountable to the company and yourself, and if you're not, you're doing a disservice to everyone. If you're not giving a hundred percent, it's not fair to you or the company."

"I really enjoy working with people in a cooperative environment, and leading the organization to achieve its mission," Chris says, summing up his motivation for why he likes to do what he does. "I've always been fascinated by how a group of people can come together and accomplish amazing things.

"I do it for the people who work with me."

Beth Perl Berman

The Rest is Still Unwritten

For Beth Perl Berman, life was relatively simple. She had been home raising her two sons and facilitating group assault prevention discussions in schools, when business opportunity knocked so loudly she could not ignore it.

In Beth's case, that call to action was an advertisement a friend passed to her for a recruiting position at a local firm. As a longtime recruiter herself, Beth's friend knew Beth would excel in the role given her natural knack for forging deep connections with people.

As she considered her potential new job, Beth envisioned connecting people with better jobs, and thus, better lives. "The work seemed like a great way to help people out and make a difference," she muses today. "It was an opportunity to help others find their way, just as I always had as a mother, confidant, and friend. I'm a big believer in making an impact, and it seemed like a perfect fit."

The reality of recruiting, however, proved a bit different. Beth did get to connect candidates with jobs—sometimes. But then there were the candidates her clients rejected. "I had pictured helping job candidates elevate themselves," Beth laughs. "But I hadn't processed having to turn them away when client HR departments rejected them! My actual job was to focus only on what the client wanted, not on what the individual needed. Far too often, the candidates I'd invested time and energy in helping ended up getting tossed. Even though I was cautioned by the company president that I was 'not a social worker,' bursting candidates' bubbles really brought me down."

After year one, Beth simply could no longer stand rejecting candidate after hopeful candidate. She did not want to be the source of constant dream-crushing. To refresh her spirits, she transitioned to the business development and marketing arm of the business using skills she'd developed in her highly successful corporate sales and marketing career.

Then, during the 2008 economic downturn, crisis became opportunity. As the demand for job candidates—and, by extension, recruiting services—fell precipitously, the business had to shift away from recruiting. "Nobody was paying for candidates anymore, so we pivoted as a job search coaching business," she recalls. "I became a partner in this business and marketed it on a shoestring. I helped develop, and deliver, our content and our coaching services."

Here, Beth hit her stride as a natural coach for job seekers, adept at helping them market their best selves. She coached them in developing resumes, LinkedIn profiles, and interview skills, all with an emphasis on communicating their value. Mostly, she helped candidates beaten down by the impact of recession and hiring freezes regain confidence in themselves and find their drive to move forward. After thriving in the role, Beth ultimately launched her own job search coaching business in 2011, setting the stage for her current successful, high-impact business model.

Today, Beth is the CEO of Compellications. Initially founded to help job seekers, it is now focused on helping business leaders, entrepreneurs, and owners build cohesive teams, and deepen their customer base by marketing themselves "compellingly." By helping them articulate their value in a way that connects, Beth helps her clients gain measurable increases in productivity, revenue, and profitability. "Compellications focuses on helping clients communicate and connect in a way that compels the right, best-fit people to buy in, buy, and advocate for your success," she says, drawing on the recurring thread of wisdom acquired in her past successes in sales, marketing, leadership, and job search coaching. "Whether you're an established leader, a salesperson hyping your wares, or a job seeker looking for your next step, you are always marketing yourself. To influence—internal or external—decision makers, be compelling. To lead others to a desired action, belief or commitment, be compelling. To win, be compelling."

To this end, Beth offers a variety of trainings and services via Compellications, including its centerpiece, the WHY-based workshops she is certified to deliver. This approach helps people answer one central question: why do you do what you do? "It's all about focusing on the question, what drives you?" Beth says. "What lights you up and places you in your zone?" She explains, "Articulating and understanding our core drivers is the basis for connecting, inspiring, and influencing others." Her work empowers people to understand one another through their innate personal makeups. This approach, applied to each member of a team, and directed at ideal clients, is the true game changer."

Beth is not shy about the secret sauce behind her clients' success. "Discovering and expressing one's WHY is the essence of what makes people feel and become successful," she explains. "My personal WHY is that I am driven, probably to a fault, to contribute and make a profound, positive, rippling impact. I want to make a difference; I want to make my mark. I love helping leaders and teams get clear about themselves and articulate so they reach their true potential."

Helping clients find and connect around their WHY is a crucial component of Beth's Compellications™ process. She believes teams and individuals simply cannot win in the current disruptive economy without forging connection. "A sustainable competitive advantage comes from providing compelling answers to the 'why you' question—answers that connect others to you and your company," Beth says. Her mantra, "Lose your value proposition and find your compelling value connection™", reflects her conviction that every win emanates from deep connection with those you want to influence.

Beth credits her success to capitalizing on her natural attributes and leveraging them, in the same way she teaches her clients to. "I'm told repeatedly that I bring a contagious, sometimes playful energy that draws people out and cultivates trust," she explains. "Within organizations, team members connect deeply when they become clear on why they—and the organization—matter. They thrive when their work aligns with what lights them up and places them in their zone. They bond and collaborate when they can see how their leaders and co-workers are driven. When team members are deeply connected to their work, to each other, to what the organization stands for, they become loyal advocates. When you create that connection and openness as a leader—with and within teams and, of course, with customers—you're unstoppable."

Beth's ability to get this kind of traction with teams is a function of her dynamic, bubbly nature. Her deep self-discovery process engages clients, while keeping things fairly light. "I then help my clients' energized, aligned teams pull together and focus on marketing to their ideal customers and ideal talent," she explains. "Together, we co-create powerful, compelling, repeatable messaging. And we have fun in the process!"

Once this synergy has been established, Beth guides the client in developing marketing messaging that emanates from the company's or the individual's unique perspective, blended with a keen focus on the target audiences. "Looking at their customers, partners, and prospective talent in a new light, clients help write their company's authentic story in a way that resonates with their ideal audiences," she says. "The best part is that leaders and teams 'own' the language they've helped develop. All levels use it to market the company from the inside out™."

Beyond WHY-based workshops and coaching, Beth's Compellications services include communications skills training, workshop facilitation, and speaker services, as well as individual coaching. Incorporating lessons learned from her diverse career, she helps clients boost their ability to influence others. From compelling emails and web content, to intergenerational communications, to marketing, to online and offline networking, Beth helps clients clarify and communicate their value and reach, and surpass, their goals.

Offering compelling communications advice, Beth recommends, "First and foremost, zip it up and listen generously. Focus on your intangibles—your inner drives. Focus on the things that connect you to others, others to you, and team members to each other. Know your target audience and what, in the end, they want. This is the path to relevance. Share knowledge and demonstrate your capabilities. Represent yourself and your company boldly. Be clear, consistent and authentic in all that you say and do. Let your unique energy shine. That's what inspires people to buy in, buy, remain loyal, and refer you."

Beth's unique methodology and perspectives were shaped by her early life in Livingston, New Jersey. All rest on the fundamental belief that attitude is huge—an idea embodied by her hard-working father, Bert Perl. He urged her to do more, dream bigger, and try harder, always modeling a resilient persistence and optimism. "My father always said 'You're a Perl, you're a winner!'" she says. "I didn't appreciate it early on, but that precise mindset has helped me see possibilities where others see limitations."

When Beth was young, Bert owned four shoe stores. "I remember riding in the back of the station wagon bouncing alongside all those shoeboxes," she laughs. "There were shoes everywhere. Even my *grandmother* hawked shoes!" Bert went on to sell land, and later, he sold security systems while promoting his private accounting practice. "He was the quintessential tin man," Beth recounts.

When she graduated from high school, Beth left home to attend George Washington University, where she discovered a love for both Economics and Marketing. She devoured books on advertising and marketing communications, becoming a sponge to soak up all there was to learn. Thanks in part to growing up around her sales-oriented family, she was a natural in the field, and after graduating with her B.B.A. in Marketing, she was recruited into what was then C&P Telephone. She excelled in sales and ascended quickly to managing the highest-billing, multi-million dollar corporate accounts, and later shifted to strategic marketing positions.

Beth refers to her leadership style as authentic above all else. "In anything we do, it's really about finding your best-fit path," she says. "My main themes are authenticity, alignment with what lights you up, and giving wherever you can to make your greatest impact. I believe in letting your true self shine… boldly. I strive to live this way. I want to reflect it in everything I do and demonstrate it in everything my company does, produces, and represents."

Careful to incorporate the lessons of her past into her present and future, Beth wears a necklace with three gems to remind her of the nature of time, and to honor the balance and importance of past, present and future. The necklace was a gift from her husband, and she considers it her most treasured possession. "From a past-present-future standpoint," she says, "I believe you have to honor your formative experiences, both in your work and in your personal life. Hard things, like the death of my mother, inform the wisdom we develop over time. We need to take the time to work through them, hold onto the hard lessons, and keep them in perspective."

"The present, on the other hand, is all about focusing on 'the now'." This is no easy feat in the age of distraction. "It's so important to be fully present, for our own benefit and, and for others," she says thoughtfully. "Being present, listening generously and connecting to what matters are powerful practices, in our lives as in communications."

When it comes to the future, one of Beth's favorite songs is Natasha Bedingfield's "Unwritten." "The lyrics are framed next to my desk," she says. "The message is that we need to live our lives fully and be willing to experiment and explore."

One extreme example of exploration gone awry was when Beth and her husband, both avid hikers, unintentionally "camped out in shorts and t-shirts, without a cell signal and without provisions" in Israel's Negev desert. They had veered way off course from their planned afternoon route. Spooked by prior warnings about the indigenous hyenas and scorpions, they spent that cold, dark night on the side of a desolate mountain, and the next day trekked for many hours in the desert sun. Attesting to the power of attitude, Beth shares, "Just before our rescue, dehydrated and feeling it was really a matter of life and death, I turned to my husband and said, 'If this is the end, I'm thankful that we've shared a good, adventurous life with few regrets.'" Beth admits, "Looking back, I'm a bit surprised I could stay positive, under such extraordinary circumstances, but I definitely don't want to test it *that way* again!"

Beth's overall philosophy aligns with the song. She shares, "Every moment, we're creating the words that ultimately write the story of our lives. My advice is: Write your story. Get real and put yourself out there. Stretch. Don't be afraid and don't give up. Make your mark… now. The only real limit in life is time, and the rest is still unwritten."

BERNHARDT
WEALTH MANAGEMENT

Kevin Beverly

Working Wonders

Kevin Beverly remembers the day he had to start working very clearly, because it was the day after his father left. "I remember coming downstairs and finding my mother crying," he recounts. "She told me he wasn't coming back, and that I had to go to work. I was ten years old."

Kevin's mother took him outside and instructed him to pick up a cinderblock sitting by the side of the road. With the cinderblock, they walked up to the church, and then back home. Kevin didn't know why. "She made me do it again," he says. "Then she told me I was going into the tomato fields the next day. I reminded her you had to be thirteen to work in the tomato fields, but she told me that if I could carry that cinderblock, I could work in the tomato fields."

The Beverlys didn't have an easy life in their tiny, rural community on Taylor's Island off the Maryland coast. They never had running water or electricity, and money was always tight. Kevin was in elementary school before desegregation, and the school for black kids on the island was poorly-resourced. When his father left, his brother Larry, ten years older and in college, didn't mince words. "He came home the following weekend and told me I had to help and work too," Kevin remembers.

Larry was the hero Kevin looked up to and the mentor he needed. A total anomaly on Taylor's Island, he was the first in the family to go to college, and hell-bent on ensuring that Kevin would be the second. He never let up on Kevin, constantly asking him about his studies and reinforcing the importance of academics. "I like to say that he walked on gravel so I could walk on pavement," says Kevin admiringly. "He always told me to sit in the front row in class. He told me I didn't have to be the smartest—I just had to outwork 'em. He said, be the first one there, and work the hardest. And if someone gives you something to do, you do it on their time, not yours. If someone's asking you to get something done, you do it as quickly and efficiently as possible. I didn't know it at the time, but he was absolutely right—hard work works wonders."

Kevin took Larry's lessons to heart and excelled in school, ultimately landing at the University of Maryland. But during his first semester, he didn't do so well. He didn't have the habits and discipline of the kids from more affluent districts and ended up on academic probation, wondering if he belonged. He even thought about going back home—until he had another life-defining moment.

Kevin was working on an oyster boat during the break between semesters when he fell overboard. "When you work on the boats, you're pushing rakes down and pulling the oysters up," he recounts. "I couldn't swim, so they always tied a rope to me—mostly to make sure they didn't lose their rakes. They don't give a crap whether you go over, or whether you're cold or freezing. That boat's not going back until it gets its haul. We went out at 3 o'clock in the morning and didn't come back in until around 10:00 AM, so I was sitting there, absolutely freezing. I thought to myself, I am never doing this again. That was my epiphany. I knew there had to be more to life, and I went back to Maryland with a whole new attitude."

Today, Kevin Beverly is the President and CEO of Social and Scientific Systems (SSS), a $100 million company that works wonders by helping to improve public health worldwide. They've worked extensively on the HIV/AIDS crisis, both in the U.S. and abroad, through clinical research services, epidemiological studies, and policy outcomes. Founded forty years ago as a small minority-owned business by Herb Miller, Dennis Ables, and Mary Francis leMatt, who was CEO when Kevin started, the company now employs nearly 500 people and is 100 percent employee-owned. "These are people who are very proud of their work, whether it's running HIV/AIDS drug trials in Africa, standing up a breast cancer epidemiological study here in the US, or doing research to help the government figure out whether Medicaid expansion is working the way it should," he says. "I'm proud to be able to lead an organization with a mission like that."

Today, the National Institutes of Health is SSS's largest client, including the Allergy and Infectious Disease Institute, and the Environmental Sciences Institute, the Cancer Institute, and the Institute for Kidney and Digestive Diseases. They specialize in clinical trials for adult and pediatric AIDS, helping to develop many of the therapies and treatments used to treat the disease today. Long-term epidemiological studies, which follow large cohorts of patients over the course of 15 or 20 years, are also a specialty, including a study of the long-term health effects suffered by workers who cleaned up the Gulf Oil Spill.

By the time Kevin began at SSS in 2003, he had an extensive background in public health, computer engineering, and business development. He was brought in by Jim Lynch, then the company's Executive Vice President and future CEO, to take over the company's Business Development operations and come up with a strategy to expand its impact. "My job was really about finding new business and creating opportunities," he explains. "SSS was very good at winning the re-competes they already had, but not as good at going out and winning new things. So that was my chore."

At that time, the company relied heavily on grants, which formed a solid infrastructure but didn't generate profit. Kevin set out to leverage it into their expertise into new contracts and transitioning their culture from a nonprofit mindset to one focused on raising share price. Thanks to this restructuring, SSS reduced its reliance on grants from 50 percent to only 10 percent, and set its sights on doing even more. "I had made it clear that I wanted to run the company one day," he recalls. "Jim was giving me more room to operate and make changes, but he was more conservative. When I told him we could be a $200 million company, he told me he didn't want to run a company that big.' But I said, 'well I do!'" His goal was realized in 2015, when Jim retired and the Board handed the reigns over to Kevin as CEO. "Jim was my biggest advocate, and I'm so appreciative that he saw something in me," Kevin affirms.

Now, with plans to double the company by 2021, Kevin is redirecting SSS toward wonders of an even greater magnitude. It may seem like a long way to go, but when measured against the ground he's already covered in life, it's nothing. "If I got to where I am today from Taylor's Island, so poor and so far out in the country that they had to pump the sunlight in, I can take SSS to the next level," he affirms confidently.

Growing up on Taylor's Island, the family kept chickens, pigs and cows, and wasn't picky about meat. "I could sit on the roof of my back porch and shoot a duck for dinner," he recounts. "We ate turtle, muskrat, squirrel, rabbit—anything that moved. We never worried much about food, but money was hard to come by."

Kevin's mother worked tirelessly picking and peeling tomatoes and shucking oysters, later picking up a waitressing job at a café. Larry had a different father, but Kevin's parents met when Larry was only five, so Kevin's father was the man he considered to be his dad. "My brother's memories of him are very different from mine," says Kevin. "He remembers when our father transported our house to the spot next to my grandmother's house, dragging it four miles with mules and a tractor. Larry remembers him working hard and being a provider. My parents were married for sixteen years, but by the time I came around, he was an abusive guy who drank too much. I thought he was a bad person when he left us, but in hindsight now, I think he just ran out of gas. It was a lot of work for me personally to start to understand him—to recognize the plight of the African-American man in the 1930s, 40s and 50s. He was one of 18 kids, with maybe a seventh-grade education. He had what skills and tools he had, and he did the best he could with them, until he just couldn't anymore."

Although his father was gone, Kevin was surrounded by extended family on Taylor's Island. His house sat between his grandmother's house and his great aunt's house, and his entire street was home to various aunts, uncles, and cousins. "We were all related, there wasn't anyone on our road that wasn't family to me," says Kevin. "It was a community dominated by our church, and especially by the women in our church. We were raised by strong, religious women who were trying to teach us right from wrong. Thankfully, with Larry charting the course ahead of me, I was following the legend."

Until fourth grade, Kevin attended the tiny one-room schoolhouse on the island. Then, in fifth grade, the black school integrated with the larger, nicer white school on the island, presenting Kevin with his first experience with inequality. "We hadn't even had plumbing at our previous school, but the white school was a two-story building with a gymnasium," he remembers. "It was definitely a change, but I didn't pay too much attention."

The summer after his father left, Kevin was preparing to go to junior high school, when Larry made a surprising announcement. "My brother told me I wasn't going to Maces Lane, where the whole black community attended," he recounts. "He was sending me to Cambridge Junior High, the white school. I said I didn't want to go, but he told me he didn't care what I wanted!"

On the first day of school, Kevin was nervous. He watched as all his cousins got on the bus to head off to Maces Lane as he hustled to get to his new bus stop. "The bus went down and picked up all the white kids, but it didn't come down to my house," he says. "I had to get to the top of the road to catch it, and that first day of school, I don't know if the driver just drove straight by. I don't know if he didn't see me, or didn't want to see me, but I started walking." Kevin was soon picked up by a farm truck heading that direction. He was dropped at the edge of town, and walked a mile to get a ride from the restaurant where his mother worked. "The school spoke with the bus driver, and the next day, he picked me up and told me to sit in the very front seat," Kevin recounts. "I knew a few of the kids from fifth and sixth grade, but not one of them spoke to me."

Getting through Cambridge Junior High wasn't easy, and Kevin was beaten up by eighth graders on his second day. But over time, he began to make friends and even managed to scare the bullies away. And by the time he headed to high school, the difference in academic quality between the black and white schools became much more apparent. "I had a real 'ah ha' moment when I saw the difference in what I had learned, versus what my cousins had learned," he says, "The difference between where I was and what I had retained, versus where they were and what they had retained, was like night and day. So I saw 'separate but equal' in a whole new light. It wasn't equal, and I had far outpaced my peers."

Kevin thrived in high school, distinguishing himself with his dedication and following his brother's advice to sit in the front row and outwork the competition. As a senior, Kevin was elected Senior Class President, a huge deal in a newly integrated school. "Looking back, the problem was the parents," he recounts. "Nobody could go to anybody's home because the parents were still fighting these battles. But the kids were figuring it out, and that was powerful and important."

Kevin had done well in his small hometown, but the University of Maryland was a whole new ballgame. He didn't get any scholarships because he didn't know how to apply, so his first order of business was to head over to the financial aid office and ask about campus jobs. The director, a man named Ulysses Glee, gave him a position shelving books in the library, and then dug a little deeper into Kevin's financial situation. "He talked to me about financial aid said he'd have to see my mother's tax returns," says Kevin. "I had been doing our taxes since I was fourteen, so I had them. My mom's annual income was about $2,500 or $3,000. I didn't have any idea what other people made. And he just looked at me and said, 'You're eligible for a lot!'"

The following semester, after his epiphany on the oyster boat, Kevin returned to campus rejuvenated. That semester, he met and fell in love with his future wife, Diane. The two were at a dorm meeting in the lounge, when he first heard her voice. "I couldn't get that voice out of my head," he says. "I went to the end of the hall to see which room was hers, and I just glanced in. I think that was a classic business-developer move because I looked for something I could connect to, and I saw knitting needles. So I ended up going up to her and starting a conversation about sewing. She said, 'you sew?' And I said, 'not very well, but my mom taught me a bit. Do you sew?' and she said, 'well, I knit and crochet.' I said I wanted to learn, so she offered to teach me. And that was that! I spent the next several weeks learning how to crochet."

The couple have been married for almost 35 years now, and while Diane has been a constant source of support, Kevin is particularly grateful for the unconditional love she provided in the early days. "She saw my potential when nobody else could," he affirms. "I was just this little, black, bowlegged boy from Taylor's Island. I had two pairs of pants, and neither of them were very good. Suddenly I was smitten but not sure how it was going to go, because nobody was giving me the time of day. But she didn't care that I had nothing. She invested in me."

Diane loaned Kevin her car when he wanted to apply for a job at the mailroom at the National Institutes of Health (NIH). Ulysses Glee had told Kevin about the opportunity, saying he'd need transportation, but that the mailroom gig paid a lot better than shelving books in the library. The job turned out to be a game changer when Kevin was asked to pick up the Director of the National Library of Medicine, Dr. Cummings, from the airport. The two chatted on the ride home, and the doctor was so impressed that he called the mailroom administrators and told them to keep an eye on Kevin.

Soon, Kevin was promoted from sorting the mail to delivering the mail. On his first mail run, he came back in 20 minutes, stumping his boss. The other employees took at least an hour on the same run. He called around the building, sure that Kevin had done a sloppy job or accidentally skipped people. But no, the mail had been delivered. Kevin was simply being efficient. He also set to work reorganizing the processes in the mailroom, translating his personal knack for efficiency to the entire operation. He remembered his brother's advice, and sure enough, the strategy paid off. When Kevin graduated from Maryland with a degree in Criminal Justice in 1979, Dr. Cummings was the first one on the phone to help.

Yet again, working hard worked wonders for Kevin, and Dr. Cummings arranged for him to meet with Mary Corning, the Director of the International Programs Library. Mary asked Kevin what he might be interested in doing, but Kevin had no idea. "My only work experience until that point was in the mail room," he says. "I had had no real contact with professional people and hadn't done anything in an office. I hadn't thought about what a career looked like."

Without direction from Kevin, Ms. Corning matched him with a World Health Organization program setting up systems to deliver biomedical literature in developing countries. He was so accustomed to working harder than everyone around him that he had no trouble exceling, soon opting to go to graduate school and later completing a post-graduate program at the National Library of Medicine.

Kevin worked there until 1989, when he took a job with PSI International as a project manager supporting the Food and Drug Administration. Then, in 1993, he moved on to Computer Sciences Corporation and developed some new skill sets. "I went from working as a project manager at a small 8(a) company, to working at a large, $2 billion organization where I had the opportunity to run bigger initiatives," he recounts. "I got to see what real CFOs, COOs, and CEOs looked like, and how they behaved."

After two years at CSC, Kevin moved to BAE Systems for a technical job, but quickly demonstrated a talent for business and business development. With a personality innately suited to the task, he began learning the craft through trainings and mentors. When an important mentor, Judy Mopsik, left to take a position with Abt Associates, he followed her there and spent the next three years flourishing in business development as he helped the company through a period of transition.

Then one day, Kevin got a call from Jim Lynch at SSS. The company needed a unique technical capability to meet a client request, and Jim thought Abt Associates might be equipped to solve the client's problem. "I was brought over to consult, and I listened to what the client was trying to do," recalls Kevin. "I didn't think Abt Associates could do it, but that had never stopped me before." With that, Kevin put together a team and set about solving the problem, leaving a marked impression on Jim. He soon reached out to bring Kevin onboard at SSS, but Kevin had some questions first. "I asked him what his growth plan was, and he said they were growing between 3 and 3.5% a year," Kevin says. "I pointed out that he'd do that just with the escalation in the rates on his contracts, so why did he need me? But he reminded me that we were two very different people. I think it takes an enormous amount of courage to go out and hire someone to replace you that looks nothing like you. Jim would say, 'Kevin will go jump off a cliff just to get the rest of us to look over the edge.' I appreciated that comment, because it really does summarize how I play. I believe you have to get people outside of their comfort zones, and he was willing to do that by hiring me."

Like his brother before him, Kevin is eager to pave the way for other underprivileged kids to achieve success. That's why he chairs the Board of CollegeTracks, a group that helps guide poor students through the college application, admission, and financial aid process. They also provide coaches to help the kids get through the tough transition into college life—a transition that almost knocked Kevin off his path to success. "My brother was my CollegeTracks," he says. "If you're from a family where nobody went to college, your chances of getting there are really low because you have no idea how to navigate everything, and nobody in your family knows how to help you. That's the single biggest indicator of whether or not you'll make it to college, so we're trying to bend that curve. CollegeTracks is an opportunity to truly invest in people in a profoundly impactful way."

Today, as a leader, Kevin stays focused on the big picture, charting a course to the future of SSS. But he firmly believes that getting there must be a collaborative process. "My first objective is to hear every voice in the room," he says. "In order to do that, you have to get everybody at the table, and you have to recognize that some people have their ideas and aren't shy about sharing them. But there are other people in the room who, unless you ask them, won't necessarily give their opinion. You have to create an environment where they know they're important too. Let everybody get their voice in, and use that information to get to the best decision. The best idea has to win."

To young people entering the working world for the first time, Kevin echoes his brother's emphasis on hard work. "No employer is going to hire you to motivate you," he says. "They're going to challenge you and expect great things from you, but it's up to you to bring your personal strength and motivation with you every day." Indeed, this philosophy has taken Kevin to heights he never imagined he'd reach. But of everything he's built through the years, his proudest accomplishment began with tearing something down. "My goal was to demolish our old house and build my mother a new one," he says. "I finally accomplished that in 1990, and I'll never forget the day she called me just so I could hear the toilet flush. For the first time, we had running water, and to me, that was one of the greatest wonders of all. Everything else is just gravy on top."

BERNHARDT
WEALTH MANAGEMENT

Richard Bodson

Teamwork Makes the Dream Work

In 1972, people didn't know much about ALS. Commonly referred to as Lou Gehrig's disease, the progressive neurodegenerative disorder was still poorly understood, and treatment options were limited. That year, Richard Bodson was a first-year student at the University of Virginia. And that year, when his mother was diagnosed with the mysterious illness, his life changed forever.

At the time, ALS patients weren't expected to live more than two years past their diagnosis. But Dick's mother survived twelve, radiating positivity and hope every step of the fight. "She had a deep love and appreciation for everyone and everything," he remembers today. "It just shined through. No matter what, she believed that life was beautiful."

It wasn't only his mother's attitude in the face of adversity that shaped Dick's outlook through that period. His entire family came together, sacrificed, and prioritized his mother in her time of need.

"We all pitched in," he says. "I would come home from school to help out on weekends. My sister and brother-in-law took a hardship transfer from Buffalo, New York, where he was an FBI Special Agent in charge, putting his career on hold. Dad sacrificed tons of time at work. It was incredibly challenging, because back then there was no support for patients and families."

Hospices were not yet common, and the few that existed were too overwhelmed to take Dick's mother. Walter Reed wasn't equipped to care for her full time, but Dick's father wouldn't take no for an answer. "The deal he struck was that one of us would be there for the evening shift," explains Dick. "That way, the nurses could focus on taking care of wounded warriors and their families."

Seven years after Dick's mother passed, his father became one of the ALS Association-DC/MD/VA founders. "That was typical of my father," says Dick proudly. "When something's not right, he took action to fix it. The way the family handled all of that—by pulling together as a team to keep mom as comfortable as possible, and then taking action to try to help families and patients in the future—that's the way you conduct yourself when you're faced with challenges."

As a leader today, Dick knows that a good team is the critical difference between success and failure. In April of this year, he acquired SysNet Technologies, a cybersecurity services contracting firm, and is now President and CEO of the company. His decision to pursue the deal was based in no small part on his feeling that he and SysNet's four founders share similar values, and he expresses true admiration for the way they grew their business. "The four gentlemen—Will Poe, Tim Irvin, Tom Schubert and John Kleinhans—were all cybersecurity experts for a large business," he explains. "Then one day in 1999, they decided to do it on their own. Their biggest customer, the Federal Aviation Administration, continued with them as a small business contractor. They had learned there were many ways that IT systems were vulnerable, and had developed an expertise in analysis and risk mitigation to protect the systems."

Thanks to their distinct methodology and excellent customer service, the business grew. Yet until Dick entered the picture, they had no formal back office infrastructure. To keep costs down and focus on customer service, they did the back-office work on nights and weekends. "They did an incredible job," Dick remarks. "Now that we're establishing contracts, finance and accounting, HR, and recruiting frameworks, we can expand our critical infrastructure protection services impact."

Thanks to the tireless efforts of the four founders, SysNet Technologies is now a respected federal cybersecurity services company that provides consistently successful methodologies for risk assessment, vulnerability analysis, and mitigation plans and recommendations to clients, as well as follow-on audits to ensure vulnerabilities have been addressed. The four founders chose to sell the business when Will Poe, the former President, announced his intention to retire. "Will did most of the finance, accounting, and contracts work by putting in extra hours," says Dick. "The other three founders decided that, rather than taking on Will's many responsibilities, it would be best to sell the company to someone who could preside over its evolution without drastically restructuring it."

But the founders didn't want to sell the company to just anyone. The FAA had been one of Dick's customers for fifteen years. He knew SysNet's contracts and teammates, and quickly proved to be a perfect complementary match. Now, as CEO, Dick has plans to expand the business while maintaining the founders' commitment to doing great work. He's brought in new administrative leadership to handle the back office work, and mapped the business plan going forward—one designed for new success while preserving its culture and values. "We've relieved the founders of some of the infrastructure responsibilities so they can focus more on customer support," says Dick. "I also want to diversify the customer base while maintaining the full integrity of our FAA support."

Dick's emphasis on working together for a higher purpose stems in part from his upbringing as a U.S. Army brat. His father served the U.S. military for forty years, with 28 years spent in the Army and another 12 years at the Department. of Army, and Dick learned early on to value service and giving back. He was born in El Paso, Texas. The family soon moved to Alaska and then Ft. Sill, Oklahoma, when Dick was four. At Ft. Sill, the Bodsons were close friends with the Brown family, and Dick was particularly taken by their daughter, Barbara. Today, Barbara Brown is Dick's wife.

A few years later, Dick's father served a year in Cambodia, while the rest of the family moved to Reno, Nevada, to live near relatives. There, Dick learned to fish and spent a lot of time appreciating the great outdoors. "I learned to play sports, and we'd ride our bikes and roller skate everywhere," he recounts. "Back then, you could ride a bike through downtown Reno. It was just a gorgeous, natural place—the desert, Sierra Nevadas, Truckee River, and Pyramid Lake. I gained a great appreciation for the environment there."

The following year, the family reunited and moved to Arlington, Virginia, where they settled. The Browns were nearby, and Dick reconnected with Barbara, but their friendship remained just a friendship for years to come. He played football, ran track at his junior high school, and in high school was a competitive discus thrower. He did well academically, got his first job working as a clerk at the photo and music counter at Drug Fair, and valued his friendships deeply. "There are a bunch of us who graduated from Yorktown High, Class of 1971, who are friends today," he recounts. "We still get together regularly, and I'm thrilled to have friendships that are so rock solid."

After high school, Dick enrolled at the University of Virginia and majored in English with an equivalent Environmental Science double minor. Between running home to care for his mother, exerting himself academically, and being a Varsity Track discus thrower, he somehow found time to get heavily involved in campus volunteering. He became a tutor for Madison House, and over his college career, distinguished himself as a leader. "In my fourth year, I was asked if I would run the program," he recalls. "It was a great experience, and the first true management experience I had. I worked with wonderful, altruistic people and coordinated 250 tutors across the Charlottesville-Albemarle County public school system."

Dick went above and beyond as the leader of the tutoring organization, setting up an orientation process for new tutors and organizing a training library while developing a process for matching student needs and tutor capabilities. "We had standard business issues, but I'd never really dealt with that kind of thing before," he says. "All of a sudden one day, I was told to prepare for a presentation to the Board of Advisors at UVa to justify the money we were getting. So I put together a presentation of the processes I had put in place. They loved it and gave us more money!"

Dick graduated from UVa in 1975 and went to work for a moving company before landing his first white-collar job as a patent editor for International Computaprint Corporation in January of 1976. "We were a federal contractor," explains Dick. "When a patent landed on your desk, it had already been approved. We edited for specific language, and computer-coded the text for master tape input. That work exposed me to the IT world."

Then, in late 1978, Dick was hired as a writer and editor in the publications department of a company called Potomac Research Incorporated (PRI). Six months later, PRI was acquired by Ross Perot's company, Electronic Data Systems (EDS). Dick stayed with EDS for the next fourteen years, rising up the corporate ladder. After he demonstrated his talent for proposal writing and editing, his boss, Bill DeHart, decided Dick should get some IT training. "The next thing I knew, I was in charge of all federal, state, and local government proposal development," Dick recounts. "Then DeHart said it was time to get me into operations, so I went to work on one of his projects as Deputy Project Manager. General Motors bought us, and my boss went off to Flint, Michigan for the transition, so I became the Project

Manager. My career just kept evolving. I kept getting more and more opportunity, and Bill DeHart was always helping me."

During his years at EDS, Dick flourished personally as well as professionally, as he finally reconnected with Barbara Brown and got the courage to ask her out. "She had gone to the University of Miami because she liked warm weather," says Dick. "She stayed there for thirteen years. But one Thanksgiving she was visiting her parents, and I asked her out. We went to the movies and saw *ET*, and me being the romantic I am, I made the ultimate offer. I asked her to go bowling! All of a sudden, this woman I had been in love with my whole life was interested in me." The two continued dating and were soon married.

Then, in 1994, Dick decided to follow Bill DeHart to a company called DynCorp I&ET, where he stayed for six good years and became a Vice President until he chose to try working for a small business called RS Information Systems (RSIS). Dick jumped at the opportunity, embracing the challenge of overseeing half of the company's operations. "It was a 115-person company when I joined, and two and a half years later, we were 1,200 people," he remarks. "The 'S' in 'RS' stands for Scott Amey, and Scott and I are still good buddies today."

Dick also particularly remembers some of the veterans he brought onboard at RSIS, especially retired Air Force Colonel Jim "Bogie" Bogenrief. "I hired Bogie for his first job out of the Air Force," says Dick. "He was a war fighter, leader, and brilliant technologist. We collaborated on a lot of things. We started with a handful of people working in Colorado Springs, and a couple of years later we had grown that to 275 people. It was all business that we bid and built, and I credit Bogie with a lot of the insights that got us there. He absolutely subscribes to taking care of your customer first. I still think about how much I loved working with those folks, and what great things we did for the Air Force and other customers. There is no greater honor."

In 2002, a former RSIS employee contacted Dick about an opportunity at a company called FC Business Systems (FCBS). It was a $60 million company at the time, and Dick relished the idea of helping another small business grow. He joined FCBS as an Executive Vice President and helped expand their operations, working alongside a great CFO named Allan Shure. "Allan did a couple of acquisitions that grew the company tremendously," he remembers. "I was enamored with the Air Force, and with Defense in general, so we expanded on that and quickly became a $150 million company."

After several years of successful growth, FCBS's owner decided to put the business up for sale. In 2006, the company sold to General Dynamics, and Dick stayed on for a few months before choosing another small business opportunity. "I love being able to just collaborate with a few people, and make a decision," he says. "I was in love with small business by that point." An acquaintance from his FCBS days, John Chapel, had bought two small companies and was in the process of restructuring them as one entity, called AVIEL Systems. John offered Dick the COO position at AVIEL, and Dick, as usual, was eager to try something new.

"I'd never been a COO, but I thought, let's give it a go!" he says. "Ninety percent of our business was up for re-compete in the first year. We won all that and then began to grow. I worked with one of the best teams ever and really loved it there. In fact, when John decided to sell it in 2008, our CFO, Vince Kiernan, and I tried to convince him not to because we were having so much fun. But John knew it was time to sell, and he was right, as the economy collapsed by the time of sale."

Dick was a big believer in John's leadership by that time, and decided to follow him on his next endeavor. "John and his wife, Jinnie, had invested in a marketing and communications company called Leapfrog Solutions, so I joined that and helped them emerge in the federal marketplace," Dick recounts. "We won a $100 million FEMA contract as a $2 million company, catapulting us into federal contracting. After setting up the company for success, I broke off to consult on my own."

During the consulting period, a company called Subsystem Technologies brought Dick on to consult for six months, and ended up hiring him to be President. The company grew and Dick left in March of 2016. Barbara was undergoing breast cancer treatment and she fell, breaking both legs and ankles. Dick employed the lessons in love and home care he learned with his family taking care of his mom. He took care of Barbara full time. "Our daughter graduated from West Virginia University, and she moved back to the area to help out," says Dick. "Our son was torn up because he was in St. Petersburg, Florida, but he supported her in every way he could. Today Barbara is again healthy."

Barbara, as well, has been nothing but incredibly supportive of Dick through his long career. "She's a very compassionate, caring, and beautiful person, inside and out" he affirms. "In one company where I worked, the owner was unethical, and even though I didn't have the next job lined up, Barbara encouraged me to quit. I've always been so appreciative of that. She's always stuck with me and encouraged me."

As a leader, Dick emphasizes honesty, loyalty, and relationships above all else. "For me, the work has always been about the customers, the employees, and the teammates," says Dick. "And a customer is not just a person at the FAA; it's people on an airplane. We are all part of an ecosystem. You don't have to study environmental science to know that we're all interdependent."

To young people entering the working world today, Dick advises finding what drives you, and building on that. "Focus on what you most enjoy," he insists. "Find something valuable and productive, not just for yourself, but for others. Then try to wrap your career around that, taking on opportunities that come your way even if they aren't exactly what you had in mind. On hard days, take a deep breath and bowl through it. Do your best and know that, ultimately, that experience is going to be valuable."

Through it all, more than any destination he's reached along the way, Dick has most valued the people that have worked alongside him, inspiring hard work and great leadership. "There's always something to learn," he reminds us. "From difficult people and situations, I've learned how not to be. And from great people, I've learned great things. I've learned to stay positive, do the right thing, and be your best. Now, SysNet Technologies is the culmination of 35 years—the dream at the end of the rainbow. Teamwork makes the dream work, and I can't wait to see what we're able to accomplish together."

BERNHARDT
WEALTH MANAGEMENT

Dr. Daniel Carlin, MD

Higher Callings

On a day in late November in 1998, it was snowing in Boston, where Dr. Daniel Carlin lived. But his thoughts were far away, 900 miles off the Western Coast of South Africa, with a man sailing solo as part of the Around Alone sailboat race. Victor Yazykov had contracted a terrible infection in his arm, and his boat was damaged. Dan knew the man was in deep trouble and needed to operate on himself, but they had lost voice communication. In a last ditch effort, he turned to a mysterious new force in the world, the internet. Dan had been working with a group of sailors on ways they could use shortwave radios to access email out at sea, developing some of the earliest theories of telehealth.

Now, those theories were being put to the ultimate test, and Dan's first challenge was to write the email clearly enough that Victor would operate on himself successfully. "I went to a well-worn paradigm for how to communicate, drafting it as a recipe," he says. "I had him lay out the supplies and follow twelve steps."

An email came back letting Dan know that Victor's arm was now lifeless. His hand was white, and he couldn't close his fingers. As an afterthought, Victor mentioned he takes Aspirin daily and that he had tied a shock cord around his arm to stop the excessive bleeding. "I immediately wrote back, telling him to remove the shock cord and apply pressure instead, because otherwise he could lose his arm," Dan recalls. "Unbeknownst to us, he couldn't communicate with the outside world at night because his solar batteries couldn't hold charge. The sun had gone down by that point, and I heard nothing back."

Powerless to do anything more, Dan joined his wife and kids at the Frog Pond, a little skating rink in the city. He remembers the surreal feeling of the snow on his face and the laughter of his family, all muted by the truth in the back of his mind: he had no way to know whether Victor was alive or dead.

At 4:15 the next morning, Dan got a call from the sailboat race headquarters. The sun was back up in the South Atlantic, and Victor had received Dan's last message in time. The procedure had been successful. "For me, that was the shot heard 'round the world," Dan says. "It was also the fruition of a lot of theoretical thinking I had done about the power of the internet and the potential of telehealth. In that moment, I saw the big picture. I knew in my heart that our world had reached a pivotal inflection point, and that I had found my higher calling."

A voracious student of history, Dan knew how the invention of the movable type printing press in the 1450s had revolutionized medicine. As books were printed and shared across wide geographical areas, Latin became the common language of medicine. Archaic, ineffective therapies were scrutinized and retired, while good therapies were honed and embraced. "Because of that inflection point, we've had more medical progress in the past couple hundred years than we had in the whole history of our species combined," Dan says.

In the 1990s, as Dan poured through books like *Being Digital* by Nicholas Negroponte and *The Discoverers* by Daniel Boorstein, he followed closely the developments of the internet and saw the world on the precipice of another medical revolution. As medicine became digitized, its new language would be binary—easily and instantaneously transmitted across great geographic and linguistic divides. At the time, Dan was testing the limits of this new technological frontier at the New England Medical Center, where he was remotely managing a large telemedicine project in West Africa. "We were serving a workforce of 2,000 men at a construction site in Ghana," he explains. "There was a trailer clinic and sick bay on the ground with a nurse practitioner who would send me cases by satellite phone and email."

As the project began to wrap up in 1998, one of the Medical Center's board members, Nancy Hawthorn, joined forces with Dan in raising $2.5 million to launch WorldClinic Inc., originally conceived as a telemedicine practice for ships and other remote places. They hit the ground running in early 1999, building the care system and then working to establish the product-to-market fit. They succeeded in securing several clients, but by April of 2000, the dotcom bust had caused the markets to collapse and constrict. "We were depending on a second round of investment that never came," Dan recalls. "I was transitioning from the world of medicine and academia to the world of entrepreneurship—a steep learning curve rendered much steeper by those tough market forces."

One of the most powerful moments of his career came days before the investors were scheduled to close the company. Dan approached them personally and asked them to hand WorldClinic back to him so he could try to make it work with what he had. At first they said no, but Dan took a hardline approach, reminding them that keeping a promise to patients was non-negotiable.

Finally, the investors agreed, setting up a compensation schedule in the event he went on to sell the company in the future. "When we closed the deal, I signed document after document and reflected on what it was like in the beginning, with so many people around offering support and encouragement," he says. "Boston isn't like Silicon Valley, where failure is a celebrated part of the process toward hitting it out of the park. It's a much more conservative atmosphere that expects immediate results. I thought about that expression—*success has many fathers; failure but one*. In that moment, I was the one father of this failure."

And in that moment that his business was left for dead, something ignited in Dan—a deep, relentless drive to become un-killable. He taught himself finance, marketing, and management while working two jobs as an emergency physician to support his family. His resolve was reinforced along the way by experiences like one he had in 2000, when he received an email about a young pregnant woman in Russia who had been diagnosed with a mysterious illness. She was told by her doctor that she had to abort her baby, but was desperate to find another way. Dan investigated, only to discover that the woman only had Lyme Disease. It posed no threat to her unborn child, and with a month of antibiotics, she would be fine. "I wrote the email in English and converted it to Cyrillic with a web translator," he recounts. "Because our communication was digital, the impossible was possible, and a life was saved."

With no money to pay employees, Dan looked at software that could help make his processes faster and cleaner. He didn't realize it at the time, but he was building a foundation for scalability. He was also undergoing the transformation from physician to entrepreneur—a mental paradigm shift that cast hard truths into nuanced ambiguities. "I had no particular desire to be a CEO, but it's the role I needed to assume, and I came to understand that it's a role of many dimensions," he says. "As a CEO, you must become adept at creating perception through information management, which was a totally new thing for me."

Dan's father grew up in Brooklyn as the son of a bar manager, fighting the odds and making it to medical school. Both of his parents taught him to be tough as nails, with no crying and no moral gray areas in life. "Their values helped get me through that trying time," Dan affirms.

Growing up in the 1960s in Dalton, a small town in the Berkshires of western Massachusetts, he learned the nuance and importance of bedside manner at an early age from his father, the town doctor. "For the average person, he was the beginning and the end of healthcare," Dan recounts. "At that time, so much of medicine was human-to-human, where it was the doctor's job to understand the patient's context, behavior, and thinking. By joining my father for house calls, I learned that being a doctor was about communicating expertly, listening closely, and being a great diagnostician without resorting to a lab or a CAT scan."

As a kid, Dan was struck by how important his father was to the people of Dalton, and how he treated everyone with the same respect and dignity, regardless of their stature in life. Farmers, mechanics, and the rural poor received the same treatment as the wealthy family that owned the paper mill in town. "The egalitarian ethos of his practice really impacted me," Dan says.

Dan was the second of six children, and the only to take an interest in medicine. He took an early interest in science and reading. When he was in third grade, his father decided he wanted to switch from general medicine to neurology, so the family moved to Boston for his internship and residency. They settled in a gritty neighborhood where kids constantly picked fights, and Dan longed for Dalton until seventh grade, when his father landed a job in New Jersey. "From then on, growing up was idyllic," he remembers. "I made best friends with a group of ten kids, and we did everything together."

To make spending money, Dan cut grass and shoveled snow. He loved working and being active, and spent three summers working as a golf caddie until he got his driver's license and got a job as a delivery boy. Though he found school intellectually boring and preferred to read smart novels about adventurers who used science to travel the world, he did well academically and especially enjoyed his brazen and unconventional French teacher. "He constantly reminded us that you don't have to take the path you think you have to take in life," says Dan. "He urged us to take risks and live our own lives. I wrote him a letter from Afghanistan years later to thank him for that."

Dan had always planned to be a doctor and pursued college at Carnegie Mellon, an engineering school that shaped his outlook and taught him how to examine today through the lens of tomorrow. He majored in chemistry with a pre-med track—a demanding course load that grew more challenging when he decided to get a second degree in philosophy as well. He also joined the Pi Kappa Alpha fraternity, which provided an avenue to unwind and develop close friendships in the otherwise high-stress environment.

Compared to Carnegie Mellon, medical school at Tufts was relatively easy. Dan secured a Naval scholarship to help alleviate the financial burden, and he spent his third year working at Bay State Medical Center in Springfield, Massachusetts. He completed a general surgery internship at Bethesda Naval Hospital and went out on the *USS Mississippi*, providing care to sailors. His Chief Petty Officer at the time, Gary McLoud, drove home the point that he was now a role model for others. "Once I grasped that point, I became the officer we both wanted me to be," Dan laughs. "Being a Naval officer was definitely one of the high points of my young life, clouded only by the passing of my father while I was at sea."

Dan left the Navy on June 21, 1998, and a couple days later set off for Peshawar, Pakistan. "After traveling the world with the Navy, I couldn't just get back to life as I had known it before," he recounts. "I decided to take a year off to do what I really wanted to do, which was becoming a refugee doctor. It was a total immersion into dirt, disease, violence, polio, leprosy, tuberculosis, and every parasite imaginable—very challenging, but incredibly rewarding. And on Friday nights we'd go to the American club in Peshawar, which attracted expats and civil servants from all over the region. It was an incredible experience."

After six months, Dan came home to the United States with plans to head to Pakistan, when he crossed paths with a remarkable young woman named Lisa. "She was happy, excited about her work, and plugged into a big world, with this gentle and kind touch," Dan remembers. "I thought she was impressive as hell." They immediately hit it off, and because she was slated to leave for a project in Kenya, he signed up for a project in South Sudan. They lived together happily in Mombasa until one day in February of 1989, when Dan boarded a small twin engine high-wing aircraft headed to Juba, Sudan. There, he was to join a UN food convoy headed to a town that had been captured by rebels and was teetering on the brink of a humanitarian crisis.

As the plane crossed the border into South Sudan, Dan looked out the port side window and saw oil hemorrhaging from the engine. They made an emergency landing in the middle of nowhere and replaced the oil return hose, which had come off the engine block. Just then, a small speck appeared on the horizon and began heading toward them. They held their breath, knowing the approaching van was either benign friend or deadly foe. Fortunately, it was a group of allies willing to drive them the rest of the way to Juba while the pilot took the plane home. Before the pilot took off, however, Dan was struck with a feeling and decided to check the other engine, just to be safe. It, too, had a loose oil return hose, and the men realized that someone had tried to kill them.

The incident had caused a substantial delay, and by the time they reached Juba by van, the convoy had left without them. Much to their surprise, however, it came tearing back several hours later. The convoy had been ambushed, with two people killed and several more wounded. One man died as Dan was administering medical care. "I think about that day sometimes, and how there's no point in trying to predict why bad things happen or how they might have been avoided," he says. "One near-death experience saved me from an almost-certain-death experience, and I'm just grateful to be here today. It keeps things in perspective, and I feel incredibly lucky."

After four months in East Africa, Dan and Lisa moved back to the United States and got married. Dan completed a three-year emergency medicine residency with Columbia in Morristown, New Jersey, and then took a job in Watsonville, California, only to realize he much preferred the East Coast. They moved back in 1995, and Dan worked as a conventional community emergency room physician until restlessness compelled him to start a medical practice for people who spent substantial periods of time at sea. "I convinced my hospital to act as a call center for me, and I started writing medical columns for sailor publications," he recounts. "I opened my first business as Voyager Medicine, providing care to people as they traveled all over the world. That effort eventually became WorldClinic."

Today, WorldClinic provides reliable medical care to globetrotting families and business executives. While the broken state of U.S. healthcare erodes the doctor-patient relationship by undermining meaningful primary care, WorldClinic embraces thoughtful, accountable, data-driven medicine, and makes it available to people anywhere in the world. The company is now transitioning from a virtual emergency room to a cutting-edge primary care practice that serves as a connected longevity platform in its ability to identify and stave off health risks. Acting as a proof-of-concept, WorldClinic is an affirmation of what's possible in the brave new world of digital medicine. "With a person's genome, I can quickly determine their lifetime plan and the things I should be monitoring, tracking, and managing so they can avoid the heart attack they would otherwise get at age 61," he says. "The future of digital medicine is absolutely transformative, and it's a future I can attest to because I've lived it."

In advising young people entering the working world today, Dan observes that most truly successful people never stop learning. With rigorous intellectual curiosity, they remain open to everything and are willing to take on even dry, dense material if they believe it's essential. "In this world that's constantly evolving, find a place where you can do your thing to your best possible expression," he encourages. "Try to find work that can't be automated or outsourced overseas, and remember that what you do is an expression of the divinity and God within you. There's spectacular stuff in all of us, and it's important to get in touch with it if you want to have a great life."

Dan also reminds us that, while jobs are certainly important, family is ultimately the most important thing in life. He and Lisa now have four daughters. "Lisa taught me how to be a good father to girls, since I grew up one of five boys," he laughs. "She rounded out my hard edges and taught me that there are times to be tough, and times to enjoy life. Thanks to her, I'm more complete in all it is to be human. We just do better when we're with someone we love."

Beyond that, Dan's work reminds us that the pursuit of a higher calling does more than change your life—it can change your world. In leveraging smartphones, technology, and advancing understanding of the human genome, he is proving that healthcare must be more than just responding to health problems—it must be about preventing them. "I'm a person of deep, abiding faith," he says. "I'm constantly driven by a sense of purpose. If I didn't have that level of spiritual, emotional, and intellectual commitment, I don't think I could do what I do. In my darkest moment, I reminded myself that if I gave up, the idea would die, along with countless people in the coming years who wouldn't get the life-saving benefit of the treatments it enables. A higher calling will carry you through the ups and downs, and ultimately into the better world you help to build with your own two hands."

BERNHARDT
WEALTH MANAGEMENT

Piper Phillips Caswell

A Champion for Every Child

Years before her father founded PHILLIPS Programs for Children & Families (PHILLIPS), a nonprofit that began as a special needs school on Old Chain Bridge Road in McLean, Virginia, Piper Phillips Caswell decided to start a school of her own. At age ten, she outfitted the small garden house in her backyard with a blackboard, bulletin board, and several small desks. She walked around the neighborhood on Saturday mornings, rounding up whatever children were willing to come. "The only admissions criteria was that you had to be a grade lower than me," she laughs today.

One of Piper's students happened to have cerebral palsy, and another had a learning disability. She welcomed them just the same, taking on the responsibility of their education without question. "I've always had a passion for giving children the opportunity and encouragement that makes for a positive upbringing and a good educational experience," she says. "Every child deserves a champion, and I've always been most attracted to those children with significant social, emotional, and behavioral challenges." Now the President and CEO of PHILLIPS, Piper continues to serve as that champion at the helm of an organization that has dedicated itself to the success of those very children.

Launched in 1967 as a school program serving four students of very different primary diagnoses, PHILLIPS began as a microcosm of the more expansive organization it has grown into today. At that time, there was no federal law ensuring every child the right to a free and appropriate education, regardless of disability, and the organization has been a trailblazer from the beginning.

PHILLIPS still operates according to the foundational model Piper's father charted out at the organization's inception, though some of its services have evolved over time. When it outgrew the small house Piper's father had bought for the program's operation, he bought the house next to it. By the third year, positive referrals had grown their enrollment to seventy students. They began renting space in the basement of a church in downtown McLean, and then expanded to locations in Falls Church, Alexandria, and Springfield, Ellicott City, and Baltimore. PHILLIPS now owns two campuses in Annandale and Laurel, and in 2016 took over a program in Fairfax to create a third campus. It also acquired a non-public career and technical education program, which allows them to teach in-demand skills to high school youth at risk of dropping out of school. PHILLIPS also provides intensive home-based services throughout Northern Virginia in their Family Partners program.

Through advocacy, education, and family services, PHILLIPS now serves over 500 youth annually, with challenges that reflect a broad range of diverse needs. Whether Piper's team is championing a child with a disorder on the autism spectrum, a mental health issue, a trauma manifesting in a difficult way, or something else, the PHILLIPS approach is unique in that it doesn't try to fit a child into a program—rather, it fits the program around the child. "The vast majority of the time, our students are referred to us and funded by the public schools," Piper says. "The county has identified them as eligible for special education services, but lacks the resources and expertise required for their level of behavioral health needs. Our partnership allows the county to provide the whole continuum of service."

PHILLIPS now has a staff of 275 people and an operating budget of $20 million, comprised of county, state, federal, and private fundraising dollars. While staying true to their time-tested strategies, the organization is also pivoting to innovative approaches to career and technical education and workforce development for youth with behavioral health needs. "We currently rely on public agencies for that work," Piper says. "The results are decent, but we can do more. Today, you're two to four times more likely to be unemployed if you have a disability. That future just isn't bright enough for our youth, so we're doing something about it."

Embracing a co-op model, PHILLIPS is adding a culinary arts and urban agriculture program, including a vertical farm for growing microgreens. "Through this 'Growing Futures' program, our students can learn work skills while addressing social justice issues like food deserts," Piper notes. "We've also partnered on a 'Designing Futures' program to help youth on the autism spectrum enter the IT and cybersecurity space. And our 'Building Futures' program allows our students to build houses that we sell on the open market. I'm so proud that we're thriving after fifty years of service, and that our leadership team and board are willing to go outside our comfort zone to pursue these new avenues that will allow us to serve even more Opportunity Youth going forward."

To her core, Piper has been shaped for the unique challenges and opportunities of the PHILILPS legacy from the time she was a young girl growing up in the City of Falls Church. Her father was a behavioral psychologist and professor at George Washington University who had studied under B.F. Skinner, and Piper's views on working with children were fundamentally shaped by his philosophy. He actively pursued his wide-ranging interests, including offering a tutoring service when she was very little and running a private practice several days a week while operating the counseling center at the University. "My father always said, 'early to bed, early to rise, makes a man healthy, wealthy, and wise,'" she remembers. "He was humble, driven, and truly dedicated to helping other people. I don't admire anyone more than I admire him and how he lived his life."

Piper also developed an early interest in activism through the influence of her mother, a member of the League of Women Voters who regularly took Piper along when she handed out leaflets. Growing up in the 1960s near Washington, DC, some of the nation's most momentous inflection points were defining moments in her own life. She was in third grade when her elementary school desegregated, and she remembers her parents' instructions over dinner to be friendly and welcoming to the new children who joined her class. "They told us what a good thing it was," she says. "Later, after Martin Luther King Jr.'s assassination and the riots that ensued, they took us into DC to see the aftermath of the riots and the subsequent building of Resurrection City on the Mall. Those kinds of experiences set the stage for my social activism and advocacy, which has been a defining aspect of my life."

As the second of four children, Piper enjoyed roller skating, bicycling, climbing trees, and exploring the woods around her home. The family ate dinner together every night at 6:45, where they would listen to the news. An avid reader, she loved elementary school. "I've always been my father's daughter in that we shared similar interests," she reflects. "I've also always been a doer, like starting my own school and setting up carnivals in our backyard to fundraise for muscular dystrophy."

By all accounts, Piper's childhood was idyllic, but her early exposure to a string of untimely deaths taught her how fragile and unexpected life can me. One of her best friends, a young boy named Davey who lived down the street, went to the school nurse one day complaining of a headache. He was rushed to the hospital and passed away two days later of a brain hemorrhage. "We were only in fourth grade, and it was a defining moment in realizing that you never really know if someone's going to be here tomorrow," she reflects. President Kennedy was assassinated that same year, and Piper still remembers her parents taking the children into DC for the funeral march.

A year and a half later, Davey's mother died of the same ailment, and several years after that, her older brother's girlfriend passed away. "Those experiences had a big impact on me, creating this sense of urgency that touches everything I do," she says. "My parents were Midwesterners who taught us to always save for a rainy day. But for me, it's equally important to seize the moment and enjoy life now because tomorrow might not come."

Amidst these traumas, life went on. When Piper was in middle school, her father bought the first PHILLIPS house, and all four children would pitch in on Sunday mornings as janitors and cleaners—work rewarded by a trip out for ice cream. In middle school, the family moved to Oakton, which was decidedly more rural and conservative than Falls Church. When Piper missed a day of Spanish class during her sophomore year to protest the Kent State shooting, her teacher dropped her grade by a full letter—a move that infuriated her parents. When she returned home that fall after a summer living in Mexico with a group led by a Unitarian minister, she finished her junior and senior years at a different school. "For my parents, activism was so much more than just dinner table talk," she says.

In Oakton, Piper became more active in the Unitarian Church and joined a group called the Liberal Religious Youth, which she helped rename the Liberal Rebellious Youth. They dove into the most pressing issues of the day, including Vietnam War protests and advocacy for young farmworkers. "It was an important time where I truly grasped that we each have a voice," she recounts. "We have a responsibility as citizens to be engaged in what's going on and to make our voices heard.

It's one of those fundamental rights that was enshrined at the very founding of our country."

Piper's activism was matched by her volunteerism—something her parents also encouraged. In middle school, she spent her summers working with underprivileged youth, and in high school she volunteered with PHILLIPS three days a week while helping out every Sunday at her church. "The importance of volunteering is something I try to instill in my own children now," she says. "You can do whatever kind of service you like, as long as you find a way to give back."

When she graduated from high school, Piper enrolled at Peabody College in Nashville, only to find that freshman girls had curfews while the boys did not. Busy with her work on the McGovern presidential campaign, she ignored the rules and had to go before disciplinary boards. After her first semester, she transferred to George Washington University, which allowed her to intern at PHILLIPS. She began working there as a floating substitute assistant teacher in her sophomore year, and when the school needed a full-time floating sub, Piper took the job and finished her bachelors degree part-time through evening and summer classes.

When she graduated with a degree in education, Piper was able to move into a full teaching position at PHILLIPS while getting her masters in special education at Johns Hopkins University. When she completed that program in 1980, she decided she needed a break from the education field. She began volunteering for Ted Kennedy's presidential campaign, where she landed a job until he lost the Democratic nomination to Jimmy Carter. After helping to close down the campaign, she worked several more years in politics before resuming her career in special education.

Over the next several decades, Piper worked with a wide range of populations in an array of capacities. Through her late twenties, as the de-institutionalization movement swept the region and clients were moved out into the community, she ran a new program in DC and began setting up community-based group homes for adults with intellectual and developmental disabilities. She then worked for a Community Services Board, and at that time, Fairfax County regulations required that she hold a meeting to essentially secure permission for such homes from the surrounding neighborhood. "The people who showed up did not understand the concept and opposed it because they were afraid," she remembers. "But we can't decide who else moves into our neighborhood, so why should people with disabilities be treated any differently? That regulation has since changed, but it was disheartening at the time, and reinforced my resolve to be an advocate."

Under a tremendous amount of pressure, Piper learned how to hire, train, and manage staff, rent houses, apply for Community Development Block Grant funding, and manage real estate. She served as Director of Residential Services for the Lt. Joseph P. Kennedy Institute, where she cemented her leadership skills as she helped expand the program. Some of the educational and community based experiences still color the way she looks at the judicial system. "It was shocking to see how many youth, who have disabilities, end up in the school to prison pipeline," she recalls.

When she wasn't working, Piper nurtured another passion, baking. She earned several certificates and trained as a pastry chef at L'Academie de Cuisine. For a number of years, she operated a catering business on the side and sold her carrot cakes to CF Folks in DC, a bakery near the Washington Cathedral and a gourmet grocery store by the State Department. "Starting that business informed her on the courage and tenacity one needs to start a small business," she recalls. "I learned a lot about what not to do, and would likely do it differently now." Piper pursued her entrepreneurial drive further in 2003 when, after searching for school programs that matched the particular needs of some youth, she established a private school which was approved by MSDE. While she chose not to continue its operation, developing the program and shepherding it through the approval process inspired another program to establish a school operating where her program did formerly. Both of these endeavors inspire her now as PHILLIPS' vision develops.

When Piper's father passed away in 1994, she joined the board of trustees for PHILLIPS, where she served for fourteen years while holding positions at several non-public special education schools. Also through that time, Piper and her husband, Phil, adopted two children. And though both children came with their unique needs, Piper wouldn't change a thing. "From the moment I met them, I was totally in love," she says. "They brought something into my life that nothing else ever had. They are both great kids, and as a special educator, it was life-defining for me to also experience this world from the side of a parent. I've lived it, and that informs me in a very different way than a lot of people in the profession."

Through her career in human services and special education, Piper had chosen not to ascend to a top executive role because the needs of her children had required her to be fully present. But when the long-time CEO of PHILLIPS retired after over forty years with the organization, Piper threw her hat in the ring amidst a national search for a successor, and was selected to fill the role in 2013. "My son had graduated from high school by then, so I thought, now is the time," she recounts. "I loved PHILLIPS because it has such a strong culture, which shaped me at the very beginning of my career. And I loved that it wasn't just about the Monday-through-Friday educational piece. I knew it would allow me to grow our services to meet the needs that are so prevalent."

Now, as a leader, Piper is oriented around mentoring and guiding her team members toward success. "This is not a one-person endeavor," she affirms. "I couldn't push any of these programs forward without our incredible team, and without the help of outside organizations who have been willing to partner with us. And I couldn't have done it without the people who have mentored and encouraged me along the way, serving as examples for how to succeed."

Piper treasures the help, growth, and support of others in her personal life as well. While the love and counsel of her childhood best friend have been irreplaceable, she also credits her husband for his partnership and care along the way. "Phil is laid-back, solid, and reliable," she says. "He has always been supportive of what I want to do. Through the emotional, psychological, and financial challenges of raising our kids, we've helped to hold each other up and make it through. That's a very special thing."

In advising young people entering the working world today, Piper underscores the importance of courage and action. "Just go for it," she says. "It's okay to make mistakes and for things to not work out, because you learn a lot from failure. I see so many people who play it safe and miss out. Don't be afraid to brush yourself off, analyze what went wrong, and try again. If I hadn't, I certainly wouldn't have my dream job today."

Beyond that, Piper's story is an homage to lifetime legacies and true callings. In the vision of her father, empowered by her own innate affinity for special needs children, she has found a way to magnify her impact and advocate better for those who really need her. "There isn't a child out there I don't adore," she affirms. "No matter how tough they are. Most people don't want to work with the most complex kids, so for those of us who are drawn to such challenges, it's important that we pursue them. There have to be champions for every kind of child, and PHILLIPS youth are it for me."

BERNHARDT
WEALTH MANAGEMENT

Brian Chavis

The Modern Fire Quencher

By now, Brian Chavis is very familiar with the look of deep gratitude that fills the eyes of the elders who come to see him when he visits family in Pembroke, North Carolina. Sometimes they come with drafting books in hand—the tools his father used many years ago in teaching them how to build a bridge out of poverty.

As one of two of the first Native American pilots in the Army Air Corps, Brian's father was a hero. He was captain of the basketball team at the North Carolina College for Indians, and because he was one of the tribe's best and brightest, he was sent to college and to Detroit, where he landed a position at General Motors. He did all this not with the goal of getting out, but with the goal of giving back. "For the tribe members who left to pursue success elsewhere, it was their duty to help others from the community with a hand up," Brian explains. "That was just how the culture worked."

One by one, his father's friends came to Detroit to live with him and his wife while they started jobs at GM. Once they made it into the factory, they set their sights on advancing to a desk job. "The only way you could really do that as a working-class person was to learn mechanical drafting," Brian explains. "So my father would have classes at his house to teach them. Now, all these years later, people still come up to me with tears in their eyes to tell me how my father changed their lives."

Brian's mother was five months pregnant with him when his father died of a chronic illness, so they never met on Earth. But for that brief interval between one's departure and the other's arrival, father and son knew each other on the other side. "The elders tell me my father and I were together in the spirit world, and that it gave me special powers," Brian says today. "They tell me I'm a fire quencher."

Now the Managing Partner of BoltMSP (formerly known as ARGroup before it was rebranded as BoltMSP), a managed services provider (MSP) with a commitment to robust, proactive care of client IT needs, Brian brings the everyday special powers of excellence, expertise, and care to companies across the DC metropolitan area. And he has become a community leader in his own rite, mastering the art of leadership and problem solving through his work as Chairman and Board Member of the Loudoun County Chamber of Commerce. When he found out there was no medical care available to poor people in the area, he became a founding board member of the Loudoun Community Health Center (Heathworks)—now the biggest in the area. As the Chairman of the County's Economic Development Authority, he signed a $195 million federal loan to finance the extension of the Metro's Silver Line to Loudoun. And today, he continues his work on a deal for a $30 million affordable housing project. This is what fire quenching looks like in modern-day Northern Virginia—a subtle kind of heroism that leaves the whole community better off.

Brian founded BoltMSP in 1986, and today, the company provides holistic computer support and security packages to companies of between twenty and a hundred people. Operating on a per-seat price rather than hourly contracts, their technicians are able to freely invest the time they need to do the most thorough, effective work for their clients. "We're not some absent MSP that only comes by when there's a problem," Brian says. "We're a high-end service that's actively engaged on a daily basis, remoting in to manage our clients' computers so that when we send someone on site, they come with a list of security items to check and re-check to ensure everything runs smoothly."

Cybersecurity is a top item of concern for BoltMSP, so they ensure their clients have the appropriate password controls. They check to make sure data is backed up and that cloud-based infrastructure is secure. Thanks to the automated systems they've implemented, BoltMSP is now a team of eight people that are exponentially more productive than the sum of their parts. "I knew tech people had a reputation for being frustrating for people who don't know tech very well, particularly very successful people who are incredibly busy and don't have the time to develop an intuitive understanding of tech," he says. "So when I started my company, I always said that we'd be the computer service guys with a smile. I wanted to teach young people in tech how to deal with all these different personalities in their moments of frustration, showing them how to diffuse stress and guide people to a place of calm and understanding. I like to hire young people that are 'people' people, not just hardware people. I love being a troop leader and helping them develop those skills."

Looking back on his life, Brian marvels at how we spend so much time fretting over the decisions we make, yet it's the random events—the ones we have no control over—that most shape our futures. Had Brian's father lived, for instance, Brian likely would have grown up in an upper-middle class neighborhood in Detroit. Instead his father passed in a Detroit hospital with a blizzard whipping outside, leaving his young, pregnant wife alone in the world. She left her life as a 1950's housewife and moved back to her hometown of Marion, Indiana, where Brian was born. "It's really remarkable that she stood up to all that and figured out a way to persevere," he says. "She got a job at a chain factory and was essentially the breadwinner through my entire childhood."

Three years later, the strong, stoic, Midwestern woman married Gene, who struggled with jobs and alcohol. They lived in a rough neighborhood in Indianapolis, where Gene later bought a small tavern. "He ran numbers, booked horses, sold liquor, and held card games," Brian recalls. "And my mother was a member of the United Steelworkers. Her fingers were always black from her work, and I remember her being active in the union."

Brian grew up with an older brother, two younger half-sisters, and a younger half-brother. Gene and Brian had daily conflicts, so Brian focused more on important relationships with his father's community in North Carolina. He remembers annual Christmas phone calls with Uncle Ray, his father's brother and the patriarch of the family that kept things together. "That was an important bond," Brian recalls. "He never let us fall out of touch and always made sure I knew I was an important part of their family."

The Indianapolis streets simmered with racism in the late 1960s. Bobby Kennedy even came to speak at Brian's school in an attempt to bring tolerance to a community that kept burning down the new housing projects being built nearby. A week later, he was assassinated. Times were tough through Brian's childhood, and as a result, he grew up street-smart and always hustling. His parents provided shelter, food, and clothes, but when he wanted anything beyond the bare minimum, it was up to him to figure it out. He sold newspapers, mowed lawns, and worked twelve-hour days on his teacher's horse farm.

His most impressive venture, however, came once a year when hundreds of thousands of people from all over the world stormed into town for the Indianapolis 500. "When I was ten, my brother Carl and I snuck into the track," Brian recounts. "By the time I was twelve, we had figured out that we could buy newspapers at a secret location at 4:00 AM for seven cents apiece. The roads were filled with cars at the time, all waiting for the gates to open at 6:00 AM. We'd walk through the traffic selling papers for 25 cents, spend the day at the track watching all kinds of crazy shenanigans, and then go to another secret location where a helicopter dropped down the hot-off-the-presses flash finals. We'd stuff 150 of those into our bags and then sell them, returning home at the end of the day with a hundred dollars' worth of quarters in our pockets. I've never felt so rich in my life as I did on those days!"

In many ways, fending for himself and looking for entrepreneurial opportunities amidst the chaotic Indy 500 crowd was a defining experience for Brian. He knew there was a world beyond Indianapolis because he saw it invade the city once a year before dispersing out to all the places he had never been. Realizing he could make money through entrepreneurship was like seeing the door to the rest of the world, and Brian wanted to open it. He joined Junior Achievement to begin honing his life experience and competitive edge.

When Brian entered high school, his family moved from the inner city, landing him in the largest school in the state with class sizes of around 900 kids. He played on the basketball team, took drafting classes like his father, and earned stellar grades, finishing second out of 700 graduates. He had wanted to be an architect from the time he was twelve, so with the scholarship money he earned, he enrolled at Ball State's School of Architecture. "At the time, I had no idea that I got my drafting skills from my father," Brian says. "He was an engineer, and I inherited that."

In college, Brian made the volleyball team as a freshman, where he had the opportunity to work with Dr. Don Shondell, a celebrated Hall of Fame coach. But architecture was all-absorbing, so he ended up quitting the team and joining a fraternity flag football league instead. In his sophomore year, he collided with another player and broke his shoulder, which meant he could no longer draft. Dejected at first, it then dawned on him that he could take computer science classes because he could type one-handed. "If I hadn't broken my shoulder, I may never have gotten into IT," he points out.

Brian graduated with a degree in Environmental Design and a minor in Computer Science, and went to work at an architectural firm in Indianapolis. He then got a fellowship to get his master's in architecture at the University of Illinois, provided that he earn a business degree at the same time. He completed those degrees in three years, balancing the work with a job developing CAD software at an Army construction engineer research lab. The work sometimes took him to CAD trade shows, where he met a startup company that offered him a software programming job in McLean, Virginia. He accepted and made the move in 1983, opting to live in downtown DC because it felt more his style.

The company ultimately failed in 1986 but was still in need of consulting services, so Brian signed on to do that. When several other companies enlisted him for CAD help, he decided he had pieced together enough money to incorporate, and BoltMSP was born. He sold and set up PCs, and because CAD was the first application that pushed people to network their computers, he learned to set up networks as well. He enjoyed running his own business for the next eighteen months, until a government contracting client convinced him to come launch a computer division in his company.

Brian made decent money at that company and liked the work well enough, but something felt off. In 1990, the same week his boss bought his second Ferrari, Brian decided to take a trip to North Carolina to clear his head with family. "It's a different culture there, where the layers are peeled back and you can see the truth," he says. "I realized I wanted to have my own business again, and that I was ready to go for it. As soon as I returned to DC, I quit my job and began sending tri-fold flyers around the city to let people know I could help with computer problems."

Offering fixed-price services for minor and major repair, and with his own hand-drawn cartoon on the front of the flyer, Brian landed ten to fifteen clients within his first couple months of business. Carrying just a backpack of cables, memory cards, other gear, and a large cellular phone, he would metro around the city to call on his clients—often small nonprofits and trade associations struggling with the advent of computers and workplace tech. "I thought I was so cool!" he laughs.

At that time, organizations were just starting to use spreadsheets and software to manage their internal list and procedures. And as they did, Brian became mission-critical. He evolved with the times, moving from custom application development to web-based services. When he realized he was making a mistake by competing with big advertising firms, he pivoted back to network and security services. He went to happy hours downtown, meeting people and handing out his card. "People were so frustrated with computers all the time, so all I had to do was stay motivated," he remembers. "I think somewhere deep down, I always had this fear that I was an underachiever—a remnant of growing up without a living constructive male role model in my life."

Brian's internal drive continued to lead him to remarkable professional success in his business, but by the time he reached his thirties, he thought marriage and children weren't in the cards for him. All that changed on a December day in 1994, when he accompanied a client to a Washington Bullets basketball game. At some point that evening, he realized they were on a date, and after the game, they ended up at a bar on Capitol Hill. But it was Amy, a different girl, who ended up getting in his car that evening, and the two have been together ever since. "I have friends that have never been married, so I just figured I was in that category," he says. "But Amy was the one, and now we're married with wonderful kids. I still have the ticket from that basketball game."

Brian's life took another dramatic turn when, in 1995, he ran into a random acquaintance who tipped him off about a tech-related RFP in Loudoun County. Though he knew nothing about Loudoun County at the time, he decided to submit a bid, and was surprised to then find out that he had a connection to the county's Head of IT. The man knew the area was poised for rapid growth, and wanted a contract for high-volume computer installation in their offices on an annual basis. Having done similar work for Prince George's County in the past, Brian landed the contract—a defining moment that changed the course of his future in unimaginable ways.

Brian and Amy were both city people who loved their lives on Capitol Hill, but they took the plunge and made the move to dreaded suburbia. And looking back, they couldn't have made a better decision. The contract transformed the BoltMSP, allowing it to scale for the first time and lending an element of security that persists even now, in its twentieth year and counting. The move to Loudoun also opened the doors for Brian to embrace his role in the community, a crucial step on the journey to becoming the leader he is today.

Along the way, Amy has always been free-thinking and artistic, and was never concerned by the risks of Brian's entrepreneurial living. Her easygoing attitude creates a positive, stress-free culture in the family, which became particularly important when Brian decided to sell the business in 2013. "I think that, at the time, I was lonely and struggling with direction," he says. "I knew that if we were going to grow, we needed a sales engine. I had paid off all my long-term debt by that time and was considering taking out a big loan to get things moving, but I was also approached by United Business Technologies (UBT). UBT had a big sales team selling copiers to an existing client base of a thousand businesses in the Washington region, so they convinced me to sell BoltMSP. All the copier companies were merging with IT companies at the time so they could handle all office tech. It was a great idea in theory, but once we went through with it, everything fell apart."

The new business struggled as it tried to merge the IT company culture of BoltMSP—more geared toward innovative, high-demand millennials—with the copier company culture of UBT, characterized by harsh sales quotas and high churn. Then, three months into the new arrangement, Brian was diagnosed with prostate cancer. He stepped aside from the business for the surgery and subsequent recovery period—a difficult time, but an experience that reconnected Brian and Amy in an incredibly deep and meaningful way. She came to all his appointments, and when he was able to walk again, they started going to noon-time movies together. Considering possible next moves, they discussed flipping houses or operating a food truck. "I came to realize, though, that I actually most wanted to do exactly what I had been doing all along—leading BoltMSP to success," he says.

A forthright, honest leader who often seems more like a coach than a boss, Brian's openness facilitates good communication and cooperation amongst the BoltMSP team. Thanks to this approach, he was honored by the Loudoun Chamber of Commerce with its Executive Leadership Award in 2013, the award's inaugural year. But his greatest achievements are the person-to-person transformation that comes from everyday fire quenching, both through BoltMSP and through his work in the community. "Life goes so fast!" he affirms. "Make your choices, but remember that the random twists and turns are the things that make us. With the right resolve and a strong spirit, you'll be able to quench the fires along the way."

BERNHARDT
WEALTH MANAGEMENT

Fred Diamond

The Heart of the Business

Fresh out of college, Fred Diamond was certain he knew what he wanted to do. He had spent his four years at Emory University solidifying his leadership role at the campus paper, advancing from sports writer to news writer to Editor-in-Chief, and planned to go into writing professionally. He quickly landed a gig at McGraw-Hill Publishing, writing and editing articles for booklets about Information Security. Fred worked in the new products department, which focused on creating and publishing profit-drivers for the company. By chance, the New Products Department was located next to McGraw Hill's Sales Department.

Fred began to take an interest in the operations of the sales team. "These guys impressed me," he recalls. "They were professional, wearing suits and taking meetings. And I realized quickly that sales was the heart of the business, even though it was a publishing company. These guys were keeping the company going. It dawned on me that, even though I was an editor, if those guys weren't successful, it didn't matter what I write. No one was going to care if we didn't get customers."

Some of the other editors were disdainful of the sales team, considering the written word to be a higher calling. But Fred was pragmatic. He understood that the sales team made his work possible, and he was drawn to their gregarious energy and sharp minds. He spent time listening to their calls and took the initiative to market some of the new products his team worked on. After moving to Apple Computer a few years later, he began to transition into what he refers to as "the art and science of sales."

Today, Fred Diamond is the Executive Director and President of the Institute for Excellence in Sales (IES), a professional organization and consulting service he co-founded in 2011. The IES helps sales professionals and sales teams improve their skills, connects speakers and organizations with each other, and provides invaluable advice to companies seeking to contract out sales work.

IES developed a series of events organized by Fred in his capacity as an independent sales consultant, driven by his vision to expand his practice by offering educational and networking events to local businesses with sales needs. "A patner and I came up with the idea of a having a series of monthly workshops, bringing authors and thought leaders to the region to speak on sales topics," Fred explains. The workshops took off, and before long, word had spread throughout the business community. Requests for more workshops were pouring in, and as attendees started asking Fred if they could become members if IES, he began to see what the Institute could become.

Then one day, about two years into the IES journey, Fred got three phone calls on the same afternoon, all from companies looking for sales speakers for events they were hosting. Fred was happy to help, and IES's reputation evolved into a tried-and-true source for great speakers and trainers. "I started asking more and more people if they thought there was a need for a sales speaker bureau and a sales training referral service," he says. "I was hearing that it made a lot of sense, so I decided to go for it."

IES operates as a professional association for salespeople, comprised of individual members, corporate members, and sponsors who pay membership fees between $3,500 and $15,000 annually. Notable sponsors and members include Learning Tree, Deltek, and Cvent. Corporate members get access to exceptional sales professionals and sales speakers, while individual members can network with sales teams and businesses, and sponsoring organizations are able to make connections with corporate and individual sales teams. "It's a win/win/win," Fred affirms.

The IES also provides consulting services to sales teams and businesses in need. "We're the only agnostic training referral source to sales leaders," says Fred. The IES fields three or four inquiries per week from entities looking for sales speakers, sales training services, or consulting related to sales—a testament to the trusted brand Fred has built.

IES is the first entity of its kind, and as Fred responds to market demand, he's found that the need is global. With hundreds of members already, he expects the organization to double in size this year, and his long-term plans includes vastly improving the IES' online platform to have a national—and then international—reach. "Because we know the full scope of sales resources out there, we're able to help our members and clients figure out the best solution for them," he says. "If you google 'sales training', a million things come up. It's very stressful to sort through the static, especially when you need to find a solution that fits your unique scenario. If you're a not-for-profit that wants to shift from a reactive to proactive model, and you have people in four different offices around the country, and you need it done in 2 months, not every company can provide that service for you. We've done the work to figure out who will fit your needs, who can make your budget, and who is available."

Fred is proud of IES because the Institute has truly brought something of value to its many members. "I had been an employee for a large part of my career, and that was fine, but I was ready to create something," he says. "I wanted to build something of substance and value—something with more of a legacy. We just signed on to sponsor someone recently who said, 'There's no one else in the world doing something like this.' That's my motivation, and I know we've only just begun to scratch the surface."

Fred's vision and success can be traced back to his upbringing in Philadelphia, where he benefitted from a stable and loving home. "I had a mom and dad who were very involved and always there for us," he says. "Both my sister and I have had happy lives because of them." All four of his grandparents were local, and Fred fondly remembers visiting them on Friday nights, spending time with extended family, and playing with the neighborhood kids on the street.

His most impactful childhood passion, however, was baseball: playing it, watching it, memorizing stats, and attending Phillies game with his dad. "Baseball was a really big part of me growing up," he recalls. "I would wait for the newspaper to arrive on Sunday mornings, and I would just scour the box scores. My dad would come home from work in a suit and pitch to me. I really looked forward to that, spending time with my dad."

Fred's father was an accountant who worked long hours. Although Fred thinks his father never particularly loved the profession, he maintained excellent relationships with his clients, and his approach to business and professionalism made a lasting impression on young Fred when he accompanied his father on client calls. "I could see that people were really appreciative of him," Fred recounts. "He would show up to do their tax return, and they were happy to see him. That struck me because I always viewed my mother as the social one."

Fred's mother was a homemaker throughout his early childhood, always busy with household responsibilities and social commitments before she started working fulltime when he reached his early teens. His parents were always invited somewhere on Saturday nights, and even today, his mother fills their schedule with activities and social engagements. "They live in Florida half of the year now, and they have something planned, breakfast, lunch and dinner," Fred laughs. "And I know my dad ain't planning it!"

It was perhaps this remarkable organizational talent that led to his mother's sudden career successes later in life. She had left Temple University after two years and never completed college, but after a great deal of volunteering for multiple charities, she was offered a job as an Executive Assistant at an orphanage. Several years later, she was promoted directly from Executive Assistant to Executive Director. "My mom is a remarkable person and an organizational genius," says Fred. "It's rare, going from a secretarial type position to the Executive Director. She always encouraged me to make friends, spend time with people, get out of the house, and schedule my days—keys to success that helped later in life."

As middle school came to a close, Fred's focus on organized sports, and particularly baseball, gave way to his participation in his local Jewish youth organization. He still enjoyed his family's season tickets to the Phillies, but he didn't play on the competitive high school team. He got his first job delivering newspapers, but it came to an abrupt end when he broke his ankle a few short months into his tenure. "It actually worked out pretty well," he laughs. "Since I was on crutches, I was allowed to get out of class early."

In high school, Fred began to earn a reputation as a writer and a comedian. He wrote and published newsletters that were passed around school, which included a satirical questionnaire called "The Quiz." A friend of his parents who worked as an editor advised him to pursue his writing at Emory, though he discouraged Fred from getting a journalism degree. "His advice was that I didn't need to learn how to write," Fred recalls. "He told me to learn about something and become an expert, so I decided to become a history major."

Most of Fred's time at Emory, however, was spent on the newspaper, where he became editor-in-chief as a junior. His newsroom acquired a bit of public reputation after a controversial editorial took aim at former President Jimmy Carter, who visited the university while his Presidential Library was being constructed on campus. Because the library was somewhat remote, a new road was being built to provide easier access for tourists. The road was being referred to as an "expressway," and local residents were livid, concerned about traffic and the impact on property values. The editorial challenged Carter to address these concerns, calling him a coward until he did.

Fred was surprised to receive a call to meet with the former President, and face-to-face Carter explained the plans in more detail. "He was very kind," says Fred. "He told me that it wasn't going to be I-95, just a four-lane road. It was cool to be hanging out with Jimmy Carter! So we wrote an article about his perspective, and it spread. People sent us cakes, and neighbors came by our office to thank us for standing up for them."

After graduating from Emory, Fred returned to Philadelphia and started at McGraw-Hill, where he first developed his interest in sales and immediately caught the attention of higher-ups. "I was assigned to this book, *DataPro Reports on Information Security*, and I wrote an article about the data encryption standard," he recounts. "I remember the day our company president came back from a trip to Russia and stopped by my cube because everyone was talking about my article," Fred says. "He told me that everyone wanted to know, 'who is this Mr. Diamond?!' At that moment I got more serious about the impact I was having."

Fred took initiative in his role at McGraw-Hill, and on a trip to visit a friend on the west coast, he asked permission to also visit clients in San Francisco. "My boss said, we've never done that before, but sure," says Fred. "It was one of the defining moments of my career. And I knew that I was invested in more than just the product—I was becoming invested in its sale, too."

Fred was also earning some extra cash on the weekends by moonlighting as a DJ. "I probably learned more about human nature as a DJ," he laughs, "I did weddings, bar mitzvahs, and everything else. I worked a few black tie weddings, but the best ones were the ones catered by Wawa with a keg in the back! Those people were appreciative." Fred did around 300 parties in a four-year period, but eventually got to the point that the work felt monotonous and mundane.

Three years after beginning at McGraw-Hill, in 1987, an Apple Computer recruiter contacted Fred about a job in Virginia, and although he had been successful in his role as editor, he was running himself ragged making ends meet with his weekend work. Apple was an exciting opportunity to move up and in the direction of sales, so he made the plunge, accepting a support role. He doggedly followed salespeople on calls, to appointments, and even into their meetings, until finally his persistence was rewarded. He moved into a marketing role and never looked back.

Apple was a great place to work, but in 1993, Fred's whole department was laid off as part of a downsizing and restructuring. He moved on to Compaq Computer, where he worked for the emerging public sector group. There, he learned about the importance of a focused and efficient sales operation from his mentor, a retired Rear Admiral named Don. "He would always ask us why we were spending money on advertising," Fred says. "I had to confront the fact that sometimes the easy way to sell—buying ads—isn't necessarily the most effective way to sell. He shifted me from being a 'just-generally-gotta-advertise' guy to a very focused, succinct, 'what's the best and smartest way to go to market?' guy. How does marketing support the sales process more effectively? That mindset eventually led to the creation of the Institute."

Fred's years at Compaq were transformative, but his then-wife was insistent on moving to Detroit, her hometown. Fred found a job there with Compuware, a large software company, in 1996. He didn't love Detroit, but working in International Product Marketing afforded him the opportunity to travel all across Europe meeting clients. For three years, Fred did sales seminars and filmed testimonials from product users like Pepsi in exotic locales like Stockholm, Oslo, Sydney, Amsterdam, Frankfurt, and Budapest.

But Detroit was too far from the tech boom action, so in 2000, Fred returned to Virginia to work for a start-up called OneSoft. "It was a classic pre-IPO," says Fred. "They raised $80 million and went out of business in the middle of the night, leaving a lot of unhappy people in their wake." After that, Fred tried his luck at an A-round funded data-storage company called Network Storage Solutions (NSS). But as the tech bubble burst, NSS too went out of business.

Tired of being an employee, Fred decided to go out on his own as a consultant. "I wanted to finally create this thing on my own," he says. "I put out a shingle and threw myself into figuring it out. There have been bumps along the way, but you have to hustle for yourself."

Consulting provided much-needed freedom, and as he expanded his sales events, Fred saw a real future. "It got to the point where I'd have 200 people in the room for a speaker, and the energy was just ebullient," he says. "Then I'd go back to consulting, which at that point meant sitting in a cube, working on an e-mail that no one was ever going to read. I thought, 'this is ridiculous.' I knew I could create more, so I did."

As a leader, Fred is focused most on value and engagement. "I want people to get real, substantive value out of IES," he says. "I'm always working to gauge what people want out of it, whether they're participating in the Institute, or coming to us as a customer, or serving as one of our speakers. What are they hoping to achieve and how can I help them succeed? It's about win/win/wins. We're creating this entity so everyone gets what they need out of it."

To young people entering the working world today, Fred points to relationships as a critical ingredient for success. "Build a list of people you could have lifelong professional engagement with," he advises. "When I look at people who've had long, successful careers, a lot of them have contacts they've worked with for decades. Many sales leaders we recognize have a whole legacy of successful people who are now leading sales teams of their own. So I always say, especially if you want to work for yourself, write a list of people you could see yourself working with as a partner in the future. Then build that core of people that you're going to stay in touch with."

Relationships are often at the heart of sales, and as Fred often points out, sales are the heart of any business. "Sales is truly the most important part of a company," he says. "If things don't get sold, there's no company. So I see IES's mission as building the heart of business, advancing business development and educating sales professionals around the globe so they can lead happier, more productive careers, and so companies can be more successful."

That legacy is coming to life here in the Northern Virginia area with every handshake that takes place at each IES event. "Nowadays, I'll go to the Tower Club and see two people I know sitting next to each other and I'll ask, 'How do you two know each other?'" Fred explains. "They say, 'Oh, we met at the Institute.' At the end of the day, those connections are my biggest achievement."

BERNHARDT
WEALTH MANAGEMENT

Bruce Ehlert

With God's Help

When Bruce Ehlert was a junior in high school, he was ecstatic to land a part-time job working for a furniture company in the Shenandoah Valley. He started at $3.35 an hour assembling desks, and he was eager to make more. "I put those desks together as fast as I could," he recalls now. "I figured that if I made more desks, I'd be more valuable to the company and could make more money. Then, one day, a foreman came over and said, 'Hey, hotshot, slow down.' He told me it didn't matter how quickly I worked, I wasn't going to be making more on his watch."

Bruce worked full-time during the summer and remembers the periodic rest and lunch breaks the employees were supposed to take. Driven by his own resolve and enthusiasm for hard work, he kept making desks right through those breaks—until his supervisor forced him to stop. "From then on, I was determined to never allow myself to be held back by that kind of mindset," he recalls. "It was an experience that was instrumental in my life and my decision that I was one day going to work for myself. I wanted to have my own company and create an environment where people are free to work according to their own drive and potential."

Bruce had the opportunity to begin contributing to a workplace like that when, around that same time, his father bought a Minuteman Press franchise. "Dad had no background in business, but he wanted to give it a try," Bruce remembers. "I was happy to pitch in part-time to help out."

Bruce's father worked hard to grow the business, but due to changes in the local market and the recession, the business had to file for bankruptcy. It was very upsetting for Bruce's father, a man with a lot of integrity who never wants to hurt or disappoint anyone. He vowed to work his way through it

During this time, Bruce and his wife, Terri, had just welcomed their first daughter into the world, and Bruce still had college classes to finish up, but he soon decided to leave school to dedicate himself full-time to helping his father revive the business. Rolling up his sleeves, and with Terri's help, he dove in. "There was so much going on, and it was overwhelming trying to think of how we were going to get through it," he recalls. "But I leaned on my faith and put the business in God's hands. We were going to figure it out."

Breaking from the franchise, the Ehlert father and son rebranded the business as Four Star Printing, and in time, reestablished credit with their vendors. They learned to deal swiftly with industry red flags and figured out what to look for when making expansion decisions or reviewing balance sheets. "When we finally got there, our lawyer congratulated us because most people in our position would have just walked away to start over," Bruce says. "But we were fully committed to righting the ship. And with God's help, we succeeded."

Through the decades, as print and paper mills have been displaced by digital utilization, Bruce has watched countless others in his industry close their doors. But many industries still need a tangible, hands-on product, and even virtual companies still need to send out mailers to advertise their websites. "The least expensive way of communicating is still by mail," Bruce points out. "Twenty years from now, that might not still be the case, but we will continue to adapt as we always have."

Now, as the company's President, Bruce has grown the business by request, expanding to accommodate the needs expressed by their customers. With seventeen employees, Four Star has evolved into a medium-size commercial printer with both small- and large-format capability, offering a wide breadth of services to include digital, web, traditional offset, embroidery, and perfect binding for books, as well as assistance with sales and marketing strategy. From mailings to data management, Bruce has found innovative ways to create value, like managing marketing initiatives for customers, brainstorming ideas, or offering last-minute solutions at competitive prices. "Our strategy has been to find the right customers and grow along with them, providing help along the way," he says.

From the moment he first got into printing, Bruce found the work to be a natural fit, allowing him to throw his energy into problem solving and helping others. This drive, and his unrelenting work ethic, come in part from the example set by his father, a Marine who served in Vietnam and later became a Seventh Day Adventist minister. "He is a very positive guy. He worked incredibly hard and helped a tremendous amount of people, both as a minister and as a businessman," Bruce recounts. "I give him a lot of credit for who I am today."

Born in Seattle just after his father's military service, Bruce led a transitory childhood as his father's ministry work led the family across Washington, Idaho, Wisconsin, and Oregon. The oldest of three brothers, he played intramural sports when he could, but they never stayed in one place long enough for Bruce to join a team. "There were certainly drawbacks," he admits. "But living on the road and out of hotels, and switching schools so often, I was constantly exposed to new environments and new people. My father drew crowds, and growing up in that environment, I developed a love of being around people. As well, it taught me to embrace change. I'm not afraid to be thrown into a new environment, and it taught me how to work with all different kinds of people."

The Ehlert family continued to travel with his father's ministry, and eventually moved to Virginia. When Bruce was 15, he started his freshman year of high school at Shenandoah Valley Academy, a boarding school in New Market, Virginia. That year, he lived with his mother and brothers just outside of town and drove himself into school, while his father continued to travel. He got a job bailing hay for a local farmer, and another working in the book bindery at school, where his supervisor refused to pay employees for the first half-hour of work if they didn't clock in by 9:00 AM precisely. Bruce worked harder and faster than anyone else on staff, but he was chronically late by several minutes, to the point that his supervisor threatened to let him go. "My work quality was the best around, but he was willing to fire me because I wasn't complying with his standards," Bruce remembers. "That was a big eye-opener for me, teaching me to respect people's time. It was character-building."

Then, when Bruce was sixteen, his life changed markedly when his parents decided to divorce. Amidst that darkness, Bruce sought out light—a defining moment that helped guide his path forward. "As a born again believer, I found myself diving more into my faith and the Word of God," he says. "I also read a lot about people in tough situations and how they got through them. The works of Zig Ziglar, Norman Vincent Peale, and Dale Carnegie were all very transformative for me at that time. I was able to draw on those positive influences to help lift me up and inspire me to succeed and help others."

When Bruce started his junior year, he moved into the boarding school, where he embraced the experience and made lifelong friends. He studied hard, did well academically, and loved the chance to finally play sports. Meanwhile, his father took a leave of absence from the ministry to pursue a variety of entrepreneurial ventures, including the purchase of the print shop franchise.

After three years at boarding school, Bruce spent his senior year at South Lakes High School in Reston, Virginia, where he lived with his father and worked at the print shop every afternoon. Working under the tutelage of a particularly knowledgeable employee, an expert with many years of experience, he learned every aspect of the business. And as his father returned to ministry, Bruce spent more and more time with the business.

Bruce's parents never pushed their children to go to college, but education was important to him, and he hoped to become a chiropractor at that point. Upon graduating from high school in 1986, he enrolled at Washington Adventist University but quickly made the decision that science wasn't his thing. "I feel entrepreneurship in my soul," he says. "I wouldn't even know the first thing about putting together a resume or interviewing for a job. I'm all about doing business, so I decided to study business."

After two years there, Bruce transferred to George Mason University in search of a stronger academic program, all the while working to be able to afford tuition. But the class sizes were large, and he found it difficult and impersonal to learn in a large auditorium where he didn't know the professor. He transferred back to Washington Adventist University for his fourth year, and then decided it wasn't enough to be studying business in a classroom. He was ready to be out in the world, working at the print shop and using his skills to help bring his father's company back to life.

Working with family can often end in disaster, but Bruce and his father operated seamlessly together, making decisions as a team and recognizing each other's strengths. "He allowed me to take the reins and guide the direction of the company, which was really great," Bruce recounts. "In the beginning stage, I was wearing all the hats. I had a lot to learn, and I had to learn it fast."

With Terri managing the books, Bruce worked hard and got the business back on stable footing. He remembers the vendors who took a chance and actually stuck out the bankruptcy with them. "We worked it out together, and I'm very loyal to them to this day," he says. "Honestly, I'm thankful I went through all that, because now there's nothing in business that I'm afraid of. Mistakes happen, but if you're honest with people and show that you're committed to coming through in good faith, things work out."

In the clear and with bankruptcy firmly in the rearview mirror, Bruce turned his attention toward development. He got involved with the Rotary Club for networking, focused on outreach to nonprofits and trade associations, and pursued key partnerships with other companies, like print brokers, to reach diverse customer bases. In 2003, they moved the company from Tysons Corner to Dulles, and Bruce and Terri bought the business shortly thereafter.

While he appreciated his dynamic childhood, Bruce and Terri have been in the same house for fourteen years now, and he couldn't be more grateful for the stable, loving home they shared with their two daughters. "Terri has made our home a peaceful refuge, and I am so grateful for that," he says. "Running your own business can be stressful, and she keeps me grounded and drama-free. She's very even-keeled, rooted, and strong in her faith, not to mention that she's great with numbers and managing money. She makes me a better person, both personally and professionally."

Now, as a leader, Bruce stays calm under pressure and never reacts in anger when something goes wrong, as it inevitably does in the print industry. When mistakes happen, he focuses on constructively finding out why things went off track so it can be fixed and then avoided in the future. More than anything, he remains driven by opportunities to help others—a priority that extends beyond serving customers and includes the well-being of his staff. "Many of them want to start their own businesses too one day, so it's important to me to take the time to guide and mentor them," he says. "I like to help them get there, even if it means I'll lose a good employee. I want to see them grow and succeed, and I always think about how I'd want to be treated if I was working for a manager."

Through the day-to-day ups-and-downs of print jobs, customer service, and entrepreneurial living, Bruce's mind remains cognizant of something bigger. In part, it's the legacy of his work. "I hope I've built a business that continues on after I'm gone," he says. Also in part, it's the thread of love that connects family from one generation to the next. "Raising my daughters, I try to be a positive, trusting influence in their lives, as my father was in mine," he continues. "Like him, I try to look for the best in people and take the time to help out. My mother, as well, imparted a keen eye for detail and a sense of awareness of what's going on around me. I use that to always look for the positive that exists in any environment, and to focus on that." And in whole, it's his faith, from which all things flow. "All my defining moments, and the things that mean the most to me, are in my life because of the Cross," he affirms. "There were so many times I wanted to quit, and times I just didn't want to be positive anymore. But if God had that kind of love for me, I knew I could get through it."

In advising young people entering the working world today, Bruce recognizes the differences between generations but underscores the timeless importance of working hard and seeking guidance. "Don't give up on things just because they take hard work," he says. "If you don't know what you want to do, it's always safe to learn a trade. But the most important thing is finding something you love, and then dedicating yourself completely to learning everything you can about that field. Spend two solid years studying, seeking advice from experts in the sector, and charting a path forward. Do what it takes to learn what it takes to succeed."

Beyond that, Bruce's example demonstrates the power of positive thinking to transcend challenges—a story he makes a point to share with young people whenever he can. Back in 1994, he and Terri joined a colleague in launching an informal Bible study group for disadvantaged youth, welcoming kids of all ages in the neighborhood to join. "They would all come out, and we'd open the Bible and just take turns reading to each other," he says. "We'd discuss it and then take the kids out for food and games. They just loved it, and so did we." Bruce has also led several youth Bible study groups over the years, equipping kids with the tools they need to nurture their faith and achieve their dreams.

"Life certainly has its twists, turns, and valleys, but we've got all we need to persevere," Bruce affirms. "If you can be a force for light in the world, you'll get where you want to go, with God's help."

Bobby Feisee

Visualizing Victories

When Bobby Feisee was a kid, his father gave him a cassette tape about visualization that he liked to listen to while falling asleep. As he drifted off at night, the calming voice on the recording asked him to think about his goals and what he wanted out of life, focusing on seeing success with the mind's eye. "My father was a big believer in the power of the mind, and I saw him accomplish so much," Bobby reflects today. "It made me a believer, too."

Bobby's first great success with visualization came when he was in sixth grade. Up to that point he had been an average student, earning mostly Cs and the occasional B. But when his sixth grade teacher read aloud the class's grades on a project, everything changed. "One of the girls sitting next to me snickered when she heard my grade," Bobby remembers. "I decided in that moment, no more Cs. I wrote it down and visualized it. And thanks to my competitive spirit, from then on, I pretty much got straight As."

Through high school, Bobby would always listen to the tape the night before a big lacrosse game as a way to calm down and focus. The biggest test of the power of visualization came in his junior year, when his brother drove him to the University of Virginia to speak with the coach about playing for the team in college. The coach barely heard him out, citing the school's policy that they didn't recruit out of Virginia. "He didn't even give me a chance," Bobby remembers. "It stirred the competitive spirit in me, and I wondered what it would take for him to look at me. I called up Roy Simmons, Jr., the coach at Syracuse University, the defending national champions at the time. He told me I probably wouldn't make the team, but I was welcome to come try out in the fall and if I was good enough, they might give me a shot."

A shot was all Bobby needed. He performed with excellence, landing a spot on the team and admission to the university upon graduating. He went on to win two national championships, and the rings from those victories are still powerful symbols for him that anything is possible. "I was always told that I wasn't good enough to make this team or that team," he remembers. "People would say, don't even bother. But I set my goal, worked hard at it, had a plan to achieve it, and it happened. If you believe in yourself, you don't have to listen to what other people think. If you can imagine and visualize it, you can do it."

It was his father's influence that gave him the tools to etch out a path of success, and his father's later decline that ultimately led him to his life's work. His father was diagnosed with Alzheimer's at age seventy, and in the ten years until his passing, his deteriorating health were accompanied by emotional and financial challenges that seemed as if they could have been avoided with some engaged and insightful advanced planning. "It seemed to me that his estate planning attorney and his financial advisor missed a lot of things," says Bobby. "The experience felt so transactional and impersonal—more about getting documents and checking boxes than about going through the process of actually understanding the situation well enough to offer truly personalized advice. I realized that it's not about the documents—it's about the family, the people, and the process."

As a lawyer, Bobby wasn't practicing estate law at the time, but he knew he was meant to use his knowledge and skills to help families in this way—shepherding them through these uniquely challenging times of life. "To best respond to the disability or death of a family member, advance communication and preparation is key," he says. Now the founder and President of InSight Law, an estate and business planning law firm in Northern Virginia, he has brought to life the relationship-based approach to service that he visualized in the wake of his father's passing, using it to better the lives of the clients who entrust him to shepherd them through their hardest times. "Every day, my work brings new challenges and new opportunities to make a difference," he says. "And every day, I rely on the basic blueprints of determination and goal-setting that help me translate visualization into reality."

Bobby first opened his firm in 2002 as the Law Offices of Robert Feisee, taking the traditional transactional approach to estate planning he'd been taught. Years passed, but real success didn't come, and Bobby felt he was just barely getting by. "It was mechanical," he recalls. "There was little follow through or relationship, and it wasn't fulfilling for me." He knew he was falling short of his potential, but was at a loss for how to take things to the next level, until he joined the National Network of Estate Planning Attorneys (NNEPA) in 2007. There, he was deeply influenced by the organization's chairman, Rick Randall, and another mentor, Scott Williams, each with decades of experience. "They really gave the me process and business management side of things I was struggling with," Bobby says. "Others in my class dropped out along the way, but I saw the value—that the tools for success were right in front of us, and it was up to us to use them. Joining NNEPA had an immeasurably positive impact on my life, and I'm now an instructor for the network."

Through his experience at NNEPA, Bobby saw the importance of naming his firm to signal that it was about something bigger than himself. With that, InSight Law was officially branded. The network also convinced him to write down a business plan. "I had spent my whole life writing down my goals, so why hadn't I done it for my biggest adventure?" he marvels. "Once I did, everything clicked."

Bobby revolutionized his business model, replacing ineffective free one-on-one initial consultations with free small group client orientation meetings several times a month. "It's a nice, easy way to introduce the firm and educate potential clients on our process," he says. "If people are interested we explore further options, but if not, at least they've gained information to be a better consumer." The next step in the process is a free consultation with the firm's associate attorney to gather asset information, do a short goal-setting exercise, answer questions, and quote a fee range. Individuals then meet with Bobby to make the final decision to work together. "We don't take our client relationships lightly, so it's important that it's a good fit," he says.

Once the agreement is signed, Bobby meets with clients to design their plans and walk through their legal documents so clients understand each component. Then the Insight team focuses on financial integration, ensuring the client's estate plan is coordinated with their financial plan to thoroughly prepare for any challenge that might arise. The InSight approach also includes a membership program with an annual group meeting, where each attendee receives a focused update on changes in the law and how it affects their plan in particular. "Things are going to change in people's lives, in their families, and in the country," Bobby says. "I give everyone an update on any upcoming changes in the law that might affect their plans and how things are going at the firm, so one-on-one meetings can be reserved only for the matters that need personal attention."

With four attorneys and three support team members, Insight Law currently serves 240 families and is able to compete with larger firms thanks to its competitive model and excellent client service. "Our clients appreciate having a relationship with a law firm that's looking after them," Bobby says. "We don't nickel-and-dime people; we just leverage economies of scale and do things in group format when we can to keep costs down."

Bobby's father grew up in a small village in a home without running water. The oldest of seven children, he learned to read the Quran—a remarkable achievement in an area where most people couldn't read or write. "He was a brilliant man with an incredible memory, and he used his mind to get into medical school," Bobby says. "My mom also inspires me every day. She has character and grace, and always taught me that having a good character is one of the most important things you need to learn. No one can take away your values, and your character is what people will remember about you. My mother succeeded in becoming a physician in a country where women were second-class citizens. That she was able to do that in Iran, where it's very hard to succeed, speaks so much to her passion and heart. Whenever things get hard for me, I think of what my mom and dad have accomplished and remember I don't have it hard at all."

Recognizing the rising oppression of the religious right, his parents immigrated to the U.S. from Iran in 1971, when his mother was pregnant with Bobby. With his older sister and brother to support, they spoke little English and struggled to get on their feet, landing their first job at a hospital in Wheeling, Virginia. After Bobby was born, they moved temporarily to Rochester, New York, and then settled in Northern Virginia when he was in kindergarten. "It reminded my father of the farm where he grew up in Iran," Bobby says. "He loved his home village and would go back every year, packing his suitcase full of medical supplies and spending his time there as the town doctor. Sometimes I went with him, and it was powerful to see. He taught me to be grateful for what I have, and to always spend 10 percent of my time and money giving back."

Bobby's parents worked long hours to keep food on the table. "We were classic latchkey kids," Bobby recalls. "Sometimes I'd watch soap operas with my dad when he came home for late lunchbreaks, but otherwise I played outside a lot with our dogs and quarter horse. There weren't really other kids that lived nearby, so I'd spend my time reading or playing sports on my own. My parents were great influences too, modeling a fire and passion that gave me an edge. They were humble and generous but also taught me to go after the things I wanted in life."

Bobby got his first lacrosse stick in seventh grade when he tagged along with his brother on a trip to the sporting goods store to get his own stick. The two would often go to the park to throw, and when his brother taught him how to cradle, his natural talent quickly emerged. He joined the youth club and joined a summer lacrosse league in Ocean City, Maryland, where his parents had a condo. "All the good kids from Baltimore played there, and I'd show up to see how I compared," he says. "That's also where I worked my first summer jobs running a beach stand, and then as a busboy, and later as a waiter. I balanced all that with summer school, since my parents placed a big emphasis on education."

Bobby enjoyed the feeling of progress and success, and though he had always been good at football and wrestling, he saw a future as a college lacrosse player and ultimately focused his energy there. "I loved the creativity of the game," he says. "It has its origins as a Native American sport, and if you can get to a high level, it's almost like art. I volunteer as an assistant coach now, and I love telling my story to these younger kids with wide eyes who want to play. I tell them they can do it if they really want to; they just have to put the work in. I believe that for any kid, no matter their size—if you have a big heart and believe, there's a place for you on the field."

Bobby made All Fairfax County in high school and received honorable mention for All Metropolitan, but thanks to visualization, he was always a national champion in his mind. He always believed he could beat the person in front of him—a reality that became harder to achieve once he was at Syracuse, playing teams like Johns Hopkins and Princeton. "When you get to that level, everyone is good," he says. "It's the same thing with business. To separate yourself, you have to have a little more mental edge."

Bobby's team won the national championship during his freshman year, and when he was a junior, they came close, losing in double overtime. He won the first overtime faceoff but lost the second, leaving room for the opposing team to win the game. It was a rough summer for him, but he eventually resolved that he couldn't let the regret consume him. He bounced back, and the next year, they won the national championship. "From lacrosse, I learned that any goal you set for yourself is achievable," Bobby avows. "Our technique at Syracuse wasn't magic, we just had consistent practices and did the same things over and over again, so our fundamentals were excellent. I apply this to business today, focusing on the importance of having systems, processes, and goals to advance progress."

In his senior year of college, Bobby decided to pursue law school—a path he wished he had settled on earlier so he could have prepared more while in school. Upon graduation with a degree in finance, he enrolled at George Mason Law School and struggled at first, finding law to be a completely different. "The Socratic method was hard to get used to," he recalls. "But I got more confident as time went on, and I went on to pass the bar on my first try."

Still unsure what field of law was right for him, Bobby took a job at a small personal injury litigation firm in Woodbridge upon graduating in 1996. He immediately began taking on court cases, quickly learning the ropes. Around that time, his father was diagnosed with Alzheimer's, and Bobby was then recruited by a bigger firm in Tysons Corner. There, he spent two years working in collections, homeowners association cases, and other lawsuits that didn't feel like the right fit. "I would win money, but I didn't like gouging people for money," he says. "I wanted to be on the defensive side or creating wealth."

He left that firm in 2000 to become a financial advisor at Morgan Stanley during the tech boom, where his entrepreneurial and hustling skills were put to the test. "It taught me that you have to be able to market and to pick up the phone to make cold calls," he says. "It was a boot camp in Sales 101, and an intense time in my life. My father was getting sicker, and finally, it clicked for me that I wanted to be doing estate planning." With that, Bobby started his own law practice in 2002. "It was a hard decision, and I was worried I might fail, but once again, my mom came to the rescue. She reminded me about who I was, and about character. She said she loved me and would always be there to help if things went wrong. She told me to follow my heart, and it gave me the confidence to take the risk and never look back."

When his father passed in 2005, Bobby accompanied his mother on a trip to Iran to wrap up his affairs. "I hadn't been there in 30 years, and I had the best time with my mom," Bobby says. "She's a legend there, and here for that matter. She showed me all the places she and my dad grew up. She was also trying to set me up, as she often did. I told her not to bother, but then I met a young woman named Newsha at a dinner party."

Bobby didn't think much of the meeting at the time, but he had needed to change shirts after spilling a drink on himself. When Newsha stopped by to return his shirt the next day, he had coffee with her, he was struck with the sudden realization that she was the one. When he returned to America, they continued to speak every day, and when he returned to Iran the next year, he asked her to marry him. "It was the best decision, and I only wish I had done it sooner," he says. "She's my partner in life and in business, and my best friend."

Newsha came to the U.S. with Bobby in the summer of 2007, where they faced a big decision—should they spend $10,000 on a honeymoon, or should they spend it on the payment for Bobby's admission to the National Network of Estate Planning Attorneys (NNEPA)? "Newsha pushed me to go for the NNEPA instead, which was really incredible of her," he says. Thanks to that choice, InSight Law took off, and Newsha joined the team to handle the client events, maintenance program, marketing, and scheduling. The couple welcomed their first child in 2016, a baby girl named Nava—the Farsi word for music. "My baby and my wife are my world," Bobby says. "They also make me better at my job because I understand on a more personal level what it means to care about family and legacy, as my clients do."

In advising young people entering the working world today, Bobby stresses the importance of hard work, a humble attitude, and business basics. "Show up on time, do what you say you're going to do, finish what you start, and say please and thank you," he says simply. "If you're patient and focus on learning and being a good person, success will come. Also, if you see a way to improve your field, go for it. Although I have a competitive spirit, I really don't think I'm in competition for what we do. There is a lot wrong with the 'traditional' approach to estate planning, and I believe we as lawyers can do a better job as a profession. That's why I became a teacher at George Mason Law School and an instructor at NNEPA. I believe estate planning should be about bringing families together, not tearing them apart. It's important to be a visionary here and consider how you can change the world for the better."

The lessons of his life, however, apply to any age, from the peers he works with on a daily basis to the young children he guides as a lacrosse coach. "It's so important to give back through donations of money, and we support Jill's House and Alzheimer's charities in that way, but I love being out on the field with the kids, telling them my story and helping them figure out theirs. I tell them to visualize, set a goal, write it down, and make it real. If you believe you're going in the right direction, keep going. Listen to what others have to say, but don't let it shake your core belief. Learn how the world works and apply it to your own experiences. My life has changed so much for the better because I didn't go with the critics—I went with my heart."

Erika Flora

All In on a Challenge

Nothing fuels Erika Flora's resolve quite like a challenge. She still remembers the day when, at five years old, she was asked by a babysitter if she knew what she wanted to do when she grew up. "I told her I wanted to be a doctor, but she told me I couldn't do that because I was a girl, and girls can't be doctors," she remembers today. "Even at such a young age, that comment made me angry. It fueled my determination that I could do whatever I set my mind to in life, and that I wasn't going to let people tell me what a girl can and can't do."

If Erika was born with the innate desire to meet challenges head-on, her parents taught her how to go all-in to overcome them. Through her formative years, they showed her how to take an interest and really run with it. When Erika's sister decided she was into basketball, their father conducted extensive research to find the best shoes to help her vertical jump and enroll her at a camp taught by Shaquille O'Neal.

Another summer, Erika got into reading, so her father took her to the library constantly and helped her learn how to speed read. "Whatever we wanted to do, it was full-steam ahead, 1,000 percent," she says. "The support was incredible."

Years later, as a young woman in a new career field, Erika was offered a job as a project manager, and though she had no idea what a project manager did, she decided to take on the challenge. At the time, her new employer was struggling to manage a chaotic mess of projects with no system and no accountability—not exactly the kind of scenario people willingly walk into with no experience and no mentor to guide the way. But Erika had spent her childhood watching her parents embrace new cities, new career fields, and new interests with enthusiasm and confidence. "If we moved away from the town where my mother owned a business, she'd just open a new one in our new town," Erika says. "And my father has had seven different careers through his life. He taught me that I could chart a new course for myself anytime I wanted."

Over the next several years, Erika took the initiative to get her official project management certification and mastered the inner workings of the company's 150-plus active projects. They were interwoven and highly complex, but thanks to the processes and tools she put in place, she could tell leadership at any point in time exactly what was going on. "It was a defining moment for me because I saw that my skill set could be used to really transform a company," she says. "I fell in love with the work of providing tools, processes, and trainings to help people do a better job and be better team members." Erika continues that work today as the cofounder and President of Beyond20, an IT service and project management firm that specializes in the elegantly simple mission of bringing out the best in people.

It is often said that employees are a company's greatest assets. Conversely, they can also be a company's greatest liability. Studies show that, when mission-critical IT systems fail in large companies, software or hardware issues are the root cause of crisis in only 20 percent of instances. In 80 percent of cases, the problem can be traced back to a failure in people or processes. "It all comes down to people and how they work," Erika says. "People make changes and don't think through the impact of those changes company-wide. We're passionate about fixing those disconnects."

Erika and her husband, Brian, launched Beyond20 in 2006 as a small consultancy in Arizona. She came from a project management track in the pharmaceutical and healthcare industry, while he had an IT and dotcom background working for companies like GoDaddy. "We were driving in the car one day, when we happened to hear a webinar about IT service management and project management," Erika recounts. "The discussion centered on how similar the two disciplines are, breaking them down to show that at the end of the day, both were simply trying to improve how companies work. We realized we were doing the same thing, so we decided to build something together."

Beyond20 serves IT departments, including thirteen of the fifteen cabinet-level government agencies, and IT leaders in large companies. It has worked with over 25 percent of Fortune 100 companies in some capacity. No matter who they're serving, the company is known for its creativity, kindness, and innovation, and was a 2015 Gold and Silver winner of the Best in Biz awards for Most Customer Friendly Company and Most Creative Executive. "We're very focused on using creativity to drive innovation in developing exceptional solutions for our clients," Erika says. "I'm also very proud of our awesome team and the great work we do together."

Though she's always considered herself introverted and often shy, Erika's career trajectory has been amplified by moments of boldness that perhaps stem from the unique strains of courage that belong to each of her parents. Her mother immigrated to the U.S. from Guatemala at the age of 18 without knowing any English and learned the language by watching TV as she worked as a nanny and attended school. She was a hair salon owner by the time she met Erika's father, a chemist-turned-professional bowler, the only time she ever set foot in a bowling alley on a night out with friends. Erika was born outside of San Francisco, and her younger sister was born shortly thereafter. When Erika was three, they moved to Iowa to be closer to family, and her father worked as a pharmaceutical salesman. Four years later, they moved to Georgia so he could go back to school, and her mother started another hair salon.

Though she was shy as a child, Erika showed early signs of leadership while playing with other kids, and some might have even called her bossy. "Our parents encouraged my sister and me in everything we did," she recalls. "Whenever we took an interest in something, they were interested too."

Her parents, as well, had varied interests of their own. After four years in Georgia, the family moved to Tampa, Florida, where her father took over a clinic and her mother opened a salon. Erika was in third grade by that time. "I was very nerdy and shy, but then I'd do these really bold things every once in a while, like run for class president in sixth grade," she says. "Nobody voted for me because nobody knew who I was, but it was still something I wanted to go after." She developed lifelong friendships with other studious girls in her class, excelled in school, and enjoyed participating in youth group with her church starting in junior high.

In high school, Erika joined the dance team, the diving team, and the debate team, but she still felt most at home and empowered in the classroom. "When I was at school and really in my element, I went from the shy, quiet one to the outspoken, bossy one," she recalls. "The teachers liked me because I always participated in class." She wasn't afraid to be herself—a gift given to her by her father's example. "He's always been best known for his colorful character and outlandish wardrobe, including a pair of brightly-striped bellbottoms that I still hold onto," she laughs. "His style was so infamous that his college named a day after him—Don Malnati Day—when everyone wore the most ridiculous, bright, mismatched stuff. He taught me to walk to the beat of my own drum, think critically and logically, question what people told me, and have fun with life by being weird."

All through high school, Erika's dream of becoming a doctor never wavered. She was drawn to the challenge of it, as well as the joy of proving wrong the babysitter who had tried to limit her aspirations all those years ago. When she graduated from high school in the top ten percent of her class, she accepted a scholarship to the University of Florida and went pre-med, as she had always planned. "College was another level when it came to academics," she says. "It was a real awakening, to be surrounded by so many other smart people and to have to study a lot harder than I did in high school. But that was a great thing." Erika majored in microbiology and also joined a sorority, though school remained her top focus. She also worked one summer selling Cutco knives—a seemingly irrelevant sales experience that would become important to her career later on.

By her senior year, Erika's interest in being a doctor had taken a turn. "I spent several summers shadowing doctors, and it didn't seem like there was a lot of joy in it," she recalls. "People told me there was a lot of paperwork, and not a lot of time to care for patients as much as they would like. It seemed like I might be able to help people more if I pursued something else."

Fortunately, Erika had an exceptional food microbiology professor whose enthusiasm was truly compelling. He worked as both a hospital consultant and a restaurant auditor, both of which supplied fascinating stories that caught Erika's attention. She decided to pursue her masters in food science with an emphasis on food microbiology, paying her way by doing work for a professor and for the U.S. Food and Drug Administration.

When she completed her graduate program in 1998, Erika decided to try a new challenge and accepted a microbiologist job for a large chicken processing plant in a small town in Arkansas. There, she tested products for bacteria before they headed to market, working for several years before opting for a new challenge yet again. "Most people my age had left town to go to college, so I really didn't have peers there," she recalls. "And I didn't want to be in a lab anymore. When I went to visit a friend who had moved to Phoenix, I loved it, so I decided to move there."

In Phoenix, Erika was hired by a company to build their pharmaceutical division through recruiting and internal sales. "They saw I had a background in science and at least some sales experience, so they thought I'd figure it out," she says. "I saw it as a challenge, so of course, I was game." For her first few months on the job, Erika learned all she could about the pharma industry and took to heart the mentorship of the company's owner, a dynamic entrepreneur. "The company was around 80 people at the time, and he would personally sit down with all new employees to train them for a week," she recounts. "It was very encouraging."

Erika worked there for three years, building a network that she then reached out to when she was ready to make her next move. One of her contacts was looking for a project manager, and though she had no idea what that meant exactly, she accepted the job and dove right in. "The company didn't know how many projects they had going on, how they were going, or when they were expected to be completed," she remembers. "I got thrown into the fire and just started figuring out what I was supposed to be doing, beginning with the basics."

That first month, the 50-person company had a staff meeting, where new employees were asked to introduce themselves and say what they do. "I was so terrified of public speaking that I stood up and managed to say my name and title, but then blurted out that I didn't know what I did," she remembers. "Who does that? It could have been a career-limiting move, and I resolved immediately that it was time to beat my shyness."

With that, Erika signed up for stand-up comedy and public speaking classes, excited by the idea of injecting humor into business presentations. She cultivated her voice and poise, learning how to overcome her fear and say out loud the things she felt should be said. "You had to stand up on stage and come up with a routine on the spot, which was really challenging for me," she remembers. It was an incredibly important professional milestone to overcome, especially for the regular public speaking obligations that would come later in her career.

Erika also joined the Project Management Institute, getting as much exposure as she could at a time when the field was much more obscure than it is today. She signed up for trainings and started taking night classes in project management, earning a certificate and then a Project Management Professional (PMP) Certification. And with the skills she learned, she tamed the chaos at the company, building out an enterprise project management system where they could view the status of projects in real time. She created monthly progress reports for leadership, tracking important milestones and charting out future projects and activities. "It was the best learning experience I ever had, and it was a joy to accomplish something so exciting," she says.

Also during that time, Erika met Brian. "He always knew he wanted to run a company one day," she remembers. "I was struck by how smart he was, and what a strong entrepreneurial spirit he had." Erika ended up working a brief stint at a medical device company, where she organized projects across multiple locations and implemented software tools that allowed for effective progress reporting to external customers, before realizing she had entrepreneurial aspirations of her own. "I decided I was ready to go out and chart my own path in pursuit of something challenging and meaningful," she recalls. With that, in 2006, Beyond20 was born. Several months later, Erika and Brian got married.

Several years later, Erika and Brian won a contract with the State Department to train the IT departments for their consulate offices. They were traveling back and forth to DC so frequently that they decided to set up an office in Washington and focus on expanding their footprint in the nation's capital. "It was a happy accident that we expanded to DC and government work," Erika says.

Erika and Brian hired their first employee in 2012, and since that time, their team has exploded to around thirty people. They were recognized for their outstanding company culture and entrepreneurial success by the Northern Virginia Technology Council in 2013, and landed their 8(a) certification in 2016. Clocking in at around 70 percent growth each year for the past three years, Beyond20 made it onto the Inc. 5,000 list in 2015, 2016, and 2017 with no signs of slowing down, and in 2017 was also named a "Best Place to Work" by the *Washington Business Journal*.

Today, Brian manages Beyond20's software development and training teams. As President, Erika oversees sales, business development, and overall strategy, including the company's consulting team. But as it is with most small businesses, there's room to be nimble and responsive to any challenge that arises. "When you're in a small company," she says, "everyone jumps in where needed."

Erika and Brian have complementary skill sets, which contribute to their exceptionally positive work relationship. Each Beyond20 employee takes a StrengthsFinder test when they join the team to determine their top five strengths, and usually Erika and Brian each share at least one strength with each employee, but the pair has no overlapping strengths between the two of them—a testament to their power as a team. "A lot of people have a hard time imagining what it's like to work with your spouse, but I couldn't imagine not working with Brian," she says. "Of course we have good days and bad days, and there are certainly times we get frustrated with each other, but ultimately we work together very well. A fellow business owner once told me that, in every relationship, there's a kite and a string. I'm the kite, and Brian is the string. Like my father, I love ideas, and 'no' is not in my vocabulary, so it's important to have him balancing me out and reigning me in a bit."

Today, Erika has more than thirty different project management, IT, and leadership certifications. As a leader, she focuses most on mentoring and empowering her employees, removing roadblocks and encouraging them to be the best they can be. "I make a conscious effort to include and teach people, and to recognize a job well done," she says. "Servant leadership is very important to me."

In advising young people entering the working world today, Erika underscores the importance of hard work to build excellence and mastery. "Get really good at your craft, whatever it is," she says. "If you're not sure yet what your passion is, just jump in and start learning. Say yes to every opportunity that comes your way and don't be afraid to try unusual things that are completely out of your comfort zone." Living by this philosophy, Erika signed up for improv classes in 2015 as a way to challenge herself, and is now a better listener and leader at work as a result. "It's helped generate ideas that have led our team to do creative marketing that no one else in our field is doing," she says. "Challenges keep us fresh, innovative, and competitive. But most of all, they show us that life always has more in store for us if we're willing to look."

BERNHARDT
WEALTH MANAGEMENT

Tom Frana

A Defining Drive

As a freshman at the University of Iowa in the 1960s, Tom Frana quickly realized he had no actual interest in attending classes. "The Vietnam War was underway at the time, and I had a low draft number," he recalls. "If I wasn't in school, I'd be drafted. I wanted to serve, but I wanted to make my own decision about where in the military I'd go."

Tom's father was an officer in the Navy, and Tom had been to enough Army-Navy games that he knew he couldn't go in the Army. The Air Force was oversubscribed at the time. That left the Coast Guard and the Marine Corps, and when he went down to the station to sign up, the office of the latter happened to be positioned before the office of the former.

Tom had learned a great deal about leadership watching his father, who had been on a fast track to an admiral ranking through World

War II and the Korean War. But his experience in the Marine Corps laid the foundation for his own brand of leadership. "I learned, first of all, how important it is to look out for the welfare of your people at all times," he says today. "The really great staff sergeants and gunnery sergeants I worked under truly did look out for us, and never asked us to do things they wouldn't do. They were strict, but ultimately understanding of small mistakes if we were shipshape 95 percent of the time."

Tom also learned very quickly that, if he showed capability, he would be given responsibility and freedom. As a 19-year-old, he found himself in Okinawa during the war, running an office and scheduling helicopter jumps and air drops. "Our gunnery sergeant would check in with me occasionally to make sure things were going well, but the rest was up to me," Tom recounts. "The Marine Corps was very good at picking people that could lead and letting them lead."

They picked Tom, in large part, because of his drive—an innate and unbendable will to get things done that was shaped and enhanced through military mentorship. "They took the time to teach me to have initiative, and really gave me the building blocks of leadership," he explains. "Once they saw that I was intent on learning and succeeding, they gave me the chances I needed to make it happen."

After over three years of military service during the war, Tom returned to the U.S. substantially behind the peers with whom he had graduated from high school in terms of career advancement, but he was determined to catch up. He completed his degree in record time, and once he landed a job in a computer room, he picked up every extra shift he could. "I got promoted because I was driven to learn and advance, always reaching for that next thing," he says. Now the President and CEO of ViON Corporation, a leading IT enterprise solutions firm serving clients in their mission to improve the security and prosperity of the U.S., Tom's success shows what happens when the kindling of drive meets the match of entrepreneurship.

Launched in 1980, ViON is a privately-held IT system integrator serving government at the federal, state, and local levels, as well as a growing commercial cliental. It provides infrastructure including servers, storage, switches, and networking capability, as well as an "As A Service" offering sprung from a Defense Information Systems Agency bid won fourteen years ago—a growing revenue stream that's still going strong today. "The model is based on consumption, allowing the agency to pay for the service only if it's being used," Tom explains. "We own the product, install it, and help the customer manage it to their requirements, with much more flexibility to scale than the traditional government acquisition process allows. Agencies can expand or contract without having to buy or get rid of product sets, which is ideal for them."

ViON's third segment of business focuses on the information security and advanced analytics marketplace. Utilizing standard information security and analytics solutions, its professional services team customizes the software package to fit the individual needs of each customer—just one example of the company's overarching commitment to exceptional service. "One very important priority for us is to train all our customer-facing employees to always ask the customer what else we can do for them," Tom explains. "Our philosophy is that we want to help in any way, shape, or form. If they ask us to do something, we'll find a way. It's been a very successful business strategy, and one of the key reasons our customers stay with us for so long."

When Tom joined ViON as President in 1992, the company had around 35 employees and drew annual revenues of about $35 million. Under his leadership, it has since grown to 195 employees and around $200 million. It has made an exceptional name for itself in the Department of Defense (DoD), the intelligence community, and U.S. Customs and Border Protection, as well as a host of other civilian agencies. As a critical IT partner, it allows these agencies to achieve their national defense missions—a strong driving force behind ViON's employees. "They feel that same sense of responsibility and esprit de corps, knowing that their work is contributing to that bigger mission of protecting the country," Tom affirms. "It's a powerful thing." Thanks to this higher purpose and to the leadership team's long-standing focus on ensuring their employees enjoy some of the best incentives, benefits, and empowerment opportunities in the market today, ViON has earned a yearly place on *Washingtonian Magazine*'s Best Places to Work list.

Even before his military service taught him to always look out for his people, Tom learned this important lesson from watching his own parents. He was born in Annapolis, Maryland, in 1946, as his father was finishing up postgraduate school at the Naval Academy after his service as an officer in World War II. The next year, his mother was diagnosed with multiple sclerosis. Treatment options at the time were severely limited, and he remembers his mother using canes to walk. As the years passed, the canes gave way to crutches, and the crutches gave way to a wheelchair, to the point that she eventually became bedridden.

Despite her condition, she was a positive influence in the lives of Tom and his older sister, and her health didn't hold the family back from a life of constant moving and adapting. His father, a devout Catholic with a strong sense of duty to country and family, was stationed in Long Beach during the Korean War to serve as the Executive Officer aboard the flagship Cruiser *Helena*. The family then returned to the duty station in Washington, DC, while Tom was in kindergarten and first grade. The next two years were spent in Hingham, Massachusetts, where his father worked at the Quincey Naval Shipyard and Tom decided he wanted some work of his own. A new housing development had just gone up nearby, and he went knocking door-to-door asking if they wanted the weekly newspaper. He bought it from the distributor for 5 cents and sold it for 10, garnering so much success that his father made him split the route with his sister.

Tom spent grades four through seven at the Naval Shipyard in Charleston, South Carolina, an idyllic environment where he enjoyed basketball, swimming, tennis, bowling, fishing, and bike riding, all within the protected environment of the base. His eighth, ninth, and tenth grade years were spent back in DC, where he attended St. Johns College High School, part of a Catholic teaching order called the De La Salle Christian Brothers. There, his English teacher and coach of the cross country squad convinced him to try out for the team. He discovered he had an exceptional talent for running, and embraced the sport as a lifelong passion.

St. John's, itself, was a life-changing experience—one that Tom was able to continue when his family moved to Cedar Rapids, Iowa. There, he would spend his last two years of high school at another Christian Brothers establishment, La Salle High School. "Through their demonstrations of faith, I really liked what the Christian Brothers did, and what they represented," Tom recalls. "The way they interacted with the students was really remarkable." Tom was also able to pursue his love of running when, with the help of his math teacher, he figured out how to lay out a track. They borrowed a truck from one of the mills in the area and purchased a ton of sawdust; built long jump, high jump, and pole vault pits; and created a track team for the school.

Tom imagined he would one day become a teacher with the Christian Brothers, and began down a path toward a religious life by enrolling at St. Mary's College in Winona, Minnesota. Within a year, he decided he wanted to pursue a different track. He transferred to the University of Iowa, where he enlisted in the Marines and was sent to San Diego for boot camp. He was then sent to Camp Pendleton for infantry training, where he was advised to ask at his next duty station for a list of positions that needed to be filled. "They told us we didn't need to waste three years of our career in an assignment we didn't like," Tom recounts. "So, when I was checking in at my first duty station, Camp Lejeune, I asked them what they needed so I could assess what my options were."

Tom, who was making $100 a month at the time, was informed that they needed dog handlers—a position in Vietnam that did not pay extra. When he asked what else they had, he learned they needed someone to do explosive bomb disposal—another position in Vietnam that did not pay extra. Finally, he was told they needed someone to do air delivery, dropping equipment with parachutes out of airplanes for an extra $55 a month. "To me, that was a no brainer," Tom says.

Tom landed the position and was sent to Fort Benning, Georgia, for jump school, followed by Fort Lee, Virginia, for Rigger School, and later a return to Pendleton jungle warfare training. Finally, his time came; he flew out of Marine Corps Air Station El Toro in California, and landed in Okinawa, where people were migrated into and out of Vietnam.

Tom spent the next year in Okinawa and then asked for a set of orders to do what he had been trained to do—actually fight the war in Vietnam. He finally received them, and in January of 1968 began packing parachutes and air dropping equipment through the Tet Offensive. He then spent the next several months with the infantry, helping to backfill for the men injured or killed during the Tet Offensive. He served the last five months of the War with Army Special Forces flying out of Da Nang, air dropping equipment along the Cambodian border.

After three years and two months of training, mastery, and war, Tom applied from overseas to finish his college education at Kendall College near Chicago, where his father was. "I returned to the states in time to start the January semester, and when I went in for registration with my blond hair and very deep suntan, the other students wanted to know where I had spent my Christmas vacation," Tom laughs. "Through the next several years, I studied anything, everything, and as much as possible. I took an extra-heavy course load and plowed through summer school, finishing my degree in economics early."

Through the college's work study program, Tom landed a job as a student parking cars in the garage during rush hour for Washington National Insurance. He was soon promoted to the night shift maintenance crew, but convinced his manager to get him an interview with the HR department. He was given a new job in data processing, which he did for a semester before being promoted to a computer room operator position. He ascended to senior operator and shift supervisor, and when he graduated from college, he became a system programmer. "That's how I got into the computer industry," he remarks.

After several years at Washington National Insurance, Tom took a systems programming job at Trailer Train in Chicago, where he took countless professional development classes. While in Chicago, his mother passed away. He married his first wife and later had two wonderful daughters. "I was working so hard that I'd fall asleep when we were out to dinner together," he remembers. "I missed my bachelor party because I was working. I was driven for the success, and I was good at it, which made me like it even more."

Soon the young couple moved to Wisconsin, where Tom ran the systems programming group at Bucyrus Erie. He was then recruited by Itel Corporation for a systems engineering job in Northern California. He was promoted to Branch Manager and Regional Manager, which meant a move down to Southern California, but headed back up North when he was named Director of Customer Support. Then, when Itel filed for bankruptcy and was bought out by National Semiconductor, Tom became Director of Systems Engineering U.S. for the new entity, National Advanced Systems. Transferring to Europe, Tom had systems engineers, maintenance personnel, and HR reporting to him. "At that point, I had about 60 percent of the firm's employees in Europe working for me," he remembers. "I became VP General Manager for Asia Pacific, which meant traveling all over Asia."

When the company was acquired by Hitachi Data Systems in 1989, Tom stayed on as VP and General Manager of U.S. Operations until 1992. Amidst the reorganization of the worldwide sales and marketing support entities, he was passed over for a top job, so he reached out to ViON, which had been a customer for twelve years. The founders of the business had worked with Tom at Itel, observing his rapid advancement to VP. "I had helped them on deals, getting products in a timely fashion when they were hard-pressed to get something done quickly," Tom recalls. "They knew enough about me to take a chance on me."

With that, ViON's leadership asked him to join them in 1992 as President for a two-year trial period, and if he didn't run the company into the ground, they would move forward with a buyout. Tom proved a perfect fit, and through his partnership with the VP of Operations and the CFO, was able to fully buy out the former owners within two years instead of the estimated six. With that, in 1996, Tom was firmly moving forward as an owner and President of his own company.

"I knew the company had potential, but I didn't know enough about the federal marketplace at that time to know how big it could become," he recounts. He succeeded in growing the company at a modest clip over the next decade, but when the 9/11 terrorist attacks transformed the national defense landscape, the opportunity to grow and meet the nation's needs expanded exponentially. "As the wars in Afghanistan and Iraq took off, the amount of data being collected was just staggering," Tom says. "The government needed high-performance servers, data storage, and analytics. That was the true engine of growth for our business."

Through that time, Tom had also reconnected with Karen, an extremely talented young woman who had been a key colleague at Hitachi. They married and in 2005 had a son, Trey. "On one side of the equation, she's my soulmate and the perfect partner for me," Tom says. "On the other, she understands the business I'm in. She's a great sounding board and will argue things out with me to help me see views that are different from my own." Both strong believers in giving back, Tom served fourteen years on the Board of St. John's College High School, where he was recently Chairman. Karen was elected to the board of The Langley School, where Trey attends, and now heads up their Development Committee. They are both founding members of the Marine Corps Heritage Foundation, where Tom serves on the board, and were initial sponsors of the United Service Organizations (USO) R&R transit facility at the Dallas Fort Worth airport.

In advising young people entering the working world today, Tom underscores the importance of picking a job but quickly moving on to the next one if it's not right for you. "Don't stay somewhere that isn't a good fit," he says. "At the same time, don't keep jumping from job to job. Be strategic and intentional about your choices, because once you find a good fit, you'll enjoy it and be successful at it."

Oftentimes, finding that fit can unlock an inner drive like the one that propelled Tom through his career of twists, turns, and rapid ascension. And along his journey to the pinnacle of business success, he has always been careful to bring others along with him, inspiring in them a similar inclination toward hard work and accomplishment. "My daughters tell me they don't know another person that's as excited about their work as I've always been," he says. "I'm glad I could leave that impression on them as they were growing up—that it's possible to make a good living and enjoy the hell out of it too. I hope Trey sees that same passion, and that all three get to experience the joy of a defining drive in their lives."

BERNHARDT
WEALTH MANAGEMENT

Francisco Gali

The Power of Persistence

Francisco Gali has never waited for opportunity to knock. Instead, he has aggressively pursued new challenges throughout his life and career. At age 13, he left Venezuela to attend a boarding school in Pennsylvania. After attending college, he was able to hop onboard the George H. W. Bush campaign, ultimately parlaying his political experience into a position with the Congressional Hispanic Caucus Institute. Still, secure though his position at the institute was, Francisco was not content. "You don't make a lot of money in Congress, and I needed to make ends meet," he explains. "I asked the office manager what they paid the cleaning company, and they were paying about $1,200 a month or so. I told them I could do it for $800, and I'd do a much better job. That was big time for me!" With that first official cleaning contract, the company that would one day become GSI Group was born.

Today, Gali Service Industries, or GSI Group (GSI), is a $30 million business employing over 1,000 staff members. The group offers a wide range of integrated facility services for clients including commercial office properties, schools, stadiums, hotels, airports, and data centers. Along with specialty cleaning services, GSI can also provide exterior grounds maintenance, moving services, daily porter services, and a myriad of other necessary upkeep services for commercial and residential buildings. "One of the unique things about GSI is that we've managed to do a wide variety of things very, very well," explains Francisco, "Most companies don't fall into that profile. They're either commercial or residential. But GSI has succeeded in meeting the needs of both verticals, amalgamating a series of services that work well together for our clients."

As founder, CEO, and Chairman of GSI Group, Francisco has worked to ensure the success of the business for nearly 30 years. The broad range of the services offered are a work in progress that has developed over time as Francisco worked overtime to keep clients happy and grow the business. As its inception in 1988, with its first-ever cleaning job, the business was called Spot Professional Services. A couple of years later, the name was changed to Argus Commercial Services. Finally, in 1992, the rapidly growing business became GSI Group, as its menu of services had already expanded significantly. "We started as a cleaning company, picking up trash and vacuuming office buildings, and then morphed into doing a lot of residential common areas and high-rise apartment buildings," he recalls, "We started providing porters in addition to cleaners, as well as assistants for light engineering. Over the years, clients would ask, can you do this or that? We wanted to provide the best and most robust service possible, so we always said yes. We started getting into carpet cleaning and floor refinishing. Last year we started a concierge service, and within a year, that offering has reached almost $2 million in sales. That's just one example of a project we launched because people were asking, which went on to great success."

Client feedback was a major motivation of GSI's continual growth and expansion. But Francisco's own ambition was another central component of the company's rise to the top. "After I got my first $800, I went out and got a contract $1,800," he recounts. "And I thought, well, if I can hit $100,000 a year, I'll be hitting the big time. Then when I got the $100,000, I thought, well, to get to critical mass, I've got to hit $500,000. When I got that, I thought, man, I won't be any good until I get to that $1 million!" No matter how much money the business made, Francisco saw success just over the horizon. He never rested on his laurels, but continued to push himself on toward that next mountain, proving the power of persistence.

Francisco never imagined the heights he would one day reach while growing up in a dusty, rural town in Venezuela. Both sets of grandparents had emigrated from Spain, so both his mother and father were immigrants to Venezuelan. His father was a businessman who owned hardware stores, and Francisco credits him with passing along an entrepreneurial gene and a drive for excellence. "He's a very determined, self-made person who I admire because he educated himself through reading," Francisco explains. "And beyond that, he educated his brothers and sisters. He didn't go to college or have the kinds of opportunities I had, but he had this persistence. My mom is very determined and hardworking as well. She's always been very much a giver, and I inherited that trait from her. I always want to help everyone and do everything, sometimes to a fault."

As a kid in Venezuela, Francisco remembers running around outdoors with friends and working at the family hardware store from a young age. He was expected to help out with the business almost from the time he could walk, sweeping the floors and killing rats with his trusty slingshot. "For the week, dad would give me a fuerte, which is five bolivars," Francisco laughs. "I used to think that if I kept killing those rats for the next thirty years, I'd be a millionaire! Dad always had me working."

Growing up, Francisco and his older sister learned a lot about the U.S., studying with American students at the bilingual school. Then, in 1977, he and his father went on a trip to New York City. It was his first time visiting the States, and his first impression was a good one. "All I wanted was to do two things: go to FAO Schwartz, the largest toy store in the world, and see Star Wars," he remembers. "When I got to New York and saw that enormous city, I couldn't believe it. It was like a dream. We didn't even have a movie theater in my hometown, and going to FAO Schwartz, I couldn't believe something like that existed. It was the biggest moment of my life up to that point."

Unfortunately, at the age of eleven, a traumatic incident affected young Francisco deeply. He was abused by an employee of the family, an older man. Afraid of what might happen if he came forward, he was silent about the abuse for decades before finally opening up. "I carried that inside until my thirties," he says. "I never discussed it with anybody, and I think it affected me and my sense of self-worth a lot in business. Sometimes I wonder how much farther I might have gotten if I didn't have so many doubts manifested from that event." The man disappeared one day, but the memories of the trauma lingered. Francisco carried this trauma with him when, at a mere thirteen years old, he began as a student at the Hill School in Pennsylvania.

Moving abroad alone at such a young age would be challenging for anyone. It was an especially steep mountain to climb for Francisco, who had so recently been through a terrible, but private, ordeal. "I was terrified," he recalls. "It was very hard, but I thank my parents for the incredible education that the Hill School gave me. It instilled a desire to learn and an ability to see things from different perspectives." The Hill School was a private, exclusive school for boys, grades eight through twelve. The school was strict—the boys were expected to wear suits and ties, and classes were held six days a week. In addition, every student was required to work a campus job. Right away, Francisco began to display the ambition that would serve him so well in adulthood.

He was assigned a job clearing tables in the dining hall, but he didn't remain in the position for long. "I said, 'I don't want to be cleaning plates here,'" he recalls, "So quickly I became a table setter, then a row captain, and then a shift captain. Ultimately, for the next few years I ran the whole dining room, serving around 1,400 people every day."

In short order, Francisco had realized that excelling in his work would ultimately place him in a better position, and he quickly rose through the ranks of student workers in the dining hall. He credits the experience as a sort of training course for managing employees, since he was responsible for directing teams of other students. Academically, he also strove for greatness, and by his senior year, he was selected to be a Prefect and awarded special privileges. Among these privileges were the ability to leave campus, and the coveted "long weekend"—not having to attend class on Saturdays. It was during this time that Francisco and his close friend, Aleco, would drive to Aleco's family home in DC, where Francisco met and began dating his high school sweetheart, Kris.

As Francisco considered his college options, Kris's location was a major consideration. They decided to both attend George Washington University (GW) together, although Francisco isn't sure GW would've otherwise been his top choice. "It's a great school, but it was my backup school and I decided to go there for her," he recounts. "But I did have a desire to come to DC because I loved that it was the seat of power of the United States. I had always really admired that, and I felt drawn to the city."

Francisco loved life at GW, but he was concerned about his parents back home. His mother was diagnosed with Stage 4 Melanoma, an aggressive cancer with a 10 percent survival rate, and the doctors in Venezuela advised sending her abroad for surgery and treatment in New York. His father poured all of his resources into saving her life, and miraculously, it worked. Francisco's mother recovered, but unfortunately, the family's savings had dwindled to almost nothing.

The following year, an economic collapse hit Venezuela, and things really got bad financially for the Gali family. Francisco's father fell into a severe depression, and Francisco describes this period as one of the defining times of his life. "I flew to Venezuela to be with him for a few weeks because I was honestly worried he might die," Francisco recalls. "I spent a lot of time with him, even though at times we had a difficult relationship. He demanded a lot, which can be good, but also challenging. Thankfully, I was able to help him snap out of it and get back on his feet. He rebuilt his businesses again and ultimately did very well."

Back in DC, it wasn't long before Francisco's dreams of working in politics came to fruition. During the 1987 and 1988 election season, he worked on the George H.W. Bush campaign. Kris, his girlfriend, went on to work at the White House, while Francisco went on to the Congressional Hispanic Caucus. In January of 1992, Kris helped arrange a photo of Francisco in the Oval Office shaking hands with then-President Bush. He still treasures the memory of that day and the photographs that were taken. "That was an incredible moment where I felt that I had truly made it," he says. "It was the beginning of my business career, and I was proud of what I had already achieved. I was able to come from where I came from in life, all the way from a poor town in Venezuela, to set foot in the office of the most powerful man on the planet. I shook his hand and spent fifteen minutes talking with him. That was something really remarkable."

By this time, Francisco's cleaning business was growing rapidly. He credits his business mentor, Herman Greenberg, with taking a chance on him as his fledging career started out. Greenberg was the father of his close friend, Aleco from boarding school, and owned several buildings in the area. He told Francisco there was a job he could take on cleaning a place called the Somerset House, if he was sure he could hack it. "Boy was he tough on me," Francisco laughs. "If there was a lightbulb that wasn't working, he'd call me up. I'd have to go on my lunch break from Capitol Hill down to change the lightbulb. But I did such a good job there, I got to bid this other big job at Seminary Towers. Once I got that job, we really started to grow."

But growing the business wasn't always as easy as that. Francisco had majored in political science at GW, and he often found himself improvising when it came to running a company. When the real estate crisis hit in 1992, there was a down period of intense cuts. "That was probably my first big professional challenge," he says, "I was learning business on the fly. When you go into these shortage modes, there's not a lot of capital, and banks don't want to lend you money when you're a small company. That was a big challenge." Thankfully, Francisco's dedication and persistence paid off. GSI's fortunes quickly revived over the next few years, and soon it was expanding faster than ever.

Meanwhile, Francisco worked closely with his father on a couple of major side ventures. "I was shuttling back and forth to Venezuela and we started a pumping services company for the oil and gas industry," he explains. "It was gravel packing, which is something you do in wells. After two years, we sold that venture because we wanted to get into cementing. We bought a company called Toucan and provided cementing services in Venezuela."

The second venture was also successful, but Francisco felt that the political climate in the country was becoming too tumultuous. After Chavez was elected, he began to look abroad for a new location. Toucan moved to Indonesia, where they again achieved success and ultimately decided to sell the operation to an Indonesian group.

Francisco was glad to have worked with his father professionally, and over the years of collaboration, their relationship had grown much closer. As the situation deteriorated further in Venezuela, Francisco decided his parents needed to relocate to the U.S.. They're both now working for GSI Group, heading up a successful new division. "They're incredibly helpful," reports Francisco of the arrangement. "They run a profitable division, and they run it very well. It's called GSI Homemade

Solutions. It caters to extended stay hotels." Francisco's father is also serving as interim President of GSI Group while Francisco addresses his ongoing divorce proceedings.

The divorce has been tough on Francisco, but he's learning to rely on the good friends and close family around him in this difficult time. "I think the important thing is, there have been great people around me reaching out—people who have been incredibly supportive," he says. "If you're a competitive person who likes to be successful in business, chances are that success is important in all aspects of life. That's how it is for me, and I especially never wanted my two older children to see me get a second divorce. Divorce hurts especially when the person you trust and love turns out to be something they are not. In my bad moments, I see it as a failure. But there's always a lesson learned, and in this case, it's the importance of taking your time to get to know people. Sometimes you learn who your real friends are during these periods. It's a journey I'm going through and a test that I'm going to have to deal with as it comes." His focus now, then, is to make his little children, Francisco III and Isabella, happy and well-adjusted kids.

Francisco's two older daughters from his marriage to Kris, Miranda and Sophia, are both high-achieving students at college. To them and to other young people preparing to launch their careers, Francisco advises the same determination that turned GSI Group from a small cleaning business into a $30 million company. "I told them that, to be successful, the number one most important thing is to be persistent," he emphasizes. "And number two, you have to be honest. Number three is, don't be afraid. As one of my favorite quotes goes, it is not your aptitude but your attitude that will determine your altitude."

As a leader, Francisco has always striven to provide a role model to the Hispanic community, and to young people in general. "I believe that empowering people to be the best they can be is the key to running a successful organization. It's all about empowering them to do the work. I wouldn't be where I am today without the hardworking people on my team."

Francisco credits one of his bosses at the Hispanic Caucus Institute with driving that important lesson home for him early on. Beverly Ellerman was the Executive Director of the group, and she served as a mentor to young Francisco. "She said to me, if you want to move up in life, you have to be confident, and you have to train someone to replace you. Because if not, you're going to be stuck in the same place, in the same spot. So don't be scared to compete, embracing all the potential that lies in both yourself and others. As long as you have a vision to strive for and the will to persist, there's no telling how far you'll go."

Francisco also credits several people who will always have a special place in his heart: His parents, Francisco and Angela Gali; Ronny Ortowski who has been a great friend, mentor, and business role model; former Congressman Xavier Becerra who is a true gentleman and role model of leadership and courage; and the great and loyal employees of GSI who have been by his side for so many years.

BERNHARDT
WEALTH MANAGEMENT

Amy Jaller Gleklen

Charting the Course to Smoother Sailing

It's lucky that Amy Gleklen's father was a doctor. He had taught her the Heimlich Maneuver when she was young, and the lesson stuck. One sunny day years later, Amy was hosting a pool party for her daughter, when one of the little girls began to choke. "A piece of watermelon lodged in her throat and she couldn't breathe," Amy recalls. "Everyone else just sat there. The girl's mother rushed over but didn't know what to do, so I took over and tried the maneuver. I thought, not on my watch! My friends remarked how I had gone into action, and I realized that, yes, that is how I'm wired—quickly jumping to action to solve the problem before me."

Amy has always been equal parts visionary, mapping out the future, and activator, making things happen. From the time she was young, she eagerly explored different paths to discover what could be, never content to pick the safe or comfortable option for herself. And as she navigated through various roles, she cultivated a deep understanding of all aspects of business, including sales, marketing, finance, budgeting, and operations. She ultimately came to find that her own circuitous route was the powerful delineator that allowed her to understand diverse contexts, experiences, and possibilities, building just the insight that today's leaders need most when facing their toughest challenges. "Executive coaching is my purpose and passion," she says. "And thanks to my own career trajectory, I can understand my client's context and offer a business perspective. Whether I'm helping people make better choices, navigate a career move, overcome an obstructive behavior, or solve a business dilemma, it's always about following their energy, exploring choices, and charting the best course forward to a better future."

Today, Amy puts this gift to work as a Chair for Vistage Worldwide, leading two peer advisory boards for CEOs in the DC metropolitan area, and as Founder and CEO of Next Game Plan, Inc. She launched Next Game Plan in 2008 and grew it through a combination of executive coaching, leadership development training, and career coaching services. "My clients are diverse but have one thing in common: they're stuck and want clarity," Amy explains. "Sometimes our work is spurred by feedback from co-workers, and sometimes it's self-motivated. They need a trained coach to ask good questions, help them understand the problem more fully, make connections, and see choices and possibilities. Once we do that, then I help them commit to new actions to lead to desired results."

Amy loved this work, but something was missing. "As a solo practitioner and executive coach, my clients are my community," she recounts. "But most clients engage for only six months or a year to tackle specific coaching goals. I missed being part of a larger, more enduring community."

In 2014, when Amy learned about Vistage, she knew it was just what she wanted. Not only could she be part of an outstanding worldwide organization with over 22,000 members in 22 countries, but she could also be responsible for building her own community through her advisory groups as a Chair. Each individual Vistage Chair builds his or her own independent boards, each structured to accommodate the specific and local needs of its executives.

The combination of individual coaching, group mentoring, and community building was perfect for Amy. Her first group launched with thirteen members, including several CEOs from larger businesses that faced challenges unique to their situations. Within the same year, she decided to build another group targeted to more experienced CEOs, all while continuing her private coaching work at Next Game Plan.

Balancing these demands has been exhausting but incredibly rewarding. She received a "Rookie of the Year" award in 2017 for her work at Vistage, but her proudest moments always come when a client tells her that the work they did together made a difference. "It's the emails I receive years later," she affirms. "For instance, I was at an event the other day, and one of the caterers notice my name tag. She told me I worked with her son, and it had changed his life. At the end of the day, I really do what I do because I know I'm making a difference."

For Amy, then, success is the joy her clients feel when their issues are resolved, measured against the frustration or sadness her clients feel, visible in a client's face in that first session or Vistage meeting. "Through that process, we become like a family," she remarks. "Over the course of my coaching career, I started working with senior management in organizations and found they don't often have people or colleagues in their lives who they can trust fully and who will hold confidentiality. Now, when I work with a client, I feel like their best friend because I have no hidden agenda and have only their best interests at heart. I feel humbled to be that person for my clients at a time when they need it the most, and the honor of helping others be happier is a great joy in my life."

In reflecting on her path, where seemingly disparate experiences and talents brought her to a place she never imagined but fits perfectly,

Amy often refers to a Steve Jobs quote that reads, "You can't connect the dots looking forward; you can only connect them looking backwards." Her work, in turn, is about connecting other people's dots, helping them figure out where they need to go next. It embraces a philosophy of forward momentum that avoids getting stuck in the present—a mindset that served her well through her own childhood spent shuttling across countries and cultures at a young age.

Amy's father, whose own father was German and mother had fled the Russian Revolution, was born in Switzerland and met Amy's mother while attending New York University. They moved to Dayton, Ohio, where he opened a successful private practice as a physician. Within a few years of Amy's birth, he grew restless and dreamed of moving to Israel. At the age of five, Amy was heading overseas with her parents, two older brothers, and three dogs, with her father's Airstream trailer and beloved boat in tow.

Amy's father was promised a job there that never transpired, and for a time, the whole family lived crammed in their little trailer. Then they got a small house, and Amy was sent to an Israeli school for kindergarten, where she stuck out like a sore thumb as the only American. "I didn't know Hebrew at the time," she recounts. "I felt like an alien. The kids had never met an American before. I made up a language that was some combination of English and Hebrew, and somehow the other kids eventually started to understand me. But I cried myself to sleep a lot. Going to school was pretty hard for me."

The following year, in 1966, Amy's parents decided to head back to the States, but not to Ohio. Her father wanted to be somewhere he could use his boat and be near friends. They parked their trailer in a trailer park in Homestead, Florida, and once again, Amy felt like something of an oddity. "Even the Southern accent was different from what I was used to," she laughs. "I went to first grade there, and then we moved to Maryland, leaving the trailer in Homestead. We'd go back three times a year, and I continued my friendships with people from the trailer park, which had a huge impact on me."

In first grade, Amy hadn't noticed much difference between herself and the other kids in the trailer park. But as she grew older, and her doctor father drove the family down in their Cadillac for visits, she began to see that she had significant privilege compared to the other children. "My life was so different from theirs, but I was still one of their best friends," she recalls. "They nicknamed me the Psychologist because I was the person everyone came to for advice."

Amy grew up a natural extrovert always eager to perform—early expressions of the creativity and freedom of spirit that she uses to serve her clients today. "I've always been a ham, and I'm not afraid to make a fool of myself in front of a crowd," she says. "Having fun, letting loose, and being creative is an important part of helping clients come up with creative solutions of their own." As a kid, she was also a tomboy who spent a lot of time outdoors, climbing trees and playing with animals. She loved to talk—a trait she got from her father, a deep thinker and great pontificator who studied art, history, and politics. Family dinner conversations were his chosen medium for expressing his thoughts and ideas, cultivating Amy's own analytical abilities and inspiring in her the same strong work ethic. Amy's mother, meanwhile, has been her lifelong support system and confidant. "Now 91, she's still my first phone call in times of trouble," Amy says. "I learned compassion and unconditional love from her, and it was a great source of strength to know she was always there for me."

After the family's move to Maryland, Amy finally settled into a less transient lifestyle. In middle school, she remembers standing up for her best friend when a group of girls began bullying her. After that, she felt more socially isolated, but Amy was glad she had done the right thing and opposed injustice. In high school, she made plenty of new friends, was involved in musical theater, played the drums for several bands, and became a leader in her local Jewish youth group, United Synagogue Youth. She spent time demonstrating for social justice, focused significant energy on community service, and was also chosen out of thousands of people to receive a regional leadership award, marking an important milestone for her.

Upon graduating from high school, Amy enrolled at the University of Pennsylvania, where her father encouraged her to pursue medicine. She had worked part-time in his medical office from the age of thirteen, but she was reluctant to commit so much time to school and initially planned on becoming a nurse instead. But in her freshman year, a traumatic experience led her to change her mind. "A couple of years prior, I had been the last person to see my grandfather in his hospital bed before he passed away," she recounts. "Then when I was eighteen, the rest of my family was out of town when my grandmother had a heart attack. I was the only one there with her telling her she was going to be okay, and I was the one there when she flatlined. I had completed one semester of nursing school, but I decided the profession was too hard, so thought I should pursue social work."

But Amy's father wasn't a fan of her new career idea. "We were in a recession at the time," she remembers. "He was worried about my job prospects, so I started looking through the course catalogue and came across Wharton School. He thought that was a great idea." To submatriculate into the business school, Amy had to achieve a 3.5 GPA in her second semester. She dedicated herself to hitting the mark and was admitted to Wharton the following year as a marketing major.

In 1981, Amy graduated and landed her first advertising job, only to realize that advertising wasn't her thing. She soon transitioned to Booz Allen Hamilton, where she had a much better experience as an internal consultant helping a partner run a 70-person practice. Her mentor there advised her to get an MBA if she wanted to gain any real traction in the business world, so she headed back to Wharton, where she also struck up a greater interest in public policy. She worked on the Hill between the first and second years of the program, but ultimately decided to accept a job offer from Merrill Lynch because it was the most coveted option at the time. "I ended up in healthcare finance on

Wall Street," she recalls. "It was pivotal for me because it was just not a good fit. It felt too empty, and I didn't feel like I was really impacting anything. I would go home and fantasize about winning the lottery to help me escape my situation. At some point, I finally worked up the courage to leave. My boss thought I would regret it, but I never did."

After Merrill Lynch, Amy was open to something new and different, and she didn't have to wait long. Interested in getting involved in politics, she booked a train from New York City to Washington, D.C., and happened to sit next to a financial consultant to Joe Biden's Presidential campaign. They conversed on the ride, and within a couple weeks, she was heading to Wilmington, Delaware, to accept a position as the National Budget Director for the campaign. "It was a great job," she says. "I had a financial role with spreadsheets and budgets, but there was a purpose behind them. I cared so much more about what we were trying to accomplish."

Also on that campaign, Amy met her husband, Jonathan. Jon was an intern, still in college and several years younger, who jokes that he was the "First Budget Director" on the campaign. The two hit it off, and at their wedding, Joe Biden commented that the pair was the best thing to come out of his campaign. The couple relocated to Chicago while Jon obtained his law degree, and then to DC, where he was hired by the law firm of Arnold & Porter. "The next ten years were kind of a blur!" Amy says. "I had a bucket list of career interests, which included television production. Then, around the time my third child was born, I went back to my roots and decided to get a Master's in Counseling at John's Hopkins."

Before she could put her new degree to work, however, fate intervened. A friend from Wharton was volunteering with an organization called Compass, and thought Amy might be a good fit for the Executive Director position. "I thought it sounded really fun because the goal was bringing together MBAs from top business schools to help other non-profits," she says. "Up to that point, my career path didn't seem cohesive, but Compass put all the pieces together. They happened to be piloting executive coaching for non-profit leaders through a one-on-one program, and the field seemed perfect for me, utilizing my MBA, my counseling background, and my yearning to connect deeper with people."

Amy kept the idea of executive coaching in the back of her mind, ultimately deciding to enroll in an intensive 6-month Executive Leadership Coaching Certification program at Georgetown. "The girl who didn't want to become a doctor because it was too many years of school, ended up getting two Master's Degrees and a Certification," she laughs. "It turns out I do love learning. I'm learning all the time, and I'm hugely passionate about it because I get to apply my knowledge and breadth of experience to help my clients move forward."

Through it all, Jon has been a partner and support system in every way. "He helps me think through my own issues, especially the curves and moments of inflection I've experienced along the way," she reflects. "He's worked at one law firm his entire career, but he's always been supportive of my bucket list and my interest in trying new things." Their four children—2 boys and 2 girls—are now happy and healthy at 24, 22, 20 and 16. "I am so grateful for my beautiful family. I am very lucky."

As a leader, Amy focuses on inspiration and collaboration. "You have to both see the big picture and set the course, and you have to invite others to help and participate," she says. She keeps in her mind life's inverted truth—its fragility and unpredictability, as hammered home when her son, Ryan, grew a tumor between his eye and nose at only nine months old. "Instead of freaking out, my reaction was, what's the big picture and what's the next step?" she remembers. "What's really going on and what are our choices for moving forward? It's the same way I coach my clients. If you only have one life to live, it's important to think about how you want to live it and the imprint you're making."

In advising young people entering the working world today, Amy underscores the importance of continued learning and growth, because we'll never have all the answers. "Know how you got to where you are, because there are plenty of lessons to learn," she says. "Once that's clear, you can get some sense of where you might want to go. Start to think not in terms of the present, but the future. It's easy to get stuck in the present, and that's when people become unhappy, seeing what is and not what could be."

Beyond that, Amy encourages everyone to seek out the energy in life that speaks to them—that which is both profound and peaceful, like water is to her. "Like my father, I've always found being on the water to be a source of serenity," she says. "It's also a place where things can go terribly wrong, like when my son almost drowned. On the water, we've been both powerful and powerless. But with the right tools, the right mindset, and the right help by your side, there's always a way to chart the course to smoother sailing."

BERNHARDT
WEALTH MANAGEMENT

Scott Goss

Proving It

Even when he wound up in the hospital after a moped accident, sixteen-year-old Scott Goss wasn't ready to admit he was in a downward spiral. It was only a couple of months later, when he re-entered the hospital for drug use, that the truth of his reality began to set in. As his peers prepared to attend Ivy League schools, he was living in a friend's car and working at a gas station. He never thought about the future because, at that point, he didn't have one.

"For the first time since I had started to fall off the tracks at age fourteen, I began to realize how bad things had gotten," he remembers now. "I had been permanently suspended from school and ran away from home. My junior year was half gone, and my senior year was approaching when I was suspended from high school permanently. What was my life going to be? Where was I going to live, and what was I going to do for a living? I can't say what spurred that moment of waking up, but I know that it didn't come from my parents, or the doctors, or any of the external voices trying to get through to me. It was a decision I, and only I, could make for myself."

Just as the decision to change was all Scott, what came next was all him as well. One year later, he was making exceptional grades at boarding school and had assumed a leadership role amongst his peers as a dorm prefect. Six years later, he graduated from a prestigious university in the top five percent of his class. And today, he's the President and CEO of Preferred System Solutions (PSS) Inc., a high-end government IT contractor specializing in computer systems, cloud computing, data analysis and analytics, and cyber security. "I remember being in high school, seeing the success of others and feeling that I couldn't measure up," he says today. "But I got past that and saw that I could be somebody and succeed. I'm driven by the feeling of being able to say, 'I can do this'—by the feeling of being challenged, and learning, and proving that I can turn adversity into success."

PSS was first launched as a staff augmentation company in 1991 by Rob Hisel. Focused mostly on commercial staffing, the company grew modestly until 1997, when it received its 8(a) certification and made its initial foray into government contracting. Rob sold the commercial staffing portion of his business to a dotcom company just in time to lose everything when the dotcom bubble burst. Despite the devastating blow, he picked himself up without missing a beat and decided to focus on growing his government contracting work.

Scott was first introduced to Rob in 1996 while working for SIGNAL Corporation. SIGNAL was acquired by Veridian, which was later acquired by General Dynamics, and after a great ride, he had begun consulting on his own. He took Rob on as a client in 2004, helping him grow PSS from $18 million to $38 million by 2006. Rob then began considering an exit strategy, ultimately convincing Scott, along with CM Equity, to step in as President and CEO in August of 2007.

At that time, 40 percent of the company's business was from 8(a) government contracts, 35 percent was from small businesses contracts, and 25 percent was from commercial staffing. The company had grown to 280 employees specializing in IT contracting. The regulatory environment was shifting along with the economic downturn, but Scott succeeded in leading the company through seven acquisitions beginning in 2009. "We've refaced the company into something brand new today," he affirms. "It's been great for the company, great for the staff, and great for the clients." Thanks to this approach and to the strong performance of PSS, Scott won a GovCon M&A award in 2015—a recognition for which he has been a finalist four years running.

Now a team of over 400 people doing approximately $100 million in revenue, PSS has advanced its focus to big data, analytics, cyber security, mobile applications, software, and high-level program management systems. Seventy percent of the company's business comes from the intelligence community, while the other 30 percent comes from other federal agencies like the Navy, Army, Department of Transportation, and Department of Homeland Security. And like the man at its helm, the company is constantly evolving. "It's important to me to have a purpose, make an impact, and learn something new every day," he says. "I believe that when you stop learning in business, or in life, you lose your drive."

This drive for constant advancement is more a reflection of his mother's influence than his father's. His father was a relaxed and kindhearted man who grew up in a blue collar family in DC and forged his own father's signature so he could enter the Navy at age sixteen. His mother, on the other hand, was a Holocaust survivor who escaped Austria at the age of seven, only after her own father was already taken to a camp. The trauma heightened her guard as a parent, and she was exceptionally protective and strict when it came to Scott and his older sister, Penny. "Growing up, I felt constant pressure to prove myself, moving on to the next thing as soon as I solved a problem," Scott recalls. "Giving up or quitting were simply not options. My mother never let me quit anything I started, and she never let me wallow. She taught me to go right out the next day and get back on the horse. I was constantly driven by the need to figure out whatever challenge lay before me so I could begin working on the next one."

Born in Philadelphia, Scott was one when the family moved to Rye Town, New York, near the Connecticut border. His father was a chemist working in the pharmaceutical industry, while his mother was a teacher, and they shared a wonderfully close marriage. Scott was a happy-go-lucky, well-behaved, well-mannered kid who enjoyed playing baseball and stickball with other kids in the neighborhood. His parents were incredibly hardworking, with his father often juggling two or three jobs, and were able to spend time with the children only rarely. "They didn't come to our ball games, and I can count on one hand the number of times we went out to dinner as a family," Scott recalls. "I decided I didn't want to live like that when I grew up. I wanted to achieve the kind of success that brings peace of mind, knowing early on that my kids would be provided for."

The Gosses were a middle-class family living in a wealthy neighborhood, and while other kids enjoyed silver spoons, Scott learned to work for what he wanted. When he turned thirteen, he had the choice between a Bar Mitzvah party like his friends were having, or a trip to Israel. He chose the latter, which became the first and only vacation his family took together while he was growing up. "They told me I wouldn't remember a 4-hour party in 30 years, but I'd definitely remember the trip," Scott says. "I convinced them to add Italy and Egypt into the mix, and they were right—I still remember that trip. I gave my own children the same opportunity, and like me, they chose the Pyramids and the Dead Sea."

Scott's mother believed in mitzvahs, or good deeds, and taught the importance of giving of yourself, doing the right thing, and keeping busy. He cut his neighbors' lawns for free, volunteered in a nearby hospital, and had a paper route. He wasn't allowed to play capture the flag with friends in the evenings because his parents thought it was a sign of bad character to be out on the streets at night. They forced him to play the piano, waking up at 5:30 AM to practice for an hour before school and then again after school, but Scott wanted to play the drums. At eight years old, he began saving up to buy his own drum set, and by age 12, he was in a band.

As Scott entered high school, his parents' strict ways began to take a toll. He dreamed of growing up to be a rock star and began gravitating toward a different crowd. He began to rebel, getting into drugs and letting his grades plummet as he headed down a path of self-destruction that led to his permanent suspension from school in eleventh grade. The gravity of the situation didn't even register with him; instead, he started working full-time at a gas station and joined a different band, practicing long hours in their studio late nights in White Plains. "I was being led by some very strong social influences, instead of a good sense of right and wrong," he reflects. "I think I was predisposed to certain behaviors, and the reigns were just pulled too tight, so I bucked."

It was seven months later that Scott hit rock bottom. "I had run away from home and continued with the drugs, living in a friend's car or wherever I could," he remembers. "I ended up in the hospital after going through the roughest period of my life, and I decided to go to a counselor with my parents. I especially remember my mother saying she still loved me because I was her son. That really had an impact on me."

The counselor said Scott needed to get away from his life in New York, where his friends were bad influences and the environment was too fraught. The counselor strongly suggested boarding school, and at first, Scott adamantly refused to consider it. But he had truly scared himself. "I finally woke up and realized that if I continued on that way, I'd be dead within two years," he says. "I needed to redo my life, and I saw that change couldn't come from anybody else—it had to come from me."

In the end, Scott agreed to go away to boarding school at West Nottingham Academy in Colora, Maryland, close enough to where his sister Penny was attending college at the University of Maryland.

Slowly but surely, he began to get his life together, studying and working hard. His grades rose surprisingly quickly, and within a month of being there, he was appointed to serve as a dorm prefect—a position of responsibility that many students never attained. His strong academic performance continued through his two years at the Academy, landing him admission to American University (AU). "I knew AU was the school I'd be able to work hardest at, and where I'd really excel," Scott says. "My parents were big, big believers in education, and sacrificed a lot to help me get there. So that meant a lot to them."

At AU, Scott majored in philosophy and minored in business and music. He continued playing gigs around town, though at that point he knew it wouldn't be his career. He worked his way through college doing construction, mostly focused on drywall. With a set of tools that included the first spackel knife his father ever owned, he went to work every single day to support himself as he made the most of the opportunity many thought he would never get. "Drywall is not a very pretty trade, and because I was working nonstop, I'd come home looking like a mess every day," he says. "But I still have those same tools today, 34 years later."

Scott will never forget the day he returned from spring break at Daytona Beach during his freshman year, when he went to see his brother-in-law, Dean Packard. He remembers fixing his car horn in the driveway when a young woman from next door came outside the house. She was babysitting and had come out to yell at him for making such a racket, but the two struck up a conversation instead. They began dating, and today, Nicole and Scott have been married for 27 years come May 2017.

Several years later, when Scott was a junior, his mother convinced him that an accounting class would be helpful no matter what he decided to do in life. He signed up and worked hard as usual, and halfway through the semester, his professor had a conversation with him. "He wasn't surprised to hear I was a philosophy major because I thought very logically," Scott says. "Then he told me that accounting is logic. I asked him if I looked like an accountant, and then he—this cool professor who drove a Porsche—asked if he looked like one. He told me he used accounting every day of his life even though he wasn't an accountant. He told me it could be whatever I made it into, and that I had a knack for it. He ended up convincing me to stick with it."

When Scott graduated from AU in the top five percent of his class, he applied for an academic fellowship for a masters accounting program. "I didn't get it, and I wasn't surprised," he says. "I gave up on that possibility and instead decided to partner with a friend to start my own construction company." Several months later, however, he got a call from the toughest professor in the whole school—a woman who taught him during his senior year. The original fellowship recipient had just dropped out, and Scott had two hours to decide if he wanted the fellowship. "It was a life-defining moment," he recalls. "I decided to go for it, shelving the company I had already gotten off the ground to go back to school as a graduate fellow working at the Kogod School of Business. In the span of two hours, I suddenly found myself on a very different path."

While working toward his masters, Scott did a significant amount of IT work on the side, and came to know the inner workings of computers like the back of his hand. At the time, tech companies were transforming old mainframe systems into client servers, and Scott found himself at the cutting edge of that market. He dabbled in databases, software, and systems, and handled network management for the accounting department at the university.

After completing his masters in 1991, he landed a position at Development Resources in Bethesda, Maryland, and commenced a period of intense learning. He spent the following six years working harder than anyone else and accumulating knowledge as his career coursed from Development Resources, to Network Management, to PRC. He then accepted a position as controller at McFadden and Associates, and then took a Director job at iNet. "My first daughter was born in

1996, and my second in 2000. Since I was working double time, it was a lot to juggle," he recalls. "Those were my years to be a sponge, learning and working as hard as I could and listening to the successful entrepreneurs I was working for."

When iNet was acquired by Wang Federal, Scott faced another defining moment in choosing between a CIO job there, or a Controller job at SIGNAL Corporation. The fork in the road was ultimately a choice between a career in IT or a career in accounting, and against the recommendations of many, he took the latter position. "I had really clicked with SIGNAL's CEO, Roger Mody," Scott says. "He gave me the opportunity to light a fire in his company, and I went all out. And I felt a lot of loyalty to him for giving me that opportunity. I was going to do all I could to make him successful." Over the next six years, Scott helped the company grow from $33 million to $320 million, taking on the CFO and CIO roles. Then, after several unsuccessful attempts at selling the company, Scott negotiated and ran the successful transaction that sold SIGNAL to Veridian.

"SIGNAL took a shot on me, and it was so rewarding to help it grow exponentially and then personally doing the sale in 2002," he reflects. "I became a President of Veridian, which had recently gone public, and I was running all of IT beneath me. It was a big defining moment in my career." Also through that time period, Scott launched a consulting practice on the side, which gave him the opportunity to work with around 160 different companies across a wide range of sectors. After Veridian was acquired by General Dynamics in 2003, Scott left to focus on the entrepreneurial thrill of consulting full-time, which ultimately led to the opportunity at PSS.

His wife, Nicole, has been by his side the whole way through the evolution from blue collar worker to CEO. "I'm a tough person with a high bar, but it doesn't faze her at all," he says. "She accepts me for who I am and has always been supportive and understanding, even in those times that I've needed to work long hours. She's my partner, my soulmate, my rock, and my sounding board. I think the world of her."

In advising young people entering the working world today, Scott underscores the importance of getting a good education and mastering the work ethic, learning, and analysis skills that spell success along any career path. Recognizing that success means different things to different people, he stressed the importance of thinking ahead, being smart, and taking chances in life. And above all else, he emphasizes the importance of hard work. "It doesn't really matter what school you go to," he says. "What matters is the work you do and what you make of it. I've watched people graduate from Ivy League schools who were very book smart, but without street smarts and common sense, they failed miserably at business. It's one thing to understand business theoretically on paper, but practical application is quite another. The world is what you make of it, and if you decide something is worth doing, give it 110 percent."

Despite leading PSS, commuting to work from Florida, and being a present husband to Nicole and father to their two daughters, Kayla and Michelle, Scott still makes time in his life for consulting—his way of giving a hand up to others. To Scott, consulting is an opportunity to see things in people that others may not see. When he recognizes a drive in someone, however hidden, he makes it a priority to use his own experience to help them achieve a level of success they might not reach otherwise. "I was the kid who wasn't going to make it," he says. "But I proved to myself and others what I was made of, and now here I am. You never know what life has in store, but in the end, it's you who gets to decide how far you go."

BERNHARDT
WEALTH MANAGEMENT

Noe Landini

Acts of Ambition

Noe Landini's father crossed the Atlantic Ocean hundreds of times as a waiter with the Italian Line, working aboard ships that transported extravagantly-dressed passengers on the several-day journey from Genoa to New York City. For them, his hard work created exquisite dining experiences. And for him, it created ambition.

He wanted more than the life he had known growing up in a poor family in Tuscany, working as a waiter, bartender, and cook for famous vacationers like Fred Astaire and Charlie Chaplin. In the early 1970s, he decided to immigrate to America to get into the restaurant business, hoping one day to find a way to open his own restaurant. He made a fresh start in the United States, sending money home to his family in Italy but still scraping together the resources to launch Pelicano, an Italian restaurant in Alexandria, Virginia. Four years later, in 1979, he parted ways with his partner, relocated across the street, and joined forces with his youngest brother to open Landini Brothers.

Noe, born two years after that, took his first formal job at the family restaurant as a dishwasher at the age of fifteen. Now, decades later, he has become its CEO and Managing Director, chasing his own acts of ambition to transform his father's legacy into a collection of successful ventures across Northern Virginia and Washington, DC. "I love what I do—the challenge, the people, the clients, and my team of 250 dedicated employees across six different businesses," he says today. "I'm only as good as my people, and I have great people. I really cherish the time I have with them—the camaraderie and the fun of putting out a great product and generating revenue. I wasn't just born *into* this business—I was born to *be* in this business."

As a kid growing up in Northern Virginia, Noe loved riding his bike and hanging out with friends. He played basketball, watched cartoons, and helped his mother by taking care of his younger brother and sister. From the age of six, his parents sent him to Italy to spend each summer with his paternal grandparents, where he learned Italian and cultivated sophisticated culinary tastes. "My siblings and I were not hot-dog-and-hamburger kids," he laughs. "My grandparents were huge influences in my life, from manners to speaking to cooking. The food at Landini Brothers is great, but my grandmother's cooking absolutely blew it out of the water. It was the best food, and it was surrounded by this sense of family since my uncles, aunts, and cousins would all have meals together. I loved those summers spent in their small town by the beach, where everyone knew everyone."

At home, Noe remembers the regimented schedule of chores that had to be done around the house. But most of all, he remembers vividly the times he would go see his father at the restaurant. "Watching my father's work ethic was a defining influence in my childhood," he affirms. "At that time, it was overwhelming trying to understand how someone could work that much—often seven days a week. But as I got older, I learned to appreciate that hard work at anything is what ultimately makes you successful."

Noe's family had a distinctly "Do It Yourself" philosophy when it came to construction and maintenance, and Noe's earliest helping hand was lent laying tile or doing carpentry in the restaurant under the guidance of his uncle. "Instead of hiring contractors, we would build the bar ourselves, finish our own rooms, plumb our own bathrooms, and do our own kitchen," he recalls. "I learned a lot through those projects, well before I started helping out in the dining room or kitchen." He also learned a great deal from his father's employees, who exhibited unyielding work ethic of their own and served as excellent role models. Through their guidance, he learned how to cook, bartend, and serve.

Outside of the restaurant, Noe's parents pushed him to do well academically, and he enjoyed playing baseball as a kid. In high school, he excelled at wrestling and enjoyed playing football with his friends. He always found ways to make money for comic books, baseball cards, clothes, and movie tickets, whether it was lifeguarding, shoveling sidewalks, or raking leaves for the neighbors. Then, at age fifteen, he formally stepped into the Landini Brothers world as a dishwasher, soon graduating to food prep and then to a job as a busboy. He worked every weekday after school except for days he had sports obligations, and through those formative years, Noe was struck by how many customers returned on a regular basis. Landini Brothers was beloved, garnering a loyal following of regulars, and Noe's father and uncle were so successful that they launched and sold two additional restaurants.

Upon graduating from high school, Noe went to New York City for the summer to work for Garage Management Corporation, a company with a Nissan dealership, retail stores, restaurants, real estate, and seventy garages in Manhattan. There, he shadowed his cousin, Gordon, in opening a restaurant on Bleecker Street and working in the dealership. "The experience was defining in giving me a sense of what it's like to be a businessman, dealing with people and applying strategy," Noe reflects. "Through high school, I had wanted to be a fighter pilot when I grew up. But that business experience, combined with the experience of watching my father excel as a restauranteur, catapulted me into a new mindset of what I wanted my professional future to look like."

For college, Noe enrolled at George Mason University and interned at the American Conservative Union for six months while still balancing his work as a manager at the restaurant. In 2000, Landini Brothers expanded from two dining rooms in a single building, to two buildings that housed five dining rooms and a new kitchen. In the process, Noe led a team in introducing a point-of-sales computer system to replace handwritten checks, helping the business through a successful expansion and modernization period.

Noe then spent two years interning with a government contractor in Crystal City, aiming to expand his professional repertoire as he was promoted from manager to general manager at the restaurant. "Through high school, I never thought I wanted to go into the restaurant business because I had all the grunt jobs, washing dishes and busing tables," he reflects. "But as I excelled, I started making good money and realized I actually could make a living doing it. I could put gas in my car, buy what I wanted to buy, and take a girl out on a nice date. I was always the one to show up late to parties because of work, but I liked that feeling of being independent and successful."

Noe found that he loved the challenge of the Landini Brothers atmosphere, where he had assumed an administrative leadership and controller role that entailed payroll management, working with the bank, and interacting with clients on a professional level. His strong work ethic earned the respect of those around him, and he could see a future for himself at the restaurant. He became a homeowner in 2002, and things were going so well that he decided not to return to college the following semester so he could focus on work full-time.

Things shifted, however, when Noe and his uncle had differences of opinion that grew with time. Noe had a vision of improving the quality of the restaurant's offerings, growing their wine list and focusing on new recipe ideas sparked by his summers in Italy. His uncle had no interest in evolving the business and refused to embrace the young man's ambition—something Noe vows never to do as a leader. "When I see young people with that kind of ambition, I make sure to welcome and encourage it," he says. "When people care and want to do more, it goes a long way, and they need to know that their ideas matter."

Unable to get through to his uncle, Noe felt dulled and unchallenged at Landini Brothers, and though his father wanted him to stay, he decided he needed to make a change. He had always been interested in going to work at the Ritz Carlton, known as a hotel and restaurant with the best customer service in the business. In 2004, he managed to land a job as the food and beverage manager at the Tysons Corner Ritz Carlton, where he helped run the steakhouse, dining room, and lobby bar over the next year and a half. He also spent time working for the Ritz locations in Georgetown and Midtown, interfacing with countless people of incredible talent as he learned about the art and science of running a large company. "Working there, I felt that my ideas were heard, appreciated, and executed," he recounts. "I was part of an active executive management team, which was a refreshing step after my experience with my uncle, where I was expected to just run through a checklist without trying new things. It was a great experience, and I learned so much about the corporate world that I still use today."

Noe's father wasn't very familiar with the Ritz prior to Noe's decision to leave Landini's, and at first was very concerned and doubtful. To help bridge the gap and calm the waters, Noe invited him to the hotel for dinner four months into his tenure there, tending to every detail to ensure his father had an excellent experience. He made sure the valet was on the lookout for his arrival and that he was promptly escorted to his table for wine service. "By the time I joined him in my suit and nametag, he was already blown away," Noe remembers. "I said, 'Welcome to the Ritz Carlton!' It was the coolest thing ever, and I could tell he was finally proud of the decision I had made. That meant a lot."

After a wonderful dinner together, Noe gave his father the keys to the presidential suite for the night. The next day, he returned to the restaurant and gushed to Noe's uncle about how well he was doing, thanks to the very ambition that had been thwarted at Landini's. "It took a lot of hard work to get to that point, putting in seventy-hour workweeks that included nights, weekends, and holidays," he says. "But that was a benchmark moment for me that was so incredibly rewarding."

A year later, Noe's expertise caught the eye of a Ritz client who owned a company doing business in the Middle East. The client needed assistance with logistics and food distribution, so Noe agreed to take a meeting on his behalf with Sysco. One meeting led to another, and before he knew it, they had formed a company together. Noe left his job at the Ritz to focus on that company, traveling frequently to the Middle East with plans to build a food distribution center in Qatar.

With that, in 2005, Noe found himself brokering a massive distribution deal, coordinating with Sysco, Military Professional Resources Inc. (MPRI), and Bonar to design and build a center to help supply 5-star hotels as they grappled to keep up with the rapid development of Dubai and Doha. "You can't run a top hotel if you can't get fresh cream, chicken or butter," Noe explains. "Additionally, MPRI planned to use our distribution center as a hub to serve their East Africa Missions. It was a huge joint effort, and I was a kid in my twenties that literally stumbled into it."

Working in that capacity, Noe also worked on brokering advertising deals for Ackerman McQueen and additional commodity deals that led him to the far reaches of multiple continents, selling copper from South Africa and the Congo to Korea, Turkey, Russia, Ukraine, and China. "Somehow I became a commodities broker," he says. "I was having the time of my life, but when I was home one day in 2007 and decided to have lunch at Landini's, my uncle told me he had decided to retire and sell the restaurant. He asked if I knew of any interested buyers. At first I thought of brokering a deal with one of my clients looking to invest in restaurants, but then it dawned on me—why don't I buy it?"

Noe pitched the idea to his father, inviting him to stay on as his partner. His father, who was still a 50/50 owner, feared his uncle would never agree to it, but Noe personally offered to pay his uncle his half of the asking price—$2.5 million. His uncle agreed as long as Noe could get the money to him in two weeks, so Noe started knocking on doors. "I thought it was half a million too much, but that didn't matter to me," he recounts. "I knew what I could do with the business, and I knew my father could be a part of it for the rest of his life. I took my ambition and idea to Peter Converse, a client and friend who worked at Virginia Commerce Bank, and he promised to get me a commitment within the two-week timeframe. He pulled through, so I was able to pull through, and a month later, we closed the deal."

Since that milestone, Landini Brothers has had an annual growth rate of ten percent—an impressive track record fueled by Noe's' focus on event business, product consistency, and quality improvement. Meanwhile, he bought the neighboring iconic venues of Pop's Ice Cream and Fish Market & Anchor Bar, refurbishing those projects room by room over a five-year period. In 2010, he built a Member's Only Club, CXIIIREX, that is now 350 members strong. "People thought I was crazy for doing that because I built it when the economy was bad, and without much precedent," he recounts. But the concept thrived, garnering praise from the *Washington Post*, the *New York Times*, *Aficionado*, and *Robb Report*. He built Washington, DC's Bar Deco in 2015, and Del Rey's Junction Bakery & Bistro in 2016.

"Through those other ventures, I wanted to expand, create, and experiment," he recounts. "Some I stumbled into, again, by accident, like Bar Deco. Others were inspired specifically by the needs of a neighborhood and the potential of a building, like when 1508 Mount Vernon Avenue seemed to be demanding a bakery. It took the help of great friends like Roy Ayers, who helped me get that lease, and Nathan Hatfield, who was willing to be a managing partner at the bakery with me."

Reflecting back, Noe's success is the constellation of so many bright stars who offered help along the way—people who began as clients but became good friends and mentors to him over time. Tony Makris, Mark Dycio, and Tyler Schropp all stick out as other successful individuals willing to coach Noe toward his own success. "Essentially, they taught me how to conduct myself, deal with banks and clients, and handle difficult situations," he says with gratitude. "You don't necessarily learn those things in school. I could always bounce ideas off of them, and they always gave me good advice."

He also has his mother to thank. Tough and entrepreneurial in her own way, she has always stood up fearlessly for the family. Compassionate and affectionate, she always pushed Noe to do better and works as his controller today. "I couldn't have anyone better in that position," he affirms. "My dad isn't a very meticulous person, but his work ethic is excellent so he makes up for it in other ways. My mom, on the other hand, is incredibly organized and neat. She's always been there through good times and bad, and I really trust her."

Today, Noe's success is measured not only in revenue and volume, but in the loyalty of his patrons, many of whom are second and third generation customers. "The restaurant business is a fiercely competitive market, and it's really unbelievable that we still have people who dine with us four or five times a week, and have been doing so for years," he remarks. This success is due in part to the caliber of his team—people Noe can trust to take responsibility and get things done.

Noe's father—still 50-percent owner and partner—is now happily retired, living in Florida and loving life. And Noe looks forward to the future, hoping to make time to settle down and have children of his own. In advising young people entering the working world today, he underscores the importance of being humble. "Nobody owes you anything," he says. "No matter how smart you are or what school you graduated from, be ready to roll up your sleeves and work hard, because that's the only way you're going to move up and gain respect. Intelligence and education are obviously important, but hard work is the key to success."

Always pursuing his own acts of ambition, Noe believes in recognizing and supporting ambition in others, whether it's combatting illness through Chance for Life and the Multiple Sclerosis Society, or honoring wounded veterans through Luke's Wings. CXIIIREX has a wall of honor commemorating pioneering individuals and the causes they support, and Landini's organizes golf tournaments and other events that dedicate 100 percent of their proceeds to charity. Noe even makes a point to support the ambition he sees in his competitors, holding bid sessions and gatherings to support other restauranteurs in the area. "The more, the merrier," he says. "Competition is a good thing, and instead of adversaries, I look to others as partners and friends. We all want the same thing—successful careers, happy customers, and stronger communities where hard work and unleashed potential create a better world for all of us."

BERNHARDT
WEALTH MANAGEMENT

Jack Maier II

A Culture of Connecting

In 1989, when Jack Maier landed at Drexel Burnham Lambert, a major investment banking firm on Wall Street, he thought he had found his dream job. But a year later, it all evaporated in front of him.

"I was only a year out of school at that time," he recounts today. "I'll never forget how the head of investment banking at Drexel called all of the employees into the auditorium. He said, 'Under the Warren Act, we're required to give you notice that you're being terminated.' I was one of those kids on TV carrying a box of personal effects out of my office. I had a lot of student loans, and Drexel was viewed as being somewhat toxic. Goldman Sachs wouldn't even interview Drexel employees."

It was a defining moment in Jack's life, and thanks to his ability to connect with the people around him, he was able to turn it into a transcendent success. At Drexel, employee surveys had consistently ranked him as the person everyone most wanted to work with on their next transaction. Roy Abbott, his boss, had taken note, and was struck by Jack's work ethic, presence, and ability to communicate effectively. When Roy joined a firm called Rodman & Renshaw, he offered a VP position to Jack, the first person he reached out to.

Now, decades later, Jack is the Head of Investment Banking at Headwaters MB, where he still prioritizes connections and relationships as the true driving force behind a productive and successful environment. "Our firm has three partners—the CEO, the President & COO, and myself—that work together very well," he explains. "Our styles are night and day in some respects. But because of those differences, we have a chemistry that works, allowing us to come together to make the best decsions for the firm."

This emphasis on teamwork extends beyond the top ranks of leadership at Headwaters, and is something Jack proudly cultivates throughout the business by encouraging a culture of transparency, communication, and flexibility. "Through my career, I've seen acquisitions go bad, mergers crumble, and profits suffer at the hands of cultural conflicts," he affirms. "But a good culture can foster low turnover, high job satisfaction, and phenomenal results. For me, a great culture comes from a focus on consensus-building. I believe in bringing people together and building trust and cooperation, treating people like adults and assuming they'll make the right decisions in the best interest of the client and the firm."

Transparency is also a key part of this equation. "Everybody at the firm knows what transactions our partners are working on," Jack says. "We have an Investment Banking Committee that reviews all transactions prior to approval, and then distributes a memo to all 110 employees at Headwater for their awareness. If somebody has previous experience they can use to add value to that transaction, they can pick up the phone and call me. Beyond these foundational principles, we also genuinely appreciate each other and believe its important to have fun together."

JACK MAIER II

Jack believes so strongly in the importance of a good business culture because, after 30 years in the investment banking industry, he's seen what can happen in its absence. He started his own firm, Legacy Partners in 2003, and while the venture was successful, their eventual sale to FBR Capital Markets was less so. "We effected the merger and lived through three painful years," he recalls. "It was a cultural mismatch, and we thought we could change things. But at FBR, I learned that cultural shifts are a multi-year process."

When his contract with FBR finally ended, Jack connected with Phil Seefried, one of the original founders of Headwaters. "He asked me to think about becoming a part of his organization, so we met at the Metropolitan Club in DC," Jack recalls. "Instead of spending one hour together, our business meeting stretched on for five hours, we got along so well. I came onboard in October of 2011, and it feels like my ideal fit. I've had a long and winding career with plenty of landmines along the way, but things happen for a reason, and I feel I can say I've grown from those experiences."

Today, after six years at Headwaters, Jack's tenure as Head of Investment Banking has completely transformed the structure of the business, for the better. For starters, he and his team led the charge to maximize the value of the firm's, referral agreements with large Wall Street banks like UBS, Goldman Sachs and Merrill Lynch. "I had had experience with these agreements while running Legacy Partners," he recounts. "In that situation, growing personal relationships was key to taking full advantage of the agreements. We travelled all over the country to make presentations to the regional offices, explaining how we could be helpful to them."

Jack's strategy of courting the big banks with personal attention and customer service paid off in spades. Business that came out of Headwaters' referral agreements used to make up a mere 10 to 15 percent of their total business. Today, it makes up a full two-thirds. "The beauty of the business is that it's annuity-like in nature," Jack points out.

"Merrill Lynch is not going away, and they pick up the phone once a week to call us about various opportunities they come across that would be good fits for us."

These relationships do more than provide a consistent flow of business via the referral deals—they also help the firm attract and retain top talent. "It creates a stickiness for our investment bankers," Jack explains. "Deal flow is the lifeblood of an investment bank, and at Headwaters, two-thirds of the deals bankers are working on have come from someone other than themselves. They might be referred in by one of our referral partners, or they might come from another partner in the firm that's run across something that falls outside his or her expertise. It's a dream come true for an investment banker, resulting in very low turnover."

Today, Headwaters is a national enterprise headquartered in Denver, with offices spanning from the Southeast, to the West Coast, to the Southwest, to New York. Servicing wide range international clients, it has no geographic limitations whatsoever. The team focuses on middle-market enterprise value clients ranging from $25 to $250 million, forming a complementary relationship with the bigger firms. They serve ten industry verticals, with an emphasis on technology, consumer, healthcare, aerospace, defense and government services, and industrials."

Jack's stunning success as an investment banker speaks to a natural talent and single-minded ambition, but growing up in Greensboro, North Carolina, he instead planned to become a lawyer, like his father. "My dad instilled in me a very strong work ethic," Jack says. "I would watch him go to work every day in a suit, and someitmes he'd let me come with him."

Proud to come from a hardworking, deeply Christian family that came to the U.S. in 1835, Jack treasures an old book with the letters his family wrote while crossing the Atlantic. "The deep faith in God and prayerful letters helped them make it through," Jack reflects. "I love being reminded of who I am and where I come from." Centuries later, his father was a patent attorney, while his mother stayed home and took care of Jack and his two younger brothers. "They were very loving parents," he remembers. "I never heard them quarrel, which is amazing after 60 years of marriage."

Greensboro was an idyllic, calm, affordable area to grow up, surrounded by rolling foothills and accessible to hiking trials. Jack fondly remembers riding bikes, playing baseball, and getting into trouble with the rest of the kids in the neighborhood. "Our lives were so much simpler," he notes. "They weren't wrapped arround technology. We'd run around until we heard my dad's dinnertime whistle. My childhood days were filled with freedom and activity."

In the summertime, Jack learned to appreciate the value of a dollar, taking on all manner of neighborhood jobs like mowing lawns, painting houses, cleaning gutters, and washing cars. His mother emphasized the importance of faith, and the whole family attended Catholic Church together on Sundays. At school, he developed an interest in soccer, eventually playing on the state championship team in high school. And his brothers were always up for a wrestling match on the porch or a football game in the living room.

Jack also began showing an interest in business early on. When he was ten, he began to voraciously read the business magazines his father brought home from work, taking a particular liking to *Forbes* and impressing parents with his knowledge. "When I was a kid, I remember my dad telling me I was the only one he could talk about business with because my brothers weren't interested," Jack recalls. "It was in *Forbes* that I learned about this job called investment banking. I knew about lawyers, consultants, and accountants, but I didn't know there was a job called investment banking, where people made transactions happen."

By the time Jack made it to college at Wake Forest University, he was planning to get both a J.D. and an MBA. As time went on, and he took a job at the Wake Forest business school library, he decided to just go for the MBA and head straight to Wall Street. "I ended up majoring in economics, and the more I learned, the more I became passionate about business," Jack says. "I knew I wanted to be in finance, but I didn't want to go work for the North Carolina National Bank, so I thought one way out was to go to a graduate school with a national reputation." When he was accepted at Georgetown University, he went directly from college to graduate school.

Jack graduated from Georgetown in 1986 and successfully landed a job on Wall Street as an associate at a firm called Dunlevy & Co. "I was a young pup, working long hours and on weekends," he recalls. "Back then, it was a thing of honor to pull all-nighters and say you hadn't slept in 48 hours. There was no such thing as a work-life balance back in the 1980s and 1990s. You worked like a dog, and if you couldn't do it or didn't want to do it, you weren't going to make it."

After a couple of years at Dunlevy, Jack moved over to Drexel, a year before the firm declared bankruptcy in dramatic fashion. Yet even after he landed on his feet at Rodman & Renshaw, the value of his year at Drexel never faded. "People never forgot their time at Drexel, and it was an instant bond," he says. "It gave me access to this vast network of relationships across Wall Street—even people I never met while there. If we share that Drexel connection, their face lights up."

Gradually, Jack and Roy built a nice middle-market Mergers & Acquisitions practice, but the times were challenging. The Savings & Loan crisis was underway in Texas, and Jack recalls that the deal environment was anemic. When he got a call from Kemper Securities a few years later, he was ready to listen. "I heard from Paul Haigney, a former managing director at Drexel that had become head of M&A at Kemper," Jack recalls. "He asked if I had any interest in helping him build an M&A practice out on the West Coast."

Conscious of the value of personal relationships and transparency, Jack met with Roy and discussed the offer with him before taking it. Roy encouraged the move, pointing out that he planned to retire soon anyway. "He taught me that the secret to success is surrounding yourself with smart people," Jack recalls. "And Paul Haigney is a very, very smart and capable guy."

Although Jack planned to stay in California only briefly, he and his then-wife remained on the West Coast for ten years, where their son and daughter were born. After several years at Kemper, Paul Hagney took an offer to lead the Los Angeles office of a firm called Wasserstein Perella & Co., and asked Jack to come along. Four years later, Jack was in the process of moving to San Francisco to open up a technology-focused office for Wasserstein, when he received another interesting offer. "In 1998, I got a call from a Drexel alumni at Donaldson, Lufkin and Jennette (DLJ), who wanted to build a West Coast M&A business from scratch," he says. "I had always thought of DLJ as a premiere platform, so I accepted."

By 1999, Jack was tapped to run the firm's middle market advisory practice, which meant moving to the New York area. Then, while he was relocating his family to Greenwich, DLJ announced it was being acquired by Credit Suisse First Boston. "It was literally as we were driving the moving van across the country," he recalls. "I stayed with Credit Suisse for two more years and was one of the last DLJ guys standing after the merger, which is generally regarded as one of the worst mergers in the history of Wall Street. The firms were culturally incompatible, which was very sad for me to watch, since the team I'd built was the best around. We were consistently ranked number one, and watching them systematically dismantle the group was a painful experience. The benefit, though, was that it created a vast network of DLJ alumni, and we still get together for lunch. It's a connection that people are very proud of and cherish."

When Jack's contract ended in 2003, he was more than ready to strike out on his own. He asked a coworker from DLJ/Credit Suisse, Jim Frawley, to come along and serve as a partner in the venture. Legacy Partners Group ultimately grew to employ about 30 people before selling to FBR Capital Markets after four successful years of growth. "We realized the world was changing pretty rapidly," says Jack. "There was a lot of crazy stuff going on in the markets—new derivatives, companies at insanely high valuations. We knew it couldn't last and felt it was going to come to a bad end. Of course, we had no idea just how bad it would be. We thought we'd be better off as part of a larger ship than as a small boutique firm."

Legacy's cultural mismatch with the buyer, FBR, was compounded by brutal markets and near-zero deal activity. Meanwhile, Jack's professional worries were compounded by the personal difficulties of going through a divorce. But although it was a troubled time, he used the turmoil to re-evaluate his priorities in a positive way. "Since my divorce, I've tried to talk to my parents every day," Jack says, "I wasn't as appreciative of them as I should have been in my younger years, but I see things differently now, and am so grateful for how they shaped me. It's easy to take things for granted through life, but I try not to do that anymore."

Jack also began to reconnect with his Catholic background. "Faith is a very important part of my life," he affirms. "I try to thank God every day for all the gifts he's given me. I pray for guidance continually, and I've become much more grateful for what I have, instead of being annoyed by what I don't have in life. I'm proud that my children know that I'm prayerful."

Things quickly began to turn around for Jack. In 2011, he joined Headwaters, where he has thrived, and in 2015 he remarried to become a committed husband and happy step-father to two high-school aged boys. "Jennifer is the best thing that's ever happened to me," he says. "We get each other, and we have these terrific conversations about life and business. She supports me in everything I do, and she provides good counsel, because she is very successful herself. We have a tremendous, loving relationship, and our kids see that. I think they're happy for both of us that we found each other."

JACK MAIER II

In advising young people entering the working world today, Jack counsels hard work, patience, and careful decision making. "Life goes by very quickly," he says. "Start saving money when you're young, and save as much as you can. Before you know it, you're going to be 65, and you'll want a nest egg to retire on. Also, choose your mate carefully. Life is long, and it presents many challenges. There will be bumps in the road, but keep going."

Beyond that, Jack's journey is a balance of loyalty to the firms that made him, measured against the ambition that led to the firm he made. "I had great runs with my past employers, like the time I took over the role of Co-Head of Middle Market Advisory at DLJ and Credit Suisse," he recounts. "We became number one in the league tables. My objective is to get to that spot one more time with Headwaters before I hang up my cleats."

Numbers aside, he's even prouder of the personal impact of the equation. "M&A is often the most significant transaction my clients will ever make in their lives," Jack affirms. "Our work isn't just about those transactions—it's about building businesses, recruiting people, and mentoring them to success. It's about serving entrepreneurs, and especially family businesses, where we can help people navigate treacherous waters to a successful outcome. It's about creating a culture of collaboration that magnifies your impact for greater good. It's what gets me out of bed in the morning, eager for the next breath and the next step."

BERNHARDT
WEALTH MANAGEMENT

Michael May

There's Always a Way

Blinded by a chemical explosion and lying in an ICU with 300 stitches in his three-year-old body, Michael May's future looked dark—figuratively and literally. But what he began learning that day, thanks to the strength of his mother's determination and the rock-solid support of those around him, is that there is always a workaround, if you're just determined enough to find it.

In fact, Mike says that this experience, as much as any other single circumstance of his life, prepared him for a life of entrepreneurship. "Television didn't interest me all that much. My friends would want to watch cartoons and I'd drag them out in the middle of a 100-degree day, saying 'Let's go play kickball, let's play baseball …' It really didn't occur to me that I had to do things their way. I could make them do things my way … So if we played football, we played tackle football; that was better for me. If we played baseball, we would play in a certain way that would accommodate me, and I just figured this stuff out as I went along. Little did I know that it was going to be instrumental in training me to deal with a life skill, which is figuring out workarounds."

Mike has parlayed his aptitude for developing workarounds into a career that has included working as an analyst for the CIA, raising almost $7 million for a technology startup that produced the world's first laser turntable, developing and marketing adaptive devices for the blind that generated $6 million in annual sales, serving as VP of sales for the company that produced the first GPS devices adapted for the blind, and, recently, being selected as President and CEO of the Lighthouse for the Blind Inc. in Seattle, Washington, a century-old organization with annual revenues of just over $80 million. Oh, and along the way, he also set the downhill speed record for blind skiers and was honored by two Presidents of the United States.

Playing in the garage of the family's new home as a toddler, Mike and his siblings got hold of a container of calcium carbide, the chemical used in miner's lamps. "It takes a low amount of oxygen to burn, so you can be underground where there is low oxygen, and the flame doesn't go out," Mike explains. "When you mix it with water, it becomes acetylene gas." Somehow, the container exploded in Mike's face, instantly blinding him and causing widespread injuries to the rest of his body that landed him in the hospital for the next six months. "I was pretty carved up. I barely lived through that catastrophic experience."

When he was kindergarten age, the family moved from New Mexico to Walnut Creek, California, largely in order to be closer to the medical resources that Mike was going to need. "This tells you something about my support network, because not all blind kids—or not all kids—have the kind of support where their parents are willing to move across the country to find a better opportunity. They figured that since my eye doctor was in San Francisco, it wouldn't hurt to be close to him, because I was continuing to have operations to try to get me some sight." Between age three and age twelve, he would undergo four cornea transplants and grafts that would prove ineffective. Much later, in 2000, stem cell and cornea transplants would give him partial vision. However, researchers believe that because of the early age at which Mike lost his vision and the forty years during which he was completely blind, his visual cortex lost much of its ability to interpret the signals coming from his eyes. So today, while he is able to discern color and motion, he is unable to recognize faces or objects, and he has almost no depth perception. "My eyes have been very healthy optically ever since [the transplants]. The real mystery has been how my brain perceives the information going to my visual cortex. They're still doing tests on me in the FMRI (functional magnetic resonance imaging) machine here at the University of Washington in Seattle."

Mike credits his mother for striking the perfect balance between providing support and encouraging him to rely on himself. "They found a school system that was fairly integrated [between blind and sighted students] which, at the time, was a big deal, because kids usually went to a school for the blind, but my parents didn't think that was a good idea," he says. "So, I grew up in a system whereby all the blind kids went to the same elementary school within the district. I was in a school with 600 sighted kids and fifteen blind kids. That really helped in participating more in the real world that I would have to integrate into."

Mike's family reinforced the importance of integrating into the sighted world with the household routine he grew up in, giving him similar responsibilities in the home to those of his sighted siblings. He says, "My mother, particularly, was a combination of supportive and tough. My father was a serious alcoholic, which is why my parents got divorced, and though he was around occasionally in a helpful way, I can't really attribute my strength in life to him, other than in a backwards fashion. When he was gone I was 13, my sister was 14, and my mother was going back to school, so here she is with five kids. My sister and I had to step up to the plate, cook meals, and take on other responsibilities that we might not have had to do otherwise. With my father gone, it wasn't really a matter of giving me responsibility; there was no other choice in life. Having had two kids of my own and knowing how hard it was to raise them, I can't even imagine what it was like for my mom to try to raise five kids."

Rather than encouraging Mike to concentrate on activities "appropriate" for a blind person, his mother never placed limitations on what he wanted to do. "The fact that I had to fend for myself and figure things out certainly was accentuated by the fact that I didn't have people in my life who knew how to do this stuff already, so I had to figure it out on my own. My mother didn't necessarily know how, either; she wasn't an [orientation and mobility] instructor or a teacher of the blind. She was just a mom, so she would tell me, 'Well, you figure it out. If you want to play with those kids, then go figure it out.'"

Mike figured it out, including the special challenges of adolescence—and being blind, on top of that. Reflecting on those years, he said, "It would be easy as a teenager, when one is so vulnerable and insecure, to blame something on blindness, and it may or may not have been due to blindness. Take, for example, dating, or even just flirting, whatever interaction with the opposite sex ... When you get rejected—which happens to everybody—the question immediately arises, 'Is that because I'm blind?' And that would be an easy trap to fall into."

Which is not to say that there were not certain special challenges associated with being blind. Getting that first after-school job, for example, was harder for a kid who couldn't see. "That was always tough," Mike says, "because it was hard to have those jobs as a bag boy or a stock boy. So I didn't really have any jobs other than the little things I might have been paid by a neighbor to do, or maybe some babysitting or something like that." Mike's first real job was working as a counselor at the Enchanted Hills Camp for the Blind, a summer camp near Napa, California, run by the San Francisco Lighthouse for the Blind and Visually Impaired since 1950. "My mother first took me to the camp when I was seven years old," Mike says. "I went back almost every year up through high school. It was the first opportunity I had to really interact with other blind people." In 1974, at age 20, Mike was hired as a counselor. A year later, his mother, who by this time had a degree in counseling and psychology, was hired as director for the camp, a position she held for eleven years. Mike worked as his mother's assistant director. "I really developed a wonderful relationship with my mom who, before, was just my mother, and now she became a colleague and my boss."

During high school, Mike became interested in electronics, and particularly in ham radio. "I think it really first happened when the shop teacher at the high school didn't want me in shop class, because he was afraid I'd chop my fingers off. I'd been in shop in junior high, but the high school teacher didn't want me. So, they pawned me off on an electronics class, which I ended up liking as well." Mike had a friend who was working on his ham radio license, and Mike became absorbed in learning about and building his own equipment. "I actually got my license, and it became a big part of my life in high school and in college." Mike built a 70-foot radio tower in his back yard and sometimes went to Santa Cruz to work on a 175-foot tower. "They figured out that a blind guy wasn't going to be afraid of heights. But let me tell you, when you're up in the air 175 feet and that tower starts waving around in the wind, it's pretty scary."

Even more dominant in Mike's memory of his high school years, though, is his experience as a wrestler. He credits his coach, Ed Melendez, with providing a strong, almost father-like influence on his character, discipline, and determination to succeed. "A lot of my life was consumed with wrestling, with working out and competing. I never got involved in smoking, alcohol, or drugs, mainly because that didn't go along with being an athlete. Our coach really emphasized being in good condition, and when we weren't wrestling, we played basketball. And I think back and wonder, 'Who taught this coach that a blind guy could play basketball?' But somehow we figured out the workarounds for playing basketball."

Mike attended the University of California, Davis, with the intention of majoring in electrical engineering. But he soon learned that getting an engineering degree was a lot more intense than being a ham radio hobbyist. He made it through a very tough freshman year and, though in his sophomore year he began to get more into the rhythm of school and study, he ultimately made the decision to leave the engineering program. "I realized that it wasn't something I was going to be able to pull off; I had multiple interests, and in engineering you have to stay very focused—you can't take classes in humanities and that sort of thing, and I just wasn't that focused at that point in my life."

Mike says that he wishes someone had guided him earlier toward studying for a career that would enable him to earn a reliable and comfortable living. "I used to always hear from the high school counselors, 'What's your passion? You should do something you really care about.' And it's fine, I think, to approach life that way, but there's also the side that says, 'What can you do that will make you productive and flexible; so you can travel around and not be restricted to one location?' I wish that someone had alerted me to the benefits of a profession like that." Ultimately, Mike completed his undergraduate studies with a degree in political science, mainly because "It was the easiest thing to get and get out of there."

It was toward the end of his time at UC Davis, however, that Mike would have one of the most formative experiences of his life. He had applied to spend a semester abroad at the American University of Beirut, in Lebanon, but at the last minute, the dean of that school was shot, resulting in the cancellation of the trip. "That was when all hell broke loose in Lebanon," Mike says. "So, I'm dead in the water. I don't want to just do another year at Davis, so I looked around and found this program." Asked if he wanted to go to Denmark, Mike responded, "I'm looking for a real cultural slap in the face." When he learned that traveling to Ghana and living with a family in the village of Kumasi was an option, he applied and was accepted. "It turned out to be very, very hard and challenging." Mike says, however, that this year of living in a culture so extremely different from the one he grew up in gave him a perspective that, he says, has driven him since that time: "We are just a grain of sand in this universe. I was living with a subsistence-level type of situation, which is really more typical of the majority of people in the world than the privileged life we have in this country. It made me much more open to other cultures, and it somewhat shaped my approach to blind and disabled people, realizing that we're all unique; we all have our strengths and weaknesses. The experience in Ghana really cemented that profoundly in my thinking."

Mike applied to several law schools, which is a frequent career direction taken by political science grads, and he was accepted to some programs on the West Coast. But he was also accepted into the master's program at Johns Hopkins University's School of Advanced International Studies. "What attracted me really was that it was close to Washington, DC. I just felt I needed to go somewhere different, and Washington, DC, sounded really exciting and different." During the time he was completing the two-year program at Johns Hopkins, Mike began working part-time for the CIA as an analyst. However, when the time came for him to graduate from the program, he didn't really consider continuing a career with the government. "Working for the CIA was fascinating," he says, "and I was the first blind CIA employee, but still, it's the government, and the government is pretty stodgy in its approaches to things, so I wanted to go back to California."

Mike spent much of the next year in a frustrating search for a job that fit his interests and abilities. "I would get lots of interview requests with a lot of banks, which is what a lot of my peers were doing—working as international loan officers. But the HR people would say, 'We don't think this department is a good fit for you,' and they would pass me off to someone else. The problem was, for a blind person with a master's degree and no job experience, there was really nowhere to get started; it was a chicken-and-egg problem." Mike describes it as "a tough year" that included two months selling Time-Life Books over the phone. "You learn to face rejection when you call people up and they hang up on you. It wasn't until some very cool managers at the Bank of California in San Francisco decided to take a chance on me that I got a job and began my career."

After working for the bank from 1980 to 1982, Mike worked with a company that specialized in high tech approaches to international political risk analysis. Mike left that company, which was subsequently acquired by TRW, to join a group of other entrepreneurs who, beginning in 1984, raised almost $7 million in order to start Finial Technology, developer of the world's first laser turntable. "As an entrepreneur, you have to be adaptable; you have to learn about workarounds. The ironic thing is, that as a blind person, you also have to know how to find workarounds. I started learning those things at age three. So, by the time I hit my career stride, I'd had thirty years of experience with workarounds and adaptability."

After spending three years and building Finial Technology from the ground up, a difference with investors over product development strategies resulted in Mike being bought out. While disappointed that his investors no longer shared his vision for the company, Mike also says that the experience with Finial was a major confidence-builder. "Number one, to be able to raise $7 million as a couple of young, naïve guys, and then to be able to accomplish the laser turntable, which both Sony and Philips were unable to do, gave us a lot of confidence that anything was possible. At the same time it was very disappointing. Fortunately, we made enough money that I was able to take a year to travel and contemplate and think, 'Do I want to go back and get a regular paycheck, or do I want to do this startup thing again?'"

During his "sabbatical" year, Mike focused a good bit of time on his passion for downhill skiing, which he had acquired after college.

"Skiing is such a visual sport, so if you can figure out how to do it as a blind person, it's really exhilarating ... I happened to enter a couple of races and won, and one led to another, leading to me being put on the US team going to Switzerland." Mike competed in the 1984 Winter Paralympics, winning medals in the downhill, giant slalom, and combination events. "It all just spiraled into more competition and became a major focus of my life. I'd been competing in giant slaloms, but I realized that the best way to compete against a sighted person would be in speed skiing, because there are no gates; you just go straight, and there's very little visual component to it. So I started competing in regular sighted skiing."

During his year off, Mike was in Europe, skiing, when he set a goal of breaking the downhill speed record for blind skiers. "Actually, it was just a practice run. We hit 65 miles per hour, and we were expecting to hit 100. But then a snowstorm came in and blanketed everything, and eventually we had to go home and get back to work, so we had to abort our attempt." Mike's 65 m.p.h. mark still stands as the speed record for a totally blind skier.

Returning to his entrepreneurial interests in 1988, Mike started Maytek Products, manufacturing specialized sports and radiographic accessories. Two years later, he and a partner began a business building and selling computer systems for the blind, CustomEyes. He eventually sold both of these companies to other investors.

While working with the computer company, Mike became acquainted with Arkenstone Inc., a corporation that produced adaptive computer equipment for persons with disabilities. In 1994, after selling his other businesses, Mike joined Arkenstone as vice president for sales. Under his leadership, Arkenstone generated more than $6 million in annual sales, increasing its software revenue by 10 percent or more each year. The company had developed an adaptive GPS product for the blind, but determined that the product was not a strategic fit. So, in 1999, Mike spun off the GPS business into what became

Sendero Group LLC. He would lead Sendero Group as president and CEO for the next eighteen years.

"We worked largely on federal grants, because in the blindness field, there's not enough volume to really fund these things [independently]," Mike reports. During his years at Sendero, he spearheaded efforts that resulted in seven federally funded grants totaling over $4 million. "This allowed us to come up with the first successful GPS [for the blind], and then over time, we just put it on smaller and smaller Braille and speech devices, ending up on the iPhone, where it is today." Mike reports that since he has left Sendero, the new frontier for development is with indoor navigation for the blind, in places like malls, airports, and hospitals. "That's what I left behind; I turned it over to my colleagues Kim Casey, Sheri Harding, and Paul Ponchillia, a blind professor from Michigan who has been working on this [technology] for years."

Mike's list of awards and honors is impressive, including the Kay Gallagher mentoring award from the American Foundation for the Blind (1998), the Da Vinci Award for Accessibility and Universal Design (2006), the American Foundation for the Blind Access Award (2009), the Louis Braille Individual Award (2012), and an honorary doctorate in humane letters from South Carolina's Coker College (2015). But two honors Mike lists as most meaningful are the 1984 commendation by President Ronald Reagan and his appointment by President Barack Obama to the 2010 White House Paralympics delegation. Attending a White House ceremony following the 1984 Winter Olympics, at which Mike skied a demonstration run, Mike was listening to Reagan speak. "I'm just listening to his speech, and all of a sudden, he said, 'I'd like to offer a special note of congratulations to Michael May and Ron Salviolo. Mike skis better blind than other sighted skiers. Mike, you and the other competitors here are a testimony to all young people that they should never be afraid to dream big dreams, and they should never hesitate to make those dreams a reality.'" Speaking of his meeting with President Obama, Mike says,

"I got invited to a meeting with the president and actually sat down at a table with him and a couple of other key advisers and discussed the question, 'What is it that disabled people need?' I also went to the meeting for the first stem cell executive order that he put out, right after he came into office in February 2009. And I had several other interactions with him."

Mike was also the subject of a best-selling 2007 book by Robert Kurson, *Crashing Through: The Extraordinary True Story of the Man Who Dared to See*. In the book, Kurson profiles Mike and the many challenges he has faced and overcome, culminating with the uncertainties of the stem cell surgery and its outcome.

Now, in his work with the Lighthouse for the Blind, Mike oversees an organization with 470 individuals working in eleven locations, including South Carolina. The Lighthouse reaches its 100th anniversary next year. Like many blindness organizations, it started as a sheltered workshop, but, Mike says, "The Lighthouse here is all about employment. The content of that employment has changed over time, from originally being piecework jobs to the point now where people are full-fledged machine operators and program managers. And of course, there's now a blind CEO." The Lighthouse, unlike many such organizations, does not rely heavily on fundraising. "This is more of a social enterprise," Mike says, "meaning that we make stuff and we sell it." Last year, the Lighthouse generated $80 million in revenue through its various enterprises. "We make seven to eight thousand different parts for Boeing aircraft," Mike says. "We make hydration systems for the military, similar to the CamelBak. We make something called an entrenching tool" (basically a foldable shovel used by the military). "We make office products, like white boards and file folders, that we sell in our stores, along with products from our other agencies. Our stores sell everything from extension cords to sticky notes. We have call centers that do contract work for retailers and catering businesses." Mike's high-tech background predisposes him to interest in providing call-center and other services to high-tech companies, and he is also interested in developing technologies and systems that would permit disabled persons to work from home. Mike identifies his key leadership trait as empathy. "I think my best tool as a leader is to understand people's strengths and weaknesses."

Despite the exciting opportunities opening in front of Mike as he assumes his new leadership role, he continues to face challenges and heartbreak. In 2016, his twenty-four-year-old son, Carson, was killed by an avalanche while skiing. "This was a parent's worst nightmare. His body wasn't found for six weeks. I have a rubber bracelet that I haven't taken off since I got it in his memory. It has one of his favorite sayings on it, which is, 'Starve the ego, feed the soul.' He was a humble guy who wasn't afraid to be a pioneer; I think he taught me some things about pioneering." In Carson's honor, Mike and others have formed Carson Technologies, which focuses on developing early search-and-rescue technologies. Mike was also diagnosed with cancer in May 2016 and endured a grueling course of chemotherapy and radiation. Though still recovering from the after-effects, he says that his doctors tell him he is cancer-free. He says he is looking forward to better things in the coming year.

Looking back on his life so far, Mike gives credit to his mother as a true hero or, as he puts it, "a testimony to the moms of the world." He also mentions his ex-wife, Jennifer, the mother of his two sons. "It was meaningful to me that she put up with my entrepreneurial roller coaster," he says. "I was really appreciative of her for doing that." Mike's wife, Gena, who is also visually impaired, is a financial advisor for Morgan Stanley. "She is joining me on this journey later in life, with other crises going on. She's really impressive in her own right; I feel that I've met my match in terms of business acumen. She's a competitive cyclist who was on the US Women's Paralympic cycling team."

When he gave the commencement speech two years ago at Coker College, Mike says he told the graduates, "There's always a way. If you go into life figuring that there's always a way, you don't have to know what that way is. You find other people to collaborate with, and you will figure it out. But you have to have the perspective on life that there's always a way."

For Michael May, finding that way has become a way of life.

BERNHARDT
WEALTH MANAGEMENT

Gregory K. McDonough

How Entrepreneurs Are Born

From the earliest days of his childhood, Greg McDonough grew up believing in the power of a positive attitude. His older brother, born handicapped and partially blind, faced considerable adversity in life, but nothing could shake his kindness and optimism. "Paul is always in a positive mood," Greg says today. "He goes out of his way to connect with strangers and is always looking on the bright side. Watching him, I learned that life really is great if you have the right attitude."

As a kid, Greg remembers being in bed at night and hearing Paul have seizures in his room next door. In those moments, his fear would paralyze him into inaction. He got in the early habit of grinning and bearing a bad situation, waiting for it to pass. But with time, Greg came to understand the importance of taking control and using his unyieldingly optimistic attitude to turn things around. "Now, I like taking on the toughest challenges, whether it's completing an Ironman triathlon or stepping up to help a business that's really struggling," he says. "I believe positive things happen to positive people, so I'm positive about most everything in life. My optimism allows me to persevere where others give up, so I'm able to help where others can't. I'm here on earth to do things that other people don't want to do, creating positive outcomes that align with the positive attitude that fuels me."

In truth, Greg feels fortunate to be here on earth at all. He can still remember a summer day when he was four years old, and he was so hot that he went walking from window to window on the second floor of their home in Fairfax, Virginia, searching for a breeze that would cool him off. The next thing he knew, he was waking up in a hospital bed with a cracked skull and a broken neck. When his mother had come out to see his broken body suspended in a bush after the fall, she screamed so loudly that his father heard it over the roar of the chainsaw he was using to cut wood out back. "That bush broke my fall, stopping my head about four inches from a concrete slab below," he says. "I consider myself very lucky to be alive."

Born in Annandale, Greg spent his formative years in the house his family moved into when he was three years old. The area was far more rural than it is today, and he remembers the thrill of playing intense games of bounty hunter—tag, essentially—that would last hours or even days. Summertime was dedicated to swim team, and Greg would play football on the weekends with the other kids in the neighborhood. He ran track and swam competitively, but soccer was his favorite sport.

Greg's father grew up in a poor family in Liverpool, while his mother grew up just outside of London. An adept construction engineer, he took a job building hotels in Vegas, where he frequented jazz clubs and hung out with Miles Davis after his performances. They moved to Tahoe, where Paul was born, and then to Virginia, where Greg's father took a construction management job building Metro Center. He was laid off just as the family had settled in, and when he was offered a job in Chicago, Greg's mother was staunchly opposed to the idea of moving. Instead, he decided to stay put and joined forces with a friend to take on consulting work.

One project led to another, so they decided to formally launch their own company, Alpha Corporation. Through his childhood, Greg watched his father grow the company into an international presence of 300 employees and $40 million in revenue—until drama in the leadership ranks prompted Greg's father to strike out on his own with two of the five partners. They started from scratch as McDonough Bolyard Peck, again growing the venture to an international force of 300 employees. "My father is an entrepreneur who's excellent at what he does," Greg affirms. "Not only can he grasp complex problems or projects, but he can also sit in front of a jury and explain those complexities in ways that others understand. I mirror that skill today when I walk my clients through the histories and trends of complicated financials and P&Ls."

Despite his obvious professional prowess, Greg's father rarely discussed business with the family. "He was the kind of guy who got the job done during the day and tried not to bring his work home with him," Greg remembers and even recognizes that he struggles to do the same. "It's very different from the relationship I have with my daughter, Sasha, who's been very engaged in my entrepreneurial work since she was only seven years old. She's very interested in what's going on, and we love having conversations about how we're going to start a business together."

Greg's mother, a caring and skillful stay-at-home mom, was the leader in the family, and the one who always made magic happen. Because Paul required 24-hour care and considerable medical attention, their parents would come up with creative ways to spend time together. For instance, they always made a point to spend quiet time together before bed—a practice that would figure prominently into Greg's success later in life. "We'd go through a kind of meditation ritual together that involved counting, deep breathing, and memory exercises," Greg recalls. "It taught me how to methodically control my emotions, which has been an invaluable life skill in managing the stress and grit of being an entrepreneur. If I wake up in the middle of the night feeling panicked or anxious, I know how to calm those voices and return to a state of rest."

Each year was highlighted by a month-long visit from Grandma Eve, Greg's pioneering grandmother who lived in Pinner, England. She embraced vegetarianism, followed kabbalah, and used homeopathic medicines—ideas that were generations ahead of her time. Greg enjoyed talking business with her through his high school years, and when he turned eighteen, he spent the summer with her in England. "I'll never forget when we hopped the Concord to Paris for my birthday that July," he recalls. "She must have been saving money for ten years to pay for that trip. Grandma always put others first."

Greg was an average student through elementary and high school, excelling in math but struggled in English, and always longed to be active outside instead of stuck in a classroom. He made his first buck mowing lawns, and he started helping out at his dad's office at the age of ten. As he got older, his dreams of becoming a professional soccer player or a fighter pilot in the Air Force evolved into an interest in following in his father's footsteps as a successful engineer. "He always taught me that getting the deal done is more important than the deal itself because walking away with something is better than walking away with nothing," Greg says. "He also stressed the importance of putting the good of the company and its culture above the good of himself. That was impactful."

Upon graduating from high school, Greg attended George Mason University, where he joined a fraternity. It was at Mason that Greg started his leadership journey, spending two years as the President of the school's largest fraternity. Greg recalls using his positive attitude and determination to motive the chapter during a time when moral was particularly low. "I told them, we were focusing on the wrong thing, and that we needed to move on," he recounts. "We couldn't go back to the ref and ask him to change the score because the game was already over. I told them the past is the past, and there's nothing you can do about it, so focus on the future and on being positive. I told them to double down on tomorrow and come prepared with the right mindset."

Greg's confidence, leadership, and vision in that moment was raw and innate, without training our counseling. And in its pure form, it touched the team. One fraternity brother approached him afterward to let him know how inspirational the words had been. "He said, 'Greg, this is who you are, and this is what you do best,'" Greg remembers. "It was a defining moment that planted a seed—one that's just now truly coming to fruition. And the next day, with our new mindset, we won."

While he began to find his footing as a leader at the fraternity, Greg continued to struggle academically. The Dean advised that he spend a year at the local community college and then return to Mason to get his degree, but Greg's father stood up for him, insisting Greg would figure it out. "I recently sent him a thank-you letter for that because it was a pivotal moment that kept me in education," he says today. "He was right, and once I figured out what I love, I took off."

Greg decided to switch his major from Engineering to Economics because it seemed like the path of least resistance out of school. In his last semester, he had to take an elective and chose Finance—the class that finally proved the perfect fit for Greg, and the catalyst that redefined the course of his future. "From my first report on Bank of America stock prices, I loved the process of drawing understanding and insight from information and data," he says. "I vividly remember sitting in class just two weeks into the course and realizing it was exactly what I was supposed to be doing."

Greg aced that class, and though he had planned to leave academia for good once he graduated, he found himself instead eagerly re-enrolling at George Mason to complete a second degree in Finance. He aced that degree as well and then immediately started a master's program at George Washington while working at Fannie Mae, focusing his studies on accounting and finance, venture investing, mortgage trading, and foreign exchange.

Greg spent five years in Fannie Mae's investor relations department before his Senior VP, Jayne Shontell, had the opportunity to start a small corporate venture capital group focused on investing in Series A and Series B venture deals. Greg agreed to go with her, jumping at the opportunity to put real dollars to use in real companies. "Through that experience, I saw that I could apply my finance knowledge to small business, solve problems, and actually see results," Greg affirms. "That's where my entrepreneurial journey really started." Greg was then invited to be an executive in residence at Dexma, one of the companies in their portfolio.

When the economy shifted and Greg's job description grew considerably more conservative, Greg decided to venture out on his own to launch a company helping startups. Grandma Eve wrote him a check to help him get started, and he named the business Pinner Financial Management, after her hometown. He picked up six clients, including a startup called Pay Rent Build Credit, a credit authority designed to capture rental payment data so low-income families could build credit while paying rent. Greg helped them raise $2.5 million in venture capital and then sell.

After two years of solo practice, Greg decided to roll his practice into Longstreet Partners, an investment bank in Tysons Corner, Virginia. Two years later, in 2006, he married Monique, a driven and talented marketing, journalism, and sales executive. The two had met in college through a group of mutual friends, weaving in and out of each others' lives for many years until sparks suddenly flew when they crossed paths at a wedding. They dated, married, and are now the proud parents of two daughters, Sasha and Simone.

Despite their busy world of work and parenting, Greg and Monique have fallen in love with undertaking Ironman Triathlons together—

ultimate tests of strength, endurance, and willpower that add new depths to their relationship. "There's something really special about having a goal with your partner," he says. "We wake up early together to train. Sometimes I watch the kids so she can get her run in, or she'll watch them so I can do my swim. We became clearer communicators with each other, and there's nothing like being there on race day and knowing she's doing it with me." Greg and Monique make family vacations out of their Ironman competitions, selecting exciting destinations like Lake Placid, New York and Zurich, Switzerland. They've also launched a website, triathlonparents.com, and authored a book with advice for other parents interested in embracing the challenging—yet rewarding—family tradition.

Also in 2006, Greg took a position as the CFO for EEI Communications, a company specializing in editorial, proofreading, and formatting services for government agencies and associations. The company experienced considerable success until 2009, when it was hit hard by the recession. For the next several years, Greg took extreme cash flow management measures and did all he could to keep the company afloat, but by 2012, it was time to decide between shutting the doors or embarking down the Chapter 11 bankruptcy process.

Greg knew he was being paid less than market rate, and he considered jumping ship for better prospects, but one board meeting changed his mind. "I remember sitting there with the rest of the management team, and the attorney pointed out that someone who experiences the bankruptcy process from the inside picks up invaluable experience that not many people have," Greg recalls. "So I decided to do the exact opposite of what most people would do in that situation. Instead of pulling out, I doubled down and recommitted to making the journey successful. I decided I was going to make a real serious play at turning the business around."

Greg spent the next several months soaking up all he could, supplementing his real-world experience with coursework that earned him a certification as a Solvency and Restructuring Analyst. As the only business owner in those seminars, he was able to see opportunities with small- and middle-market companies that most people overlook in their efforts to serve bigger companies. And thanks to his hard work, EEI improved. "I wish I had known in 2009 what I know now," he reflects. "I see now that when you're going through dire straits, it's best to get in, stop the bleeding, and get reorganized so you can emerge stronger. If you're spending today's profits on yesterday's problems, you can't prepare for a better future. It's a hard process, but with the right advisors, you can make it out on the other side. I also would have taken bigger risks and made bigger changes at the time. We had a great core business with clients that loved us, and we just needed to get back to the fundamentals. That guidance is one of the value-adds I bring to clients today."

As a leader, Greg brings passion, positivity, and energizing solutions to difficult situations. Looking toward his next tough challenge, he has set his sights on helping entrepreneurs get the most out of their efforts. With a focus on business leaders living month-to-month and payroll-to-payroll, his rich and nuanced bank of firsthand experience will provide the tools, mindset, and methodology entrepreneurs need to skip the turbulence on the road to success. "It's incredibly helpful to begin with a clear understanding of your business's core, and with an ultimate exit strategy in mind," he says. "Once your business is whittled down to its fundamentals, you can model out according to your vision, strategically aligning every decision with where you want to go. This approach makes a big difference in cutting out incremental missteps that compound to a big impact down the road."

In advising young people entering the working world today, Greg echoes the lessons learned from his parents, who taught him to genuinely appreciate what he has. "Gratitude is truly a freeing, empowering thing," he affirms. "Of course there are times in life when I want what I want, and I want it now. But you have to put that kind of thinking out of your mind. Accept that you might not get exactly what you want now, or ever. Stop complaining, put your head down, and get the job done. Focus on being the best you can be at what you do, and have faith in the process. If you can open yourself to gratitude, you'll have a better experience along the way."

It's this simple, unassuming gratitude that fuels Greg in his mission to take on the toughest. After a full day of confronting complex business challenges or triathlon competing, he finds rejuvenation and contentment in the small miracles that define his life. He and Monique support Innisfree Village, where his brother Paul lives, and the Challenge Athletes Foundation, which buys prosthetic limbs for paraplegic individuals who want to compete in Ironman events too. "I believe in helping people achieve their goals, whatever they may be," Greg affirms. "And in my own life, I'm just grateful that I can get in my car and visit friends, or go hit golf balls, or go for a run. Gratitude for small things helps create opportunity for great things, fueling the stamina it takes to succeed."

BERNHARDT
WEALTH MANAGEMENT

Michael N. Mercurio

Calming the Chaos

Michael Mercurio obtained a master's degree in international affairs because he wanted to impact the world around him and help calm the chaos on the international stage. "When I graduated, the Balkan and Bosnian Wars were going on, Yugoslavia had broken up, and the Cold War was ending," he recounts today. "I took a job at a think tank, where I wrote and thought a lot about the problems of the world. But I'm a problem solver who likes to be in the trenches, roll up my sleeves, and dive into issues that are here and now. I wanted to make a difference that could be seen and to impact the world today, not just think and write about what we should or could have done. I wanted a career that was hands-on, solutions-oriented, and immediately tangible."

In search of a different kind of chaos to calm, Mike pivoted and earned his law degree. Now a Principal with Offit Kurman, P.A., a full-service law firm serving entrepreneurially-minded clients and families of wealth, he's motivated by the feeling of coming to work every day knowing he helps everyday people solve real problems in real time. "Bringing empathy to chaos is still what drives me, but now, it's immediate impactful solutions to tame the chaos," he says. "When people reach out to our law firm, it's often because something really good or something really bad has happened. Regardless, they are stressed and looking for advice. Their heads are spinning, and they can't sleep at night. I'm incredibly passionate about the fact that my empathy, knowledge, and pragmatic skill set is the thing that can calm them down and bring them some relief. It's very rewarding that my clients can sleep at night again knowing I've got their back." Mike takes this relationship of pure trust very seriously.

Offit Kurman was launched thirty years ago by Ted and Maurice Offit and Howard Kurman as a Baltimore County general practice firm of solid, reliable lawyers specializing in the core practice areas often sought by businesses and individuals. From those beginnings, the firm added skillsets, practice areas, and industry knowledge like government contracting, evolving into a one-stop-shop for all legal needs. From transactional such as corporate, employment, and intellectual property, to litigation such as business disputes, domestic disputes, and insurance recovery, the firm works with entrepreneurs and families of wealth to assist with their life cycle needs and help families achieve their goals.

Ted, a shrewd businessman and entrepreneur in addition to being an excellent lawyer, had envisioned targeting the lower middle market, entrepreneurially-driven business niche as a full-service local firm alternative to the big DC and Baltimore firms. "We've settled on that niche, so we don't chase the larger clients like Under Armour or IBM," Mike explains. "Small and mid-sized entrepreneurial businesses are our focus."

Ted Offit's vision proved a powerful one, and since the day Mike came onboard as the firm's twelfth attorney in 2003, he watched it expand to 135 attorneys today. It grew from a single office in Baltimore County to twelve offices along the corridor from Northern Virginia to New York, earning it a regular spot on the Inc. 5000 list of fastest growing companies. "I think we've been so successful because we match the entrepreneurial mindset of our clients," Mike points out. "In simple terms, a lawyer's job is to manage risk. When you're dealing with an entrepreneurial clientele that regularly accepts all sorts of risks, traditional legal approaches can clash. But we're very adept at understanding and respecting the elevated risk tolerance of our clients. We don't try to convince them to care about a risk when they don't. Instead, we see our role as shedding light on the risks that exist so our clients can decide for themselves whether they care about them or not. We believe in cutting out nonsense and giving our clients what they want, without all the extra baggage they often face in working with other firms that don't understand the entrepreneurial frame of mind."

Offit Kurman's success also stems from the caliber and experience of the attorneys it hires. Most come from big law firms where they've already cut their teeth and gotten substantial experience under their belts. They come onboard ready to take on the often unpredictable and inconsistent legal issues that arise with their clients, from employment issues to succession planning. "We're not a training ground," Mike affirms. "When our clients come to us, they don't get someone who's learning on their dollar. They get someone who's been around the block—someone who already has a lot of tools in their toolbox to address their needs, and can do so at an effective price point."

Mike specializes in corporate transactions, heading his firm's practice in this regard. He focuses most his time on the life cycle issues of his clients, especially end stage considerations such as mergers and acquisitions, succession and equity transfers. In the summer of 2016, Mike took on the challenge of building out the transactional practice of the firm's Tyson's Corner office, using his leadership and networking skills to obtain market share in the area. "I enjoy working with business owners, especially driven leaders who have put their businesses on a growth curve that's evolving toward a conclusion, like a sale," he says.

"I enjoy the transactional side of law and the work of M&A deals, as opposed to litigating, which can be adversarial and destructive. Rather, it's about building something and working with people who are incredibly smart, creative, and innovative when it comes to making money and changing the world. From companies that make drones, to companies that do up-dos for wedding parties, it's amazing to see the visions of these entrepreneurs, who are truly the engines that drive this country."

As a leader at the firm and within the community, Mike is known for his genuine, passionate, straightforward manner, where what you see is what you get. He treats a receptionist the same way he'd treat the CEO of a $200 million company—a hallmark of his upbringing in a traditional home with strong values in a suburb of Philadelphia. "My parents taught me to be down to earth," he says. "They're still alive today and have been married for over fifty years. They always taught us to do what we say and mean what we say. They were great role models, showing us that our word is our bond and that it's important to go out of your way for your dedication to family and to doing what's right. And they always follow through to the end."

Mike's father, always quick-witted, spontaneous, and fun, worked for Unysis, a global information technology company that often sent him to Asia to work on Air Force contracts and procurements in Japan, Korea, and Taiwan. He enjoyed a good party and a cigar, was very passionate about sports, and rarely worried about anything. Mike's mother, on the other hand, was more reserved and refined. She graduated second in her high school class, but her parents—first generation Italians from the old country—had already sent her older sister to college, and weren't able to pay to educate another girl. So Mike's mother was left to sacrifice her professional potential for the good of her family, staying at home to raise Mike and his younger brother and sister until they entered high school. She always considered it her calling, and took great pride in the role. When her kids were older, she took a job with Merck & Co.

Growing up in a duplex with his cousins living next door, sports were a big thing for Mike's family, as they were for most families in Philadelphia. "We lived and died by the Eagles, the Phillies, and the Flyers," he reflects fondly. He played baseball, basketball, and football, laying the foundation for many of the sports analogies he would later use as a businessman. "My father coached my baseball team, and I remember many happy days on the field together," he says.

The Mercurios were a very traditional, Catholic family, and Mike attended parochial schools all the way through undergraduate school. Despite their love of sports, his parents made sure that academics always came first, and good grades came relatively easily to Mike. As a young kid, he was at times shy and reserved, though he grew into a more outgoing and aggressive leader over time.

When Mike was in fifth grade, the family moved to Herndon, Virginia, where his father was transferred for work. The transition was difficult at first, but soon showed its silver lining as Mike made new friends and came to know the area. His Italian American neighborhood in Philadelphia had been relatively homogenous, and the international flare of the DC metropolitan area struck a whole new cord with him. "I spent a lot of time visiting the city and going to museums, and I met a lot of international movers and shakers," he says. "We attended President Reagan's inauguration, and I still remember the parade. I cultivated a deep appreciation for the cosmopolitan nature of the city."

After his freshman year of high school, the family decided to move back to the Philadelphia area. "I was really gaining momentum and doing well in Northern Virginia," he laughs. "But we integrated well at our new school in Lansdale, Pennsylvania." There, Mike played varsity baseball and lettered in multiple sports. He also got a job at a pizza place, joined clubs at school, and participated in the honors program. The interest in international affairs sparked by his time in DC was further cultivated by joining Model UN and working with a particularly passionate history teacher, who encouraged his pursuit of politics and global issues. He also appreciated his baseball coach, who taught him that sports come down to having the confidence to play your best and not hold back.

Upon graduating from high school, Mike enrolled at the University of Scranton, a Jesuit school, where he got a Bachelor's of Science in International Affairs. He worked as a waiter and a bartender, and when he graduated, he took a semester off to save money and work in construction. "I learned a lot about the value of hard manual labor, and that I didn't want to spend the rest of my life doing that kind of work," he says. "Many of my fellow workers would get paid Friday afternoon, head to the bar, and were broke by Monday morning. It was a sad lifestyle."

Instead, Mike decided to pursue international affairs in graduate school and returned to the city that had catalyzed his love for the subject in the first place—Washington, DC. He enrolled in American University's School of International Service, hoping to serve his country through a career in the State Department or the CIA. The program afforded him an opportunity to visit South Korea on a Congressional Exchange Program—an experience reminiscent of the business trips he saw his father take when he was young.

Working full-time to cover the cost of school, Mike graduated on time with a masters in international affairs and a minor in technology, and took the job at the think tank. But two years was all it took for him to reassess the best context for his skills, recalibrate to a path that could solve more immediate problems, and he pivoted to the American University, Washington College of Law. He took classes at night and found a day job as a paralegal and clerk at a law firm, which was extremely useful in putting the theoretical and conceptual lessons of his coursework into action. He then landed another clerkship at another large law firm, Epstein Becker Green, and stayed on as an associate after graduating. "I spent my first couple of years bouncing around several different practice areas, but I knew I wanted to eventually work in business," says Mike. "I was always intrigued by the stock market and what truly makes a business tick."

Mike worked a short stint at Gallagher Evelius & Jones LLP doing tax and low income credit work, and then decided to make the jump to business when he became the first corporate associate hire at a small firm in Bethesda. There, he spent a year working for the named partner and did a great job—until the partner decided he was ready to semi-retire. He had absolutely no negative critique of Mike's work, but because of his life decisions, Mike was let go. "Through no fault of my own, and after a great performance review, I was laid off, with a wife and kids to support," he says. "No matter how hard I worked, my destiny was tied to someone else's life decisions. It taught me that I had to be the captain of my own ship because I never wanted my success to be controlled by the whims of others. From then on, I focused on developing my own book of business and creating my own practice."

From then on, Mike built a practice despite having comparatively few connections in the DC area, gaining each client through hard work, commitment, and hustle. He accepted the job at Offit Kurman, and under Ted Offit's excellent mentorship, he was a sponge. Success at work stemmed in large part from mastering the art of truly delivering what the client asks for—something easier said than done. "I call it the 'good enough' standard," he says. "You can put in a lot of time to go above and beyond for a client or a partner, but those efforts often backfire because what you end up delivering is not what they hired you to do. It's important to be a good listener and deliver exactly what's asked of you, not what you think they need or want, and not what you would want."

By that point, Mike had become single but was blessed to have a young son and a daughter to raise. Determined to make the most of the situation, Mike embraced his role as the single father of two young children. And when the children spent time with their mother, his time was freed up to focus on work more than he might have been able to do in a traditional family environment. "I remember having to figure out how to braid my daughter's hair and get her ballerina costumes," he laughs. "When my kids were with me, I was wholly present. And when they weren't, I could be wholly present with work. It was a tremendously defining experience for me, being a single dad while building a practice. I count myself as very fortunate to have been successful with both."

Then, in 2008, Mike met Liz. By that time, he had learned a lot about relationships, and about himself. He knew not to rush into anything, and he knew what he really wanted out of a partner. "We're very similar in that we like to do everything together, but we also complement each other in every way," he says. "She's my partner and the rock that keeps me grounded. We really get each other. Liz has two daughters, and we worked carefully to blend our families into a wonderful unit." Liz and Mike got married on the beach in 2014, surrounded by family and friends—a day that he remembers as one of the happiest of his life.

Perhaps their greatest strength as a couple is their spontaneity—a trait that allows them to truly live life to the fullest together. They enjoy outdoor enthusiast activities such as riding motorcycles and ATVs, scuba diving, and shooting together, while also enjoying the finer pursuits like attending live music shows, festivals, wine and bourbon tasting, and travel. They are also generous with their time for their children's and extended families' activities. Mike also plays competitive ice hockey—a sport he loves for its fast pace and action-packed speed—and is a long-standing season ticket holder for the Philadelphia Flyers.

In advising young people entering the working world today, Mike underscores the importance of working hard and working smart. "You don't have to reinvent the wheel," he says. "All the knowledge you need to be successful in the world is already out there—you just have to discover it. That means you've got to be a good listener, and you've got to be coachable. Know that you don't know it all, and listen to the people who are willing to mentor you."

Beyond that, his story shows the power of staying true to your driving force, but remaining flexible enough to find the context that best fits your strengths and interests. Had he stuck with the international affairs think tank world, he may have wrestled the rest of his career with an ambiguous form of chaos that could never really be tamed in a sense that would be rewarding to him. Instead, he took a risk and found a path that affords the face-to-face effects of his efforts, and is a better lawyer and entrepreneur because of it. "Because of my work, people in my community sleep better at night," he says. "They're happier, more effective, and more successful as leaders and job creators, and to me, that's the most rewarding part of all."

BERNHARDT
WEALTH MANAGEMENT

Clyde Northrop

A Can Do Attitude

Sitting in their small apartment across from his mother and stepfather, thirteen-year-old Clyde Northrop knew his life was about to change—though he couldn't have guessed how much. After living in Japan for six years, his parents had parted ways subtly, as divorce often occurred back in the 1950s. Clyde and his younger brother had returned to America with their mother, who went to work and had neither the time nor the energy to keep her sons disciplined and in line. Stuck in low-caliber classes where he had already learned the material, Clyde was bored and often skipped school. Then, after a year of being a wild child, Charles Roberts entered the picture.

Charles had a daughter and son of his own, around Clyde's age. Only a week after he married Clyde's mother, the newly-blended family gathered so the parents could announce the news that they had decided they would never work for anyone again. Instead, they were pooling their money to start a family business, in which the kids were expected to play integral roles. "By then, I had already learned that questioning the old man was not a good idea," Clyde laughs today. "So we readied ourselves for a wild ride."

Charles Roberts hailed from Appalachia with an eighth grade education, while Clyde's mother had finished high school and was trained as a secretary. They had no real expertise to speak of, but that didn't stop them from trying their hands at business after business. "In rapid succession, they started a delivery business, a food service business, and a furnace cleaning business," Clyde recounts. "My stepfather had this unbelievable confidence that he could muscle through anything, figure it out, and make it work. It was a mindset that was passed on to us kids."

Clyde still remembers vividly the day one of their delivery trucks blew a transmission. He and his brother called up to their stepfather, who told them to go to the parts store on the corner and take care of it. When the boys told him they didn't know how to fix it, Charles disappeared back in the apartment and returned with a transmission manual. "Well, read about it and figure it out!" he shouted, hurling it at the two boys. "That was our whole thing," Clyde says today. "If we didn't know how to do it, learn. My stepfather taught me everything I know about work, drive, and initiative, and I became sure over time that there was literally nothing I couldn't do." Now a Master Chair of Vistage International, Clyde brings that same "can do" attitude to the CEOs and executives he works with, opening doors to new successes and new heights.

As the world's largest executive coaching organization, Vistage provides leadership training and guidance to the visionaries and innovators who shape the businesses that put the world to work. The program acts as a success accelerator, helping business leaders across seventeen countries take their companies further, faster. CEOs and C Suite executives are divided into groups of around fifteen people, which are led by Chairs that facilitate the sharing of perspectives, wisdom, and best practices. "Vistage helps people succeed by de-leveraging an individual's risk, spreading it around so it's not all on the shoulders of one person," Clyde explains. "Rather, you get a range of perspectives, which illuminate your blind spots and help lead to better decisions. I believe in the wisdom of crowds—that none of us is as smart as all of us. By that logic, you benefit not only from the people in your group, but from over 20,000 Vistage members in our network worldwide. To me, it's that multitude of perspectives that makes Vistage truly invaluable."

As a Master Chair, Clyde has done over 10,000 hours of one-on-one coaching for Vistage, and has a proven track record of strong retention across the four groups he leads. In the twenty years he's been with the organization, he's worked with around 1,200 leaders, each a top influencer in companies that average around 50 employees. By that math, his work has touched around 60,000 employees—a legacy that magnifies exponentially when accounting for the families and communities that depend on those people. "I'm a big believer that Vistage Chairs attract people like themselves," Clyde says. "My groups tend to have people with high confidence and high drive."

Vistage brings value to its members through various avenues, including one-on-one sessions, group sessions, and speakers. Clyde sees the greatest value, however, in connecting the information that comes from those various dots. "When you take what you learned in one training and share it with someone else, they add their piece to it by giving their perspective, which means you've just learned something else," he says. "New value is generated through exponential connection, which I find very powerful."

In part, Vistage is about understanding and leveraging the power of your own story—something Clyde first learned through watching his father. A native Washingtonian, Clyde grew up thinking his father was a globetrotting laundry expert who taught clothes cleaning best practices across Asia. In reality, the story was a cover for his father's work as a spy for the Defense Intelligence Agency. He spent eleven months out of the year overseas, returning to the U.S. to "learn new techniques" once a year before heading out to his new duty station. When Clyde was six, he moved with his mother and younger brother to Japan to finally live with his father, and still remembers vividly the eight-day trip on a troop transport vessel that took them from Seattle to Yokohama.

The family lived on base in Sendai for a year, and then moved into a village. His mother worked as a Red Cross volunteer, and he remembers the nanny, Yoko, who continued to expand his mind and experience with the foods, cultural practices, and tone of post-World War II Japan. When he was nine, the family moved to an air base several hundred miles north. Clyde played in Little League and rode his bike, but couldn't develop long-term friendships due to the transitory nature of the military schools. He remembers his relationship with his father, however, as especially good. "He'd take me out to the rice paddies in his '49 Studebaker, set me in his lap, and teach me how to drive," Clyde recalls. "I couldn't quite reach the pedals, but he'd clutch it while I'd change the gears and steer. I loved that."

When Clyde was twelve, he and his younger brother returned with their mother to the U.S., allegedly so she could undergo surgery. In reality, his parents had drifted apart and decided to divorce. Fortunately, his father was a spectacular letter writer and storyteller, and would send Clyde and his brother eight-page masterpieces covered front-and-back in his compelling scrawl. When they arrived in the mail, Clyde would read them aloud to his younger brother and cousins. "The stories were so crazy and exciting that the kids would all stop playing to come in and listen," he says. "Years later, when we finally found out he was a spy, we were shocked to realize that his stories were actually true."

Clyde had attended parochial school through sixth grade, but made the switch to public school for seventh. The coursework was far less advanced, and Clyde was bored senseless. He began skipping school and was ultimately expelled for absenteeism. By that point, his mother was remarried to Charles, and when Clyde broke the news at the dinner table that evening, he braced himself for a firestorm. His stepfather, however, remained completely calm. "That's actually great news because I need help with the new business," Charles said. "You can work with me now. We'll start tomorrow morning at 3:30 AM."

When Clyde was allowed back at school, he was the most dedicated student imaginable. He and his siblings adopted a highly regimented lifestyle, working paper routes first thing in the morning and working at the business in the evenings. "We were the only kids on the block that couldn't wait to go back to school and do extracurricular activities," Clyde laughs It was a grueling upbringing, but Clyde took to it well. "As kids, we all lamented the work and dreamed of growing up to get normal jobs where you clock your eight hours and enjoy weekends and vacations," Clyde says. "But now, all of us have our own companies and still work crazy hours. We owe that to my stepfather's influence."

When Clyde turned 18 and neared graduation, he knew the drill. The second he received his diploma, his parents would expect him to head out on his own, as they had with his older step siblings. "The drinking age was eighteen back then, and on the day of my graduation, he took me and a friend out for our 'first beers,'" Clyde says. "My stepdad asked me what I was doing tomorrow, and I said I didn't know. But then he clarified and said, 'No, where are you *living* tomorrow?' Fortunately, I was ready for the question and had joined the Air Force."

Clyde had made the decision hoping to avoid being drafted directly into the Marines and sent to Vietnam. With a friend, he joined the Delayed Enlistment Program, which opened the door to his first real forays out of town. He spent the summer in Florida and then reported for basic training in Texas, where his squad was completely torn down and reconstituted, both physically and mentally. "It was an extraordinary experience that my stepfather prepared me well for," Clyde says. From there, he was sent to his first duty station in Illinois, where he spent a year in tech school. There, he was offered the opportunity to take over a makeshift fatigue tailoring business, and though he had never sewn anything before, he eagerly accepted. "For the next ten months, I made about $3,000 as the station's tailor," he says.

Clyde was then transferred to Arizona, and then overseas to Vietnam, where he served two tours. "The last movie I saw stateside was The Green Berets, which is a lot of shooting and killing as these guys are trying to protect this base in the middle of some godforsaken jungle," Clyde remembers. "I saw that movie and thought, I'm toast! Reflecting on it during the flight over, I fully expected to be killed."

After landing at the air terminal in Vietnam, waiting to be transferred to his duty station, Clyde bought a soft serve ice cream and remembers seeing a group of dusty, battle-hardened servicemen lugging their weapons. Suddenly, rockets started raining on the terminal, and Clyde ducked for cover as the building shook. He came up when the coast was clear, to find the group of soldiers in the same place, unflinching. He knew he was in the big leagues.

When he arrived on base, Clyde was relieved to find a sizeable, solid compound, much more secure and comfortable than what he had seen in the movies. After enough guerrilla attacks, he too learned the calm and composure displayed by the men in the trembling air terminal. After serving his twelve-month deployment, he volunteered to serve an additional six months—a period cut abruptly short when President Nixon initiated a troop drawdown.

Back stateside, Clyde arrived in Seattle and took about a year to make his way back to the East Coast, hitchhiking across the country. Charles agreed to rent him the basement floor to sleep on for a hundred dollars a week, and he enrolled full-time at Prince George's Community College on the GI Bill while working odd jobs on the side. He started a modest home improvement business, moved in with friends, and remembers driving to New York City in 1972 in a van to see a concert protesting the atrocities in Bangladesh. Unable to get tickets, he didn't make it into the concert, but he did meet Mary Christina, the lovely young woman he married the following year. "We were poor as church mice," he laughs. "Our wedding bands cost maybe $50 apiece, which was a king's ransom to us back then."

Clyde finished his degree at the University of Maryland and picked up a large territory distributing the *Washington Post* to paperboys on weekends. He planned to complete graduate school to become a criminal psychologist, but then realized he could make just as much growing the delivery business he was running out of his kitchen. "We had a baby on the way, and it dawned on me that I could either save the criminals in the state of Maryland, or I could save my family," he says. "Criminal psychology was interesting, but not that interesting, so I left that behind and looked forward."

With that, Clyde and Chris decided to take her accrued government retirement of $5,000, plus whatever money they could scrape together, and turn their kitchen business into an actual company. They incorporated Southwest Distribution in 1974 and set to work expanding their customer base by disrupting the market, which was already comfortably divided amongst their two competitors. Chris handled the books and finances, while Clyde went out to grow the business. "I put on a suit and a smile and went everywhere I could—NYC, LA, Chicago, Dallas, Miami—to tell publications we could distribute them in DC," Clyde says. "People wanted to take a chance on us. By 1980, we had captured the market and brought in this flood of out-of-town newspapers to the DC area that was very well received."

In this way, Southwest Distribution evolved into a logistics company that moved and transported product across the country. At that time, papers were printed in their cities of origin, so Clyde would negotiate how to get them to DC. "We went after every newspaper in the country that was published in a market of over 300,000 people," Clyde explains. "We became the official newspaper distribution contractor for the White House and most of the federal government." It was the perfect challenge for Clyde's can-do attitude, and the company grew to $10 million in revenue.

Business was good and continued to grow, but as the world evolved, electronic transmission and "Print on Demand" papers disrupted Clyde's model. Yet he managed to adapt over time, drawing on traits and skills he had picked up from important figures in his life. He employed the extreme focus on craft and mission that he had learned from his paternal father, who was able to compartmentalize and perform perfectly in the moment without getting caught up on what he would have, could have, or should have done. He demonstrated the unflagging work ethic, self-confidence, and drive he had learned from his stepfather, believing always that anything was possible. And he maintained the absolute loyalty he had learned from his mother, who supported and defended her children no matter what. "When the market asks, 'Can you do this?', my answer is always, absolutely!" Clyde says. "I overpromise but never under deliver, pulling all-nighters and giving it my all to figure it out."

When Clyde joined Vistage as a member in 1989, he only wished he had found the organization sooner. Nine years later, he turned fifty and hit his 25-year mark at the helm of his company. He felt ready for a shift, and a friend suggested he become a Vistage Chair. "Vistage had done so much for me and my company," he recalls. "I'd met some of the smartest people on the planet and learned more than I'd ever learned before. I've always been compelled toward personal optimization, continually learning and trying to better myself, so I knew it would be perfect for me. And my life's mission is to build community through listening, caring, and sharing, which is what being a Vistage Chair is all about."

Clyde and Chris sold their company to their two sons in 2005—men who, like Clyde, grew up in the family business and swore they'd never return to such grueling work after heading off to college. But they both found their way back to the company, rose through the ranks, and initiated a ten-year buyout of what is now a much more technologically-oriented company. Their involvement, as well as Chris's support, allowed Clyde to fully step away and focus on his work at Vistage. Thanks to this focus, Clyde won the distinguished Hyndman Award in 2015. One of the organization's most prestigious awards, it honors individuals with strong chairing capacity who have exemplary ability to lift others through help in the community and support for younger chairs. Clyde and Chris mirror this giving focus in their personal lives, supporting a host of philanthropic goals that include support for abused children in Montgomery County and The Hunger Project (thp.org), an organization focused on transforming conditions that give rise to hunger and poverty..

Beyond any doubt, Chris's support has been absolutely integral to Clyde's success in life. "Without her, there's no way I could have lasted in business," he says. "My 'can do' attitude is great, but unless it's balanced with fiscal discipline, it can easily spin out of control. When anything is possible, money is no object—until you need to make payroll. Chris's ability to be fiscally prudent is unquestionably why that company is 42 years old and still successful today. Beyond that, she is extraordinarily caring and compassionate and always smooths the edges out for everyone. I'm so lucky to have her."

In advising young people entering the working world today, Clyde underscores the importance of confidence. "Whether in the military, in school, in family life, or in business, it's important for leaders to convey absolute confidence in themselves," he says. "Not arrogance or authoritarianism, but feeling good about themselves and the direction they're headed." Confidence must be balanced, however, with open eyes and an open mind. "Technological shifts are changing the game all the time, so stay alert and agile so you can respond swiftly," he says. "You can't know what's going to happen, so you have to be open.

When things are evolving faster and faster, the goal is to adapt and keep up. But never forget how attainable that goal is. You can learn to do literally anything if you believe you can. Failure is unacceptable, so your mindset must be resolute: you can, and you will, so you do."

Dawn Peters

One More Step

Standing at the base of a telegraph pole that seemed to be a hundred feet tall, Dawn Peters saw more than the very top rising high above her, and the trapeze to which she'd need to leap—she saw her fear. She had always been afraid of heights, but also always one to face her fears. So when her Life Coach Group committed to doing this unique team-building exercise, she had agreed.

Now, as the assistant helped secure her harness, she wasn't so sure. "Will you do me a favor?" he asked. "Go as far as you can, and then take one more step. Can you do that?"

"Yes, I can do *that!*" Dawn replied, and through her fear, she was able to grasp the defining lesson that would come to characterize her work ethic. "From that moment, I realized that we all have self-imposed limits, whatever they may be," she says today. "How many phone calls will you make today? Make one more. How many miles will you run? Run one more. Anytime we think we've reached a limit we perceive for ourselves, either personally or professionally we can always take one more step."

Now the founder, owner, and CEO of ConneXion Hub, a multi-level, multi-touch marketing platform and network for connecting B2B and B2C clients, a lifetime of "one more steps" has led Dawn around the world, exploring new cultures and ways of life to find the perfect one for her. 'One more step' led her across the Atlantic Ocean from her home country of England to lay down new roots in a new country. And step by step, opportunity by opportunity, and person by person, she has built a life, a business, and a professional ecosystem that has helped countless individuals and businesses take their own next steps too.

When Dawn arrived in America from England in 2000, she knew two people in Washington, DC. Since that time, she's organically grown her network and reach to over 300,000. "In the beginning, I didn't do that with any thought or intention," she says. "I just wanted to meet people in my new country, and I had a corporate job that required me to network."

As time went on, and driven by her innate love of people, Dawn joined a number of networking organizations, a national speaking network, and nonprofit boards. "I've always been fascinated in what makes people tick," she says. "I'd find out what makes one person tick, and then I'd discover that same motivation or purpose in someone else, so I'd connect them. I had this 'rolodex' permanently at work in my head, and in time, I came to realize that people really valued and appreciated these connections."

In 2009, Dawn decided to start her own coaching business, which allowed her to see even more connections between people's stories and their businesses. She decided to start doing workshops and networking lunch-and-learns, which required her to develop a method of consistently getting the word out to as many people as possible through various platforms, and with multiple touches. She developed an impressive marketing platform that centralized all her connections in a single database, quickly realizing just how many people she had come to know over the years.

As the business networking lunch-and-learns began to pick up momentum, people began approaching her to co-host the events. Those individuals and companies would then promote her business in their networks, which expanded her network, and vice versa. As the ripple effect compounded rapidly and required more and more of her time, she made the decision in 2013 to professionalize her connection work for incorporation under her company umbrella.

Today, individuals and companies partner with ConneXion Hub for six-month or year-long increments, and select 'a la carte' out of the available avenues for being connected, marketed, and promoted with others. They might choose introductions, leads, and connections, or they might opt to get access to the social media networks Dawn has developed over many years. Other options include business networking lunch-and-learns, speaking opportunities, vendor table opportunities, 'Connecting With a Twist' evening networking events, or partner-only boutiques, which come in three different formats. Partners can also choose to be featured in Dawn's online magazine, in her newsletter, or on her website. Keenly aware of the viewership and impact of video in the business world, she also launched the 'Connect Live' show to showcase businesses. "Through professionally videoed interviews, the show enables owners to tell their story, explaining their services and solutions and what makes their business unique," Dawn says. "These are live to tape, with the option to take questions or testimonials from callers, or to live-broadcast to clients' Facebook and YouTube sites. Clients leave with four web TV broadcasts that can be repurposed for a variety of marketing sites," Dawn is further adding to her 'offerings' by partnering with Microsoft to help get the company's IT educational materials out into the marketplace.

In this way, ConneXion Hub works with small to medium-size businesses typically between $200,000 and $10 million in revenue, and across all industry sectors. "I believe that business is best built through connections, engagement, and relationships. When businesses plug in to my multi-platform, multi-touch 'machine,' they leverage my eighteen years of networking and relationships in this area to work for them, therefore compounding their marketing efforts without any time input from themselves," she affirms. "Many businesses I work with traditionally market to their *own* network, and therefore their exposure is limited to those in their orbit or connection space. With ConneXion Hub, they're exposed to, and engaged with, an additional huge and diverse body of connections that's constantly growing, in a number of very strategic, systematic, and highly effective ways."

Through this rather unique methodology for enabling businesses to connect, market, and grow, ConneXion Hub is as independent of rules and convention as its founder has always been. Even as a little girl growing up in England, Dawn's childhood was shaped in part by the profound frustration she felt when her father would always tell her to go help her mother in the kitchen. "My two older brothers were right there and equally capable, but because I was the girl, he always told *me* to do it," she recounts. "It's fascinating to me that this was my world at the time, and I didn't know any differently—yet it simply seemed instinctively and inherently wrong. There were a lot of arguments around this discrepancy when I was growing up. I believe that was defining because it helped me grow into a very strong woman with a keen awareness of right and wrong—or simply of fairness—in the circumstances."

Born in South England as the youngest of three children, Dawn grew up in Petersfield, a large town in Hampshire County. Her father worked as a District Sales Manager for a national domestic, commercial, and industrial ventilation solutions company, while her mother was a Regional Sales Manager for Avon cosmetics, recruiting and managing over two hundred sales representatives across her region. Their home-based careers allowed for flexibility, and they passed up promotion opportunities in the interest of not uprooting their children and lifestyle. "Looking back, I'm so appreciative that we did a lot together as a family," Dawn says. "I remember a lot of day trips and vacations, and even something so basic as always sitting down together for meals as a family. I really appreciate that I was taught and brought up with the right values, ethics, and behaviors."

Dawn also grew up with an innate passion for art and creativity, her main interest both in school and at home. When her family watched TV together, she always had to be busy creating something. When it came to sports and adventures, she tried to keep up with her brothers, but being the youngest and a girl, she usually came up short. Still, it never dampened her spirits. "Anytime we played sports, they'd usually turn it into a battle or a fight, and I'd often end up getting hurt or losing," she says. "But I remember never feeling defeated. My father was very encouraging about me just joining in and doing my best. I think it gave me an enduring fighting spirit, and when I fall down in life, I simply just get back on up! And because I couldn't beat them physically, I learned to beat them verbally instead. That's got to have advantages in life, surely!" she laughs.

Though they were never wealthy, Dawn's parents made a point of taking the children to lots of theater performances and shows, and Dawn dreamed of being a dancer one day. "I always had the strong urge and feeling that I wanted to be on the stage, not in the audience," she remembers. But she didn't like her ballet lessons, and though she wanted to be musical, she unfortunately didn't like the violin, the only instrument her parents could afford at the time. But she stuck with it, reaching Grade 4 and playing in the school orchestra for several years.

As Dawn got older, she got various summer jobs, including at IBM headquarters in Portsmouth, England. After completing secondary school and college, the equivalent of high school in America, she went on to Swansea University in Wales, where she decided to focus on

Psychology due to her fascination in human behavior. "I had no idea what I wanted to do and considered pursuing art, but my parents cautioned me against it because they thought it was too risky for a stable future," she says. "Looking back, I do wish I had followed my passion for the arts or dancing. But as it turns out, running your own company certainly involves a lot of creativity."

Upon graduating in 1985, Dawn decided to gain a few more active and creative skills. She got certified in therapeutic massage and as a nutritionist, and she also wanted to learn to ski, so she spent the next year working as a cook at a ski resort in France and then on a Greek Island. Then, having always dreamed of living in the big city, she moved to London and landed a job as an IT Recruiter. The field aligned perfectly with her love of people, matchmaking, and connecting, yet she couldn't shake the feeling that there was more to discover. She wanted to explore the world. "I had an undying desire to experience different cultures and how other people live—a yearning that has helped drive and define me ever since," she says. "I ended up meeting a friend of a friend for coffee, and after over three hours of nonstop talking, we decided to travel the world together."

With that, Dawn spent almost two years backpacking from country to country, having the time of her life. After exploring Egypt, India, Nepal, Thailand, Singapore, and Malaysia, and Australia, they settled in Sydney, Australia, and got jobs at global conglomerates, travel companies, restaurants, and bars. She loved being immersed in so many cultures around the world, appreciating life and how others live. One particular awakening and realization, though, will never leave her. It occurred during the last two months of her time in Australia, when her middle brother, John, was a fighter pilot in the Royal Air Force preparing to go fight in the Iraq War. One day, as Dawn walked to her job as usual in Sydney, she happened to pass a telephone booth and was struck with the strongest and most inexplicable urge to call her parents in England. So she did, knowing she'd be late for work. She was surprised when her oldest brother, who was married and didn't live there, answered the phone. "What are you doing there?" she asked. He responded, "John's just been shot down."

Dawn will never forget how she fell to the floor of the phone booth, the world blurring and spinning around her. "I had no idea that I had such emotions for my brother," she says. "We'd never been close. In fact, he was always the annoying one growing up. For the first time in my life, I felt and realized how deep-set and strong blood ties are. From that moment on, I never took my family for granted again, because in the end, they're what matters most. I started to see my parents and grandparents as people, not just elders, and I also realized the finality of life. I've focused on learning more about the lives they led, and valuing aspects I never saw before. My maternal grandmother, especially, was a vibrant woman who didn't have an easy life, and I feel and believe she's watching over me. I've also come to be so incredibly grateful that I have the caring, endearing, loving qualities of my mother, paired with the strong, disciplinarian, straight-shooter qualities of my father. They brought me up with the right ethics and values, and I carry those qualities with me in all areas of life—in work, in play, in how I treat my clients, and in how I operate my business."

Miraculously, after 42 days of imprisonment and torture, Dawn's brother was released, prompting her return to England in 1991. She went back into IT recruitment, but by that point, she craved something new. When a Sales Trainer came in to train her team, Dawn was instantly drawn to the profession. She left to join that woman's company as a National Sales Trainer, soon mastering the skills and knowledge base so well that she could design and deliver rigorous, engaging 8-hour training courses. She then landed a position with an International IT recruitment firm in 1996. "I was thrilled to find myself the Global Sales Training Director for their 22 offices around the world, and set up their entire sales training department," she says.

All the while, Dawn harbored a burgeoning interest in working in television. On her frequent business trips to the U.S., she saw that

America was her best bet for making that happen—not only because there were more channels, but because of the culture itself. "I truly believed, and still do believe, that America is the land of opportunity," she says. "Here, people give you a chance."

With her company, Dawn was offered a Regional Director position in either Atlanta, Boston, or DC. She chose DC because it was closest to home, and as she quadrupled the office's sales, she got headshots and began guest-hosting on local cable shows. After a year, however, the industry took a nosedive, and her company wanted to her back to Europe. "That was a defining moment for me because I had moved my entire life here to follow my dream," she says. "I was determined to stay and make it work. I had no idea how I was going to do it, but I wasn't going back to England."

Dawn knew it wouldn't be easy, but her challenge was made exponentially harder when she then found out that she was exempt from getting a work visa in TV since she had no prior experience. So she decided to instead pursue sales training in a TV/video production company—one more step closer to her goal. With the opportunity to work in that environment, she focused on gaining significant experience on and off camera in her spare time—especially as a host and segment producer interviewing C-Suite executives in fast growing companies, creating segments that aired on ABC and Tech TV. She also joined a one-year coaching course taught by Tony Robbins—an experience she found incredibly enriching. "I was especially compelled when he said, 'All that you need is within you now!'" she recounts. "So often through life, we look outside of ourselves for the answers or resources we need. When you take the time to look inside yourself, you realize there's a hell of a lot more than what you're accessing. That was a pretty powerful realization."

By that time, Dawn had found her way to Atlantic Video, where she worked fully immersed in a larger TV production environment. Finally, in late 2008, she landed her Green Card—just in time before the company closed soon afterwards. "It wasn't clear to me how to break into a hosting and presenter role in TV at that point," she says. "But coaching came naturally to me, and I saw that as a dynamic way to make a difference in people's lives. So I decided to see what I could do with that and started my own business."

At that time, Dawn had little idea how to start a company or run a business, so she sought advisors and signed up for courses that might light the way. In one such class, she remembers the presenter declared that anyone planning to undertake such an endeavor should be ready to give up their nights, weekends, and 'life as they know it!' "I remember thinking, '*Ha—that won't be me!*'" Dawn laughs. "But as it turned out, everything she said was right. Had I known then what I know now, I would have gotten more help earlier. I always try to do everything on my own, which I suppose is a great quality in a lot of respects, but it also has its downfalls."

Now, as a business owner, entrepreneur, leader, and mentor, Dawn is happy to seek outside resources and expertise to help resolve any problem that arises. Focused on charting optimal paths forward, she also embraces the constantly-changing landscape that comes with ownership and leadership. "Running your own small business, and managing people, means you have to wear every hat and be responsible for every aspect," she explains. "Decisions have to be made and action has to be taken. You have to be your own constant motivator, picking yourself up when things don't go so well and patting yourself on the back when they do. It can be tough and lonely. But you are in control. You have no one to report to. You can decide how you want it to be and the changes you want to make, which is very exhilarating and empowering!"

Dawn also marvels at how life finds a way to come full-circle and realize the dreams we thought we put aside. Thanks to her 'Connect Live' show, she was recently asked to host a similar show for other channels. "Every day is one more step toward realizing my dreams," she affirms. She also uses her 'platforms' of connecting and communicating with many to address the limitations experienced by others in her community.

Dawn works to support Devotion for Children, the National Kidney Foundation, and the Red Cross, and plans to get more involved in efforts to combat human trafficking, a major human rights tragedy that pervades the Northern Virginia region.

When advising young people entering the working world today, Dawn points to the power of believing in yourself and following your passion. "If you've got a burning desire to go after something, go for it," she says. "Don't let other people put you down. There are plenty of people out there who will want to help and mentor you. Don't let anyone talk you into doing something just for money, because unhappiness isn't worth any amount of money. As you consider your career, it's far more important to focus on how you can follow that passion or desire using your own unique gifts."

Beyond that, Dawn has always felt an urge to make more of an impact in the wider community. "I think it's human nature to want to have an impact and make a difference," she says. "I've always had the urge to make people's lives better by telling them what I've learned so they don't have to go through the hardship I went through to learn it. Any knowledge I acquire, I've wanted to shout it from the rooftop so others can acquire that knowledge, use it to make their lives easier, and then pay it forward. I know that my coaching made a huge difference in people's lives. Now, in a way, ConneXion Hub is one big rooftop for people to use to inform others about how they can help them. And thanks to that 'one more step' that helped me face my fear of heights, it's a rooftop I'm proud to stand on top of."

Kathleen M. Poorbaugh

Taking Charge while Taking Care

Even as a little girl growing up in Philadelphia, Kathy Poorbaugh was never afraid to jump in and take charge. In Girl Scouts, she was always organizing things and earning badges. In swim club, what she lacked in raw athletic talent was made up for in competitive drive that earned her ribbon after ribbon. When the nuns at school launched fundraising efforts for orphans, Kathy would volunteer to manage the collections, and she was the one who stayed after school to help the teachers clean the chalkboards.

"The nuns would have described me as driven," she says today. "I grew up in a blue collar area, and I saw most high school graduates go immediately into the workforce or military service. My parents didn't go to college, and I definitely wasn't raised thinking about my transcript and college marketability. I was just a go-getter who liked to lead."

While taking charge, Kathy also took care of others—especially her brother, six years younger. She still remembers when he started first grade at her school and came to find her in class one day just to ask her a question. When she'd go out shopping with friends, she'd always bring him back a present. "He still refers to me as his second mom," she laughs. "I looked after him a lot and always made sure he was okay."

Now the Principal and President of Homes, Lowry, Horn & Johnson, Ltd. (HLHJ), a CPA firm providing a wide range of accounting, tax, and consulting solutions in the DC metropolitan area, Kathy has come a long way from those days growing up in Philly. But her leadership style still revolves around the core tenets of taking charge while taking care, both at home with her family and at work with her fellow partners, employees, and clients. "I'm driven and inspired by the fact that our work helps people all throughout their lives," she says. "It's not about the number crunching. It's about being with our clients through life's great inflection points, easing the ensuing adjustment in any way we can."

HLHJ was launched by Gene Homes in 1956 and has grown organically ever since. Serving both businesses and individuals, multigenerational family clients are a big key to their success, including estate and trust work. They also have a strategic three-year succession model for their retiring partners, where clients are co-managed by the retiring and new partner to ensure continuity. And after that three-year window, the retiring partner is free to continue assisting with the firm. "Mr. Lowry stayed on semi-retired for nineteen years," Kathy says. "It's so helpful to our staff because they get to see the firm's history and benefit from the mentorship of those who have lifelong experience to share."

As a leader, Kathy ensures the firm is always cognizant of its up-and-coming talent, and is firmly committed to a silos-free organization. The firm's five full-time partners share clients freely and help wherever needed, a model that shores up any blind spots or weaknesses for the benefit of the clients. "Rivalry doesn't have a place here," she says.

"We're not a sweatshop where people log 80-hour weeks. It's not the up-and-out mentality of a lot of the bigger firms, where people burn out and move on. Our employees tend to stay with us a long time, and we like to help them grow if they want to move to the partner level."

Today, HLHJ is a team of 35. It serves the four business niches of government contracting, real estate, car dealers, and retirement plan audits, but also has expertise in a range of other professional services and organizations. "I especially love when startups come to us with an idea and ask, 'now what?'" she remarks. "It's very rewarding to help cultivate those ideas into successful businesses. But my proudest accomplishments are those clients who have followed me over the years and through my various career transitions. It says a lot about the relationships we've built."

HLHJ's culture is remarkably inclusive and places a high premium on work/life balance. Each month, the company does a "jeans day for charity" day, where employees can decide how they want to give back. They do an annual afternoon of service working on a project together, and they support Toys for Tots. On both the professional and the support staff, they have more women team members than men, a true anomaly in the industry. Thanks to these factors and the firm's remarkably family-friendly vibe, it was named one of the best firms to work for by *Virginia Business Magazine*.

From her earliest days growing up in Philadelphia, it's always been about family for Kathy. Her father worked as a service representative and then a sales representative for an equipment company, while her mother was a homemaker. Both sides of her family lived in the area, and Sundays were always spent with cousins and grandparents. "One grandparent died when I was little, but the other three were around and always there to listen," she remembers. "That was very special."

Everything changed, however, when Kathy was thirteen, and her parents decided to move to Northern Virginia, where her father had to travel often for work. They settled in Chantilly, at that time a rural area, when she was in eighth grade. Kathy was devastated to leave the only life she had ever known, and especially worried about leaving her grandmother. Her parents promised that if she still hated it by the end of the first school year, she could move back to Philly to live with her grandmother, but her grandmother passed away shortly thereafter.

Kathy's Catholic School experience in Philly had been very stable, where families rarely moved and many students graduated with the same kids they started first grade with. But as a military area, Chantilly was transitory, where many students had lived around the world and would only be there for a few years. It was also a brand new school that embraced an open-classroom model, so there weren't walls, desks, or chairs when Kathy first started. "It was a big shock to go from a very structured environment to something so fluid and different," she remembers.

Fortunately, Kathy made friends in the first couple months, and she had much success in launching a babysitting network in her new neighborhood. She also responded to the new environment by focusing even more on academics. She saw that the open classroom experience could be whatever she made of it, so while other students slacked or goofed off, she seized the opportunity to learn more and get involved. When she got into high school, people began asking where she wanted to go to college. "I was a good student, so I thought to myself, maybe I should start thinking about that," she says. "My parents encouraged me to do well and think about what I wanted to do. College was never a given, but it became a consideration."

Contemplating her future career path, Kathy had an affinity for math but didn't know what to do with it. She was advised to sign up for a high school accounting class, which she loved. "I took bookkeeping and saw that maybe I had a future in it," she remembers. "I saw many of my classmates struggle to understand, but it came very naturally to me, and I liked the order of the numbers and the fact that everything worked out."

Kathy accelerated through the school's math classes, balancing her school work with Honor Society, Government Club, and other extracurricular engagements while volunteering as the manager of the cross country team and working a part-time job at McDonalds. She earned straight A's except for two B+'s during her senior year, which she still regrets today. She thought she might pursue a career in teaching, but a few key conversations curbed her path toward accounting. "I enjoyed doing spreadsheets, and a friend's father took the time to tell me all the things I could do with an accounting degree," she recalls. "Even then, I thought about how it would be a really good job to have as a mother because I could go part-time and still be very successful."

Upon graduating, Kathy enrolled at the College of William & Mary with the goal of majoring in accounting. Her best friend enrolled as well, and the two were roommates for three of the four years there. Kathy helped cover costs by doing work-study during the school year and working full-time in the summers. In fact, it was the summer after her freshman year, while working for AAA, that she met Sam, the man she has now been married to for over three decades.

For the most part, Kathy's college days were happy, filled with studying, synchronized swimming, accounting club, and dates with Sam. But her worldview underwent a profound shift during her junior year, when she found out her parents were getting divorced. The news broke the weekend before Thanksgiving, and though Kathy had her coursework to think about, she immediately took charge to take care of her family. "I was always very financially literate, keeping close track of my money and always making sure my checkbook was balanced," Kathy says. "My mother had never done any of that. When my father left, she had no money and no credit card. I could tell she was kind of falling apart, so I rushed home to help."

At that time, it was difficult for a 40-year-old woman with no credit history to open a credit card, but easy for a college student. Kathy didn't know much about credit at the time, but she opened a card and added her mother's name. She helped her mother open her own checking account and made sure she was okay with each step forward. Her mother increased her part-time hours working for the Fairfax County School System, and with time, things stabilized. But Kathy's perspective and priorities were forever changed. "I didn't want to ever find myself in that position," she says. "I wanted to know I could stand on my own no matter what happened, and that I could provide for my family. It really drove me to make something of myself."

As she neared graduation, Kathy interviewed at all the big accounting firms and chose KPMG because it seemed the most grounded and family-friendly. She spent the next two years working in audit and ultimately decided she wanted to look for a role that allowed for more personal connections with clients, so she took a position with MCI. It was just as the company decided to divide from one corporate office into a handful of regional offices, and she managed key training programs while mastering the world of revenue accounting. By that time, she and Sam were married, when she had their first child, she left to spend time with her newborn daughter.

Hoping to make a little money on the side, Kathy answered an ad in the paper and went to work several hours a week doing bookkeeping and payroll for a man who had taken over the small business of his deceased son-in-law. "I'd bring my daughter to work with me and she'd sleep in a crib in the office," Kathy remembers. "They were like grandparents to her."

Kathy also worked part-time during tax season, and soon switched from accounting and audit to tax, taking a job at the small CPA firm where her brother worked. Her son was born soon thereafter, and she would get work done at night while the kids were asleep. "It was so flexible," she says. "I had as many hours as I wanted, which was great because I still had this drive to provide so my kids could have the best in life."

Several years later, the tax division of her firm was sold to a larger firm, and Kathy was sold along with it. Her son had just started kindergarten, so she picked up more hours, working under the vision and leadership of Will Soza. From 1994 to 2001, she watched as he grew the modest CPA practice into a 1,500-person government contracting firm—without losing the culture that made the company great. "He taught me how to be great to clients," she says. "Even though we had these multi-million dollar contracts, the $500 individual client was valued just as highly. Later on, when I worked in bigger firms, I remembered the lesson that everyone is important, not just the clients bringing in the most money. He also taught me that, while it's easy to be somebody's friend, business is business at the end of the day. You've got to stay pragmatic and do what's best for the company overall. I'm lucky to have had a lot of great mentors through the years—people who believed in me and helped drive my career forward."

By the time her kids were in high school, she was still working part-time but was racking up so many hours that she was close to being made partner. After consulting together as a family, Sam decided to leave the world of programming to stay at home, freeing up Kathy to fully embrace the career opportunities before her at HLHJ. "Family has always been number one for me," she affirms. "Going full-time and becoming partner was just another way of showing that and ensuring I could provide for them."

When Will was ready to retire, he sold the government contracting group to Perot Systems. The firm's small CPA practice, then around twenty people, went to Kathy and a fellow partner. "He was the stern fatherly type, and the accounting firm was near and dear to his heart," she says. "He made us rent a space in the building he owned and would drop by to make sure we were doing everything right and taking care of his clients. It was a great experience, but we were twelve people with some really big clients, and it got hard to manage."

In 2005, they merged with a regional firm, where Kathy worked for the next three years under the excellent mentorship of Clark Childers. Then, in 2008, she got to know HLHJ and saw that it was the perfect fit for her. "I wasn't actively looking at the time, but I was very impressed by their constructive and supportive workplace culture," she says. "People were working insane hours at my firm, and there was a lot of strain. They also wanted me to focus on selling and bringing in more clients, rather than serving the clients we did have. That just wasn't working for me."

Kathy loved the idea of a medium-sized firm where she would know all her staff, meet with any client she wanted to meet with, and do practice development on her own terms, so she accepted the position. Several years later, she stepped up to assume the role of President—a pragmatic choice that made the most sense for the firm's succession plan and for Kathy's own skill set. "It's a great position where I'm working to implement ideas that will help us move forward," she says. "As a firm, we're always thinking about longevity and how we can improve our processes. It's also important to transition the leadership team just as we transition the clients, so I look forward to passing my role on to a younger partner in the future."

In advising young people entering the working world today, Kathy underscores the importance of lifelong learning, and of nurturing relationships. "Be a sponge," she urges. "Stay in touch with people you went to school with or knew at other points in your life, because those relationships matter. Remember that life doesn't have to be all work, though you do have to put in the time. Keep growing and learning, like I did several years ago when I got my Master of Science in Taxation degree. There are lots of ways to keep learning, whether it's formal education or simply observing and asking questions of the people around you."

Beyond that, Kathy drives forward without ever losing sight of what matters most. Her two children are now grown up and married, and Kathy and Sam were thrilled to welcome their first grandchild into the world in 2016. "Family is what keeps me going, and it all stems back to the relationship I have with my husband," she says. "We've been very supportive of each other throughout our careers. Sam is my rock—quiet, even-keeled, and always there to listen. He makes sure everyone is taking care of, from our parents to our kids to our dog. We take charge and take care of things together as a team, and it's made all the difference."

BERNHARDT
WEALTH MANAGEMENT

Sherri Renée Romm

Your Perfect Look

Sherri Renée Romm has always had a passion for art. To this day, she spends four mornings a week in her studio, paintbrush in hand as she careens over the canvas set up on her easel, her most meaningful and treasured possession. She painted and sculpted through school, and even took classes at night for nine years to complete a degree at the Maryland Institute College of Art.

Studying art at night kept her sane as she spent her days doing computer engineering consulting work. But learning how to use her gifts professionally was a journey—one that slowly pushed Sherri Renée in a direction she never anticipated.

In the early 1990s, Sherri Renée received the bad news that a close friend had been diagnosed with cancer. In many ways, Sherri Renée felt powerless, but when her friend began experiencing severe hair loss from her medical treatment, Sherri Renée saw a way she could help.

"My friend went to the local wig shop and bought an auburn wig," Sherri remembers. "It was hideous, and she never left the house."

Coincidentally, Sherri Renee's then-husband was working on putting together a men's hair restoration procedure at the time. Self-conscious about his own receding hairline and determined to put better options on the market, he already had a palette of hair-replacement materials and color swatches on hand, which proved perfect resources for Sherri Renée's vision. "I didn't know exactly what I was doing," she admits today. "But I set my mind to trying to make a wig my friend would be happy to wear."

Sherri Renée started by taking a cast mold of her friend's head, and though it was her first try, she made a perfect fit. She designed a wig based on selected materials and hair colors and texture. Six weeks later, the finished product arrived. Sherri hired a stylist to cut the wig, and when the process was finished, her friend looked spectacular. "It was her perfect look, and that was a pivotal moment for me," Sherri affirms. "Her whole spirit lifted up when she put it on. For the first time since her diagnosis, she seemed herself again. She started going out again, free from the self-consciousness and worry she had felt before. In a way, it was the stepping stone that allowed her to move forward. And it was the pivotal moment that inspired me to move forward too, applying my background in sculpture, painting, and engineering to empower others through beauty and image recovery."

With that, Sherri Renée and her then-husband co-founded a hair replacement manufacturing and design business, Versacchi USA. Sherri Renée handled the hair design and application, while her husband became the "face" of the company and oversaw the manufacturing of the business. She continued to work at her day job as the breadwinner of the family as the business grew, but by 1996, Sherri Renée was able to leave her consulting work to become a hair loss designer and architect.

Over the next few years, Sherri's situation evolved. She and her husband ended their marriage and sold the manufacturing arm of Versacchi

USA. Sherri Renée formed her own hair specialty salon, Versacchi Studios, to pursue her love and passion for personal transformation. "I never doubted myself or thought that I couldn't do something," she says. "At the time, I didn't think too much about it. When something interested me, I'd express that interest, and I'd just do it."

As the business grew and her offerings expanded, Sherri decided she needed one more tool in her arsenal. "I felt inept because I didn't know how to cut the hair myself," she says. "It was like carrying a child for nine months and not seeing the whole thing come to fruition. So I apprenticed in my own shop for two years under another stylist and got my license in cosmetology. Then I got my senior cosmetologist license so I could train others."

Since that time, Sherri Renée's talent and confidence have paid off in spades, and Versacchi Studios has helped countless men, women, and children get their confidence back via custom hair enhancements. She also founded Sherri Renée & Co., a line of Parisian hair enhancement products that are now available at salons internationally. Launched in 2014, Sherri Renee & Co. is taking some of the technological advancements and artistic achievements from her experience at Versacchi Studios, and mass marketing them through partner salons. "About eight years ago, I took a trip to Paris with my mom and was inspired by the beautiful Lingerie Parisian silk, lace, and cotton lace fabrics," she recounts. "I was inspired by their aesthetic beauty, touch and 'lightness' and started incorporating them in almost all of my designs. My Parisian Hair Enhancement Collection was born. Their light bases, coupled with a scalp replica and chiaroscuro color rendering, were so unique and realistic, that they were incredibly well-received by my clients—better than anything I had ever done before. It was at that time that I had decided to patent by designs in order to help protect what took so much hard work, innovation, and infinite experience to achieve."

It didn't take long for word to spread about Sherri Renée's popular Parisian Hair Enhancement Collection. Soon, salons were knocking on her door, asking about the products. "I didn't really have anything to show them, so that's what spurred me to develop the branding, packaging, literature, and catalogues," she says. "Obviously, I don't sleep much!"

Relying only on word of mouth, the business continued to expand. Sherri Renée & Co. is now international, with 21 salons stretching from East to West Coast, and with new studios opening up in Barbados and Canada. "I have high hopes for what the line can accomplish in a mostly-stagnant industry," she affirms. "Part of that success comes from the fresh fine art approach we're taking, even down to the vocabulary we use. There's a lot of stigma and negative connotation attached to wigs and hair pieces and toupees, so we focus on the concept of accessorizing to get a 'better me.' I want to take away the stigma and make it something convenient and fun. Steve Jobs had the vision that 'there's going to be a computer in every home', and I have a vision that every woman will have at least one of these Parisian enhancements in her beauty arsenal."

Sherri Renée is on the cutting edge of hair enhancement design, fusing aspects of hair restoration with the modern freshness and innovation of fine art and fashion. "My goal is to incorporate the top 150 salons in the country," she avows. "We're a partnership with salons that are interested in providing a highly specialized service, since 26 million women have issues with hair loss. We provide solutions for everyone struggling with this issue, regardless of what they're looking for."

Sherri Renée also provides trainings to the salons that carry her line, ensuring that the stylists are able to properly design, color and cut in the hair enhancements. "When a salon purchases our hair enhancements, they receive marketing, social media, and specialized training to start them the next day," she says. "From there, we offer a portfolio of workshops to assist from business building, marketing, design and artistic couture."

Sherri Renée's focus on bringing her vision to life comes in part from the example of her father, who loves to draw and possesses a unique gift with people. "I have never met a person that has met my dad and has not fallen in love with him," she affirms. "He has a way of making you feel like you are the only one in the room." Artistic talent also stems from her mother, who flourished when she finally found her way to a career in interior designing. "My mom is such an out-of-the-box thinker," Sherri says. "She's incredibly creative, with no age and no limitations. She's not an artist in the drawing and painting sense, but she's great with color and texture and fabric and putting things together in an intuitive and inventive way."

Sherri's mother also deserves credit for Sherri's early fascination with hair and transformation. Growing up in Baltimore County, Maryland, Sherri often snuck into her mother's closet to examine her stock of falls and hairpieces, and was blown away by her ability to change her whole look with some make-up and hair enhancers. "She had really short fine hair," Sherri recalls, "but on nights when she went out with my dad, she would come down in a gown and beautiful make-up, with a long blonde fall on, just like a fashion model. I remember being so impressed by that transformation."

Sherri Renée didn't have any sisters, and her two older brothers had no interest in playing dress-up in their mother's closet. Fortunately for Sherri, her younger brother was malleable and agreeable enough to play guinea pig in Sherri's first makeover experiments. "I pretty much watched him all the time, so when I was about 8 and he was 5, I would bring him into my mother's closet to dress him up and put these beautiful long falls on him," she laughs. "Wigs and falls were really in in the 60s, and my mother was no exception. She had an entire walk-in closet of falls and hairpieces, so I had a lot to work with. That was so much fun for me, and my brother was so sweet to be so tolerant."

All through her childhood, Sherri Renée's father worked for Romm Press, the family publishing and newspaper printing business. Publishing had been in the family for some time, and back in Ukraine, the Romms had had the first printing press that was permitted to print

Jewish publications. "I used to go with him to the printing press," remembers Sherri. "Back then, the machinery was massive. There were guys there missing a finger or two, and the smell of glue and ink is imprinted in my mind."

Sherri was 8 when her parents divorced, and her mother began working 14-hour shifts to help make ends meet. "A lot happened to my mom by the time she was 26," Sherri recalls. "She had 4 young kids, and her mother had died. She had a hard time after the divorce, and I made a mental note that I never wanted to struggle like that. I decided I'd never depend on anyone else for my livelihood, because if they walked out, then what?"

Although the relationship between her mother and father had become contentious, her father stayed very involved and was always present at Sherri's sports events. Sherri played soccer and tennis, for which she had a particular affinity. "My father was a total gentleman through the separation and was always there for me," she says. "There were some negative feelings on my mom's side because he went on with his life, while she was still trying to find her way. But they're friends today, which is wonderful. Somewhere along the way, they made up, and we all get along."

In elementary school, Sherri made scenery for all the school plays and began to cultivate her artistic talent more seriously. "In middle school, I had two great art teachers, Mr. Simon and Mr. Smith, who both told me I needed to do something artistic in my life," she says. "That stuck with me."

During high school, Sherri didn't go through the typical rebellious teen phase because she'd had a lot of independence from her parents at an early age. She did, however, establish some independence from her peers as she navigated adolescence. "I became an independent thinker," she says. "Drugs were incredibly rampant, and when I was in tenth grade, I just decided that I wasn't going to participate. That's important when you're at that age and you're easily influenced. I focused on other things, including my art."

Sherri's dream at the time was to attend art school and eventually make her way as a professional painter. "I thought I'd become a famous painter and be commissioned by the wealthiest people in the world," she laughs. "I dreamed that they'd pay my way to travel around Europe as I painted their portraits, so I pursued a Fine Arts degree at Towson University upon graduating from high school."

Without money from her parents, Sherri qualified for a Pell Grant to help her get through her first semester, but after that, she had to work nights to pay her way. Her boyfriend at the time convinced her to be pragmatic and enroll in a data processing class at the local community college over the summer—a defining decision that changed the course of the next twelve years of her life. The school offered her a job working in their Operations Center, and Sherri recognized she had some talent in the field. She decided to transfer to the University of Maryland, Baltimore County (UMBC), and switched her major to Information Systems and Computer Science. In 1984, she graduated with an Information Systems degree and a mathematics minor.

After graduation, Sherri got a job with Computer Task Group (CTG) as a consultant. In that capacity, she spent the next decade consulting with various companies and working on everything from project management, to coding, to business processes, to computer systems. "I was all over town, working with different people and different personalities," she recounts.

By day, Sherri excelled at CTG, but she was happiest at night, when she went to her classes at the Maryland Institute College of Art. She enrolled immediately after leaving UMBC, determined to continue pursuing art. She was only able to take a class or two each semester, and it took her nine years to finally complete her Bachelor of Fine Arts, but having an artistic outlet helped her get through her days as a consultant.

Eight years into her time at CTG, Sherri's then-husband began looking into hair replacement technologies, and the rest is history. By 1994, Sherri was involved with the business and incorporated Versacchi

Studios. By 1996, the money had begun to come in, and she quit consulting altogether. "My husband at the time was an entrepreneurial spirit," she says. "He introduced me to that philosophy of risk taking, where you know you'll regret it if you don't go for it."

When Sherri gave birth to her two wonderful children, her relationship with her business took on a new dimension. For the first time in her life, she experienced some hair loss of her own, allowing her to relate to her clients' struggles on a whole new level. "They don't tell you before you get pregnant!" she exclaims. "Your hair is really nice when you're pregnant, but about three months later, you start shedding. I began working on smaller pieces for people that are going through hormonal changes, or people who have surgery and lose a little bit of hair. This also drew on my fine arts background, because in drawing and painting, you have to study the underlying anatomy. I'm addressing where something sits on the head, what's surrounding it, the coloring, the tone, the shading, all of that stuff. I developed these methods over the course of years, observing what makes something look real and applying techniques to take my products to that level."

Her post-partum shedding wasn't the only time her personal experiences shaped the direction of her businesses. A few years later, Sherri was diagnoses with a thyroid tumor, and again experienced hair thinning. It was right around this time that she took her trip to Paris and began working on the line of enhancements that would become the Parisian Hair Enhancement Collection.

Kids are often the most heart-wrenching—and the most rewarding—cases. "A boy named Dylan had a particularly strong impact on me," she says. "He had a tumor surgically removed from his head, which left a visible scar. In elementary school, it was no problem, but when his parents brought him in, he was 11, going into middle school and concerned about teasing. So I designed something for him, a puzzle piece that matched his hair color, texture, and density. He went from being an introverted, self-conscious kid to a normal, outgoing kid, even after just one session. It really meant a lot to be able to help him like that."

In advising young people entering the working world today, Sherri offers the same career advice she gave her own sons. "Follow your heart," she says. "Do what you're passionate about, and you'll find that gusto for life—your purpose and why you're here. If you just go after the money, you're going to feel something's missing. But if you go after your passion, take some chances, and try some things, you'll find your path. If you feel like you're one with whatever it is you're doing, then that's exactly what you should be doing. Prosperity and abundance will ultimately follow."

Beyond that, as a leader, Sherri seeks to empower people to use their own skill, talent, and intuition to just do it, whatever "it" is for them. "I've seen so many people put off their dreams because they don't think it's the right time," she says. "But I tell them not to wait, because you may not have the 25 years you think you have to make your dreams come true. Just do it! You just might look in the mirror one day and find that, somehow, you've found your perfect look."

BERNHARDT
WEALTH MANAGEMENT

Lee Self

A Transformative Faith

Before 2000, Lee Self was a VP with Bell Atlantic, now Verizon. Her workload was intense, and her schedule was exhausting; she was constantly hopping between New York, Boston, Philadelphia, and her home base in Virginia. Her young children were five and ten years old, and spending time with them was becoming more and more difficult as she rose up the corporate ladder. Then one evening in New York, Lee finally reached the end of her rope. "I was at a meeting that went late," she recalls. "Then when it was over, my boss said we had to have another meeting. It was just brutal."

The second meeting wasn't productive, and didn't accomplish much other than delaying Lee's return trip to DC. "My boss was just a bulldog," she says. "He was a great guy, and I learned a lot from him, but when he got focused on an issue, he wouldn't let go. Sitting there, knowing I needed to get home to my kids, I became livid."

Lee didn't quit her job that day, but in retrospect, she pegs that moment as a defining one that put her career on a different course. She left the meeting upset and remembers calling her sister in tears. "I just said, 'this is NOT a good use of my time!'" Lee recounts. "It was the end of my career with Bell Atlantic. In the weeks and months that followed, God spoke to me. At the time, I was all about me—where I was going, what I was doing. And then I remember very distinctly, sitting at my desk and hearing God say to me, 'It is not about you.' His voice was transformative, and I left to be accessible to my family. I had no idea what I would do next, but I was done. Done with playing the game. Done with moving up the ladder."

Following her faith, Lee took an unlikely path forward. After a stint working remotely for a web hosting business in Atlanta, she happened to hear about franchising from her financial advisor. "I found out that his firm was actually a franchise, and he described what it takes to get his business up and running," she says. "I didn't feel like I had the patience for that, but he encouraged me to talk to a franchise coach."

Today, Lee is the founder and President of four successful Northern Virginia Renaissance Executive Forums, a national franchise business with around fifty chapters across the country. "For each Executive Forum, we bring together 10 to 12 business owners, CEOs, and Presidents from similarly-sized companies," she says. "They're not competitive because the groups are confidential. We come together monthly for a half-day, and I facilitate a discussion that helps them learn from each other. We also bring in thought leaders on leadership and business issues that are important to our members. It's very interactive and experiential, and the results can be transformative for both the members, as well as their businesses."

Lee personally runs two CEO Executive Forums and presides over two Key Executive Forums facilitated by colleagues to serve COOs, CFOs, and VP-level executives. "My colleagues do their own work in leadership development and management training," she explains.

"They're both experts in executive coaching, so I benefit greatly from them. We worked on building those groups together, but a lot of the early members of the Key Executive Forums came from the CEO Forum members."

Lee feels the franchise arrangement is beneficial for all parties involved. She can run her chapter independently, but she's grateful for the community of practice Renaissance provides. She feels certain she never would've made the initial push to create her own forums without the guidance of the national organization. The national organization provided sales training when she was recruiting her first group members, facilitation training when she was holding her first meetings, and still provides materials for the group's annual two-day retreat—Strategies for Success. "It's a venue for getting together annually where we really dig into what's changed, and what needs to change both personally and professionally," she explains. "Renaissance puts together the retreat curriculum based on current leadership and business works. I learn it and then deliver it in an environment where my members can learn from each other. I would never have done all this if I'd had to make it all up from scratch."

Despite the guidance, getting her groups up and running was hardly smooth sailing. For one thing, Lee's only past sales experience was selling Girl Scout Cookies. "At first, I wasn't as good at recruiting members," she says. "But it was a lot of fun meeting with business owners and hearing their stories. I made up for the skills I lacked by doing more, working really hard to create two groups that first year."

Lee expanded to three groups after a few years, but later combined two of the groups when her husband, Mid, lost his battle with cancer. During that time, Lee struggled to balance her personal loss and professional responsibilities. Her faith, combined with the personal fulfillment she found in her work, helped her keep going. Now, Lee is glad she only runs two groups, which allows time for her participation in a number of faith-based service opportunities.

Lee loves working with her groups because the benefits are tangible, making a marked imprint in the world that is up close and personal. She remembers one group member agonizing for months over letting go of a leader who had been with his firm for over twenty years, but was not able to take the organization to the next level. After months of discussion, he finally took action. While the decision was painful, it was ultimately good for both parties. "Then about six months later, I met with another Forum member, who announced he had let his VP go. I said, 'wow, that was quick!' And he said, 'Oh yeah, I wasn't about to let that happen to me!', referring to the other member's experience. I realized the members pick up on things that aren't currently their issue. While it wasn't a problem he brought to the group, he had been able to learn from someone else's experience in a way that served him well when his own time came."

Lee's Executive Forums provide a space for leaders to learn from each other, listen to new ideas, bounce problems off one another, and receive some much-needed support. She remembers another member who used the group to work through his retirement and succession process, striving to ensure his departure was properly managed. "He decided he was leaving in three years," Lee says. "He had a long way to go to make it happen, but he went ahead and announced it. Every month we would work through it with him. What's the next step? You need a board of advisors. You need a leadership team. Wouldn't you know it, three years later, he met his goal and promoted one of his leaders to fill his shoes. His successor is now a Forum member and continues to learn from the group. It's a great example of how using the Executive Forum to hold yourself accountable can help you make changes you're committed to."

Lee has certainly seen her share of change. She grew up in the tiny town of McCormick, South Carolina, on the Savannah River, with her parents and four older siblings. "We had one traffic light at the time," she laughs. "Now we have two!" Her father worked over at the textile mill, but would have preferred farming. "He realized he wasn't going to feed five children doing that," she says. "So farming was relegated to a hobby, and we had cows, chickens, pigs, and horses."

Lee's parents met teaching high school, but neither one of them stayed in the field long. When Lee's oldest sister was born, her mother left teaching to stay home and raise the kids. Three more daughters and one son later, her mother decided to go back to work when Lee entered first grade—an unusual move for women in that area at that time. She took a job as the County Extension Agent and advanced to become the first woman in the state of South Carolina to serve as the County Extension Leader. "She was very unique in our town because she worked in a professional role," Lee remembers.

Although both worked hard, Lee's parents were different in some ways. While her mother was high-energy and emotional, her father was steady and quiet. She was close with both, but considered her father to be her hero. "He wasn't trying to impress anybody," she says. "He always tried to do the right thing, and he was dedicated to his family. He loved us and was always joking around with us. He didn't talk a lot, but when he said something, it mattered."

Lee's mother always stressed the importance of faith—something Lee values highly today. She remembers, at the age of seven, when she first heard the Bible verse John 3:16: "For God so loved the world, that he gave his one and only Son, that whoever believes in him would not perish, but have eternal life." She was too young to fully comprehend the meaning, but she knew it was important. "I remember very clearly talking to my sister about it," she says. "I sat right there and prayed to God, and told Him I believed in Jesus. That experience was an important beginning in my relationship with God. I didn't know at the time the impact that would have, but in hindsight, it was like putting an anchor down in my life." Today, she still treasures the Bible her parents received at their wedding.

The whole family attended church on Sunday mornings, and as Lee got older, she was active in the church youth group. She also sang in the choir, participated in Girl Scouts, went to camp, and joined the 4-H Club led by her mother. She was editor of her high school yearbook, a cheerleader, and a member of the basketball and softball teams. "My siblings and I were all pretty involved in whatever was happening," she says. "It was just a part of life growing up in a small school and a small town." She also spent plenty of time at Clemson football games, cheering on her father's alma mater.

Chores were also a big part of life in Lee's family. As a young child, she often felt grateful she hadn't been born a boy, since her brother got the worst of the farm duties. Her older sisters ran the household for years, but by the time Lee was 14, all her older siblings had moved out, so much of the housework fell to her. "By the time I was in high school, I was buying all the groceries, washing clothes, ironing my father's shirts, and cooking meals," she says. "That is, if you could call them meals. I didn't really enjoy any of it, but it wasn't optional. Both my parents were working hard, and they'd gotten accustomed to their other children helping out, so it all fell to me."

In high school, her best friend's father was President of the local bank, and he hired the two girls as tellers during the summer. When she wasn't busy with work, chores, school, and her many extracurricular activities, Lee spent time with her high school sweetheart, William Middleton Self III, or "Mid" for short, who went on to become her husband. Mid was a year older and went off to college at Washington & Lee in Lexington, Virginia. Lee's brother had gone to Clemson, and her three sisters had all attended the University of Georgia, but Lee was determined to go to school near Mid. "My parents were always adamant that all five of us were going to college," Lee remembers. "And we didn't have to pay a penny ourselves. They didn't make a lot of money, but they put it all aside for our college since it was a huge priority for them. That's no small feat."

Lee settled on UVa as her college choice, and although her out-of-state tuition was far higher than her siblings' had been, her parents agreed. She and Mid spent every weekend together, alternating between Lexington and Charlottesville. Her friends partied hard, and they both joined in, but Lee always prioritized her schoolwork. "I was very driven, both in high school and in college," she says. "I had to get that A."

Mid graduated in 1983, and when Lee graduated in 1984, the two married and decided to move to the D.C. area for the career opportunities. Mid was an engineer and quickly found work with the government. Lee's first job was with the McDonald's Corporation's accounting center in Fairfax, Virginia, but after three months, she landed a more dynamic job with Bell Atlantic.

Years went by, and Lee rapidly rose through the ranks at work, but cracks began to appear in her marriage at home. While faith had always been central to Lee's life, Mid did not share that commitment. Her relationship to God took a backseat for a while, and even when she began attending church regularly again when their daughter was born, her day-to-day concerns took priority. Finally, in 2005, she had an experience which transformed her life, her faith, and ultimately her marriage. "I was invited to the High Tech Prayer Breakfast," she recalls. "My life, and my marriage in particular, was a wreck."

Adolph Coors IV, the heir to the Coors fortune, was speaking that day, and the story he told resonated deeply with Lee. "He talked about how, even though he had been groomed to take over the Coors Empire, his life was empty," she recounts. "His marriage was in deep trouble. And he said that God used that to reorder his priorities, teaching him to put God first and his wife second. And it really hit me—I knew that was what I had to do. I left that day and put God first."

Lee started reading the Bible, which she had not done with any intensity before. She also joined a Working Women's Bible study, where she found the support of a group of inspiring and committed women. "I learned that I had to pray for my husband—not for me, but for him," she says. "That was a big shift."

Then finally, after years of denial, she was able to come to terms with a hard truth. "I finally admitted that Mid was an alcoholic," she says. "He was so much more than that too, and I loved him deeply, so I couldn't believe it could possibly be true. For 25 years I denied that it was a problem. He and I both loved each other, and there was always loyalty and commitment, but when I went to that breakfast, I was holding on to my marriage for dear life."

Lee joined Al-Anon, a twelve-step program for families and loved ones of alcoholics, which provided the support she needed to make some necessary changes. "That's where God really humbled me," she says. "I had never been honest with myself or anybody else about what was really going on. But there, you have to be honest. I don't know what would have happened if I had never turned back to the Lord and started going to Al-Anon, but it wouldn't have been good. Ultimately, Mid found the end of his rope too, and got sober. I'm not saying that what I did directly caused him to stop drinking, because he found his own path. But I got out of God's way, and Mid also turned his life over to God. So there you go. I had been sure all hope was lost, but God transformed."

Mid lived only a few more years before dying of cancer, but Lee is so thankful for the healing process they were able to go through together, and for the years of peace and happiness their shared faith afforded them at the end. "When he died, it was hard, hard, hard," she admits. "But how grateful I was, that I didn't lose him—I know where he is! Now, I'm able to help others by sharing that story. It's hard to tell, but it's redemptive and powerful. It's a story of humility because we don't have all the answers, but a story of hope because we're willing to learn and change."

To young people entering the working world today, Lee advises that same humility, hope, and openness. "When you're young, you try to map out the next ten to fifteen years, as I did," she says. "But things don't go as planned anyway, so recognize that all you have in front of you is that next decision you need to make. Try to make the best decision you can at the time. You'll have a chance to make other decisions, so just learn from it and do your best."

At its essence, it's the same kind of thoughtful, patient transformation that Renaissance Executive Forums is all about. "I love doing what I do for my members," she says. "When we're all together, members get epiphanies from each other, or from themselves, and I see how they put them to work changing their businesses and their lives. I love connecting people and seeing something meaningful happen as a result. I love seeing somebody transform right before my eyes."

BERNHARDT
WEALTH MANAGEMENT

Mark J. Silverman

Doing the Deep Work

When Mark Silverman arrived in DC on September 1, 1989, he was a 130-pound vagabond battling addiction and homelessness. He had driven across the country with no money, sleeping in his truck and living off of Diet Cokes and cookies he bought with a gas station card. "Before that, I had been living with a group of people that practiced a very strict lifestyle and morality together," he says today. "It was somewhat like a cult, with good things and bad things about it. But I was ready to say goodbye to that life for good, so I left. On my own for the first time in my life, I was shell shocked and had no idea how I was going to live in the real world. All I knew was that if I didn't drink, it was going to be okay."

Mark had always been good at starting over, and he was ready to do the deep work it would take to pull himself out. He moved in with his brother, who had three requirements for Mark: he was to join

AA, enroll in college classes, and go to the gym. And with those basic building blocks, Mark set to work creating a new life.

Mark had no life skills to speak of, but through his work living with the group for the previous nine years, he had established a core of strength and a strong ethical foundation. And through his experience with homelessness, he gained an impermeable humility that eroded any inclination toward self-centeredness, opening him up to truly caring about others. "That changed everything," he affirms.

Over the next decades, Mark embarked on a whirlwind journey of discovery that led him to a career in the high-tech startup industry selling multi-million-dollar hardware and software solutions. The success and affluence was dizzying, but the pressure and pace became maniacal. Each year, he was expected to blow last year's achievements out of the water. In 2007, he overachieved his goal by 200 percent, landing a $380,000 commission check and the honor of top sales rep in the region. "For me, that was the bar that meant I had finally achieved success," he remembers. "It was the finish line that told me I was good at what I do. But then the clock struck midnight on New Year's Eve, and the counter reverted back to zero, and the treadmill started all over again. It was a defining moment where I realized that there is no finish line, no moment of arrival in that kind of life. It just goes on and on."

That year, the company doubled his goal again, but Mark's focus was elsewhere. In search of ways to cope and thrive in the grind, he began a journey of self-discovery and deep introspection. He attended workshops, read books, took courses, and learned to meditate. He began training with some of the world's top coaches in 2012, and in 2013, he formally launched his own transformational executive coaching business, Mark J. Silverman and Associates. "I work with CEOs, VPs, and high-level executives because I've been in business and I understand it, but I go a lot deeper," he says. "If I do my job right, it changes a client's life with their kids, spouse, and colleagues, and completely transforms how they show up in the world. It's about helping them access their own core strength and wisdom, so circumstance does not influence well-being."

Through speaking, writing, and direct coaching, Mark's deep work helps people thrive in the world when it asks the most of them. He gives them tools and strategies to be able to get past the presenting problem, like wanting to make more profit or wanting to do more sales. Five layers beneath that, he unleashes what's really in the way of them doing what they need to do. "At the beginning of their careers, it all seems to work no matter the hours or demands. But as time wears on, as good and put-together as everyone looks on the outside, with their Hugo Boss suits and nice houses and BMWs, it becomes unsustainable. They're actually fraying on the edges," Mark observes. "Inwardly, they're just hanging on. They let off steam through smoking or drinking or other destructive habits. Then, as people get older and take on more responsibility with spouses and kids, they have less energy, and success becomes even more difficult."

Looking around, Mark saw his contemporaries choose one of three coping mechanisms, all equally caustic. Some put themselves on the backburner, neglecting their health and well-being to the point that they were a heart attack waiting to happen. Some ignored their relationships with their spouses or kids, often breaking up homes. And those who prioritized their families and their health had no choice but to sabotage their careers, because there simply wasn't time for all three and the pressure was too great. "These are good men and women, and there's no reason it has to be this way," Mark affirms. "Success shouldn't come at such a dark cost."

For the high-powered, strung-out, but eternally earnest executive just trying to do what life expects of them, Mark is the perfect portal to a better way, because he himself used to be that person. Even as a troubled kid, he was drawn to the peace and perspective of a higher power and thought he might one day be a rabbi or a teacher. Mark was born in Brooklyn and raised on Long Island in a lower middle-class neighborhood of predominantly Irish and Italian families. His father ran a Burger King, while his mother worked in a furniture store. His brother was a full seven years older than him, and his sister a full eleven, with both engrossed in their own lives. "I was the traditional latchkey kid," he says. "Nobody was home to raise me. I was on my own, free to get in trouble—and I did."

Left to his own devices, Mark and the other neighborhood kids stole bicycles, started fires, and beat each other up. As the only Jewish kid in his neighborhood, he was scrappy and tough, and though he was small for his age, he never lost a fight. "My brother teaches hand-to-hand combat and shooting, and says I'm still the toughest person he's ever met in his life," Mark says.

By the time he was thirteen, Mark was drinking and doing drugs. He stole alcohol from people's houses and drugs from his brother, which he sold for spending money. His parents were clueless, and assumed that anytime he got into serious trouble, it was someone else's doing. "They did the best they could, but were just really out of touch," he remembers. "I had no role models for a successful life."

Despite this disruptive lifestyle, and though he rarely did homework or studied, he always did well in school. His report cards always took note of his potential, lamenting his refusal to apply himself. "Sales guys know how to get stuff done," he remarks. "They see the shortest distance between Point A and Point B. I knew that as long as I went to class and listened, I could do well on tests." He also always had a job, whether it was working in fast food restaurants, a supermarket, or later as a waiter and bartender.

When Mark graduated from high school in 1980, he enrolled at Central Connecticut Community College and got a bartending job in nearby Hartford. Spending all his time at the bar, he flunked out after the first couple weeks—something he didn't tell his parents until he was supposed to come home for Christmas vacation. Instead, he leaned into the hedonistic frenzy of his current lifestyle. "I would bartend from 10:00 AM to 6:00 PM, eat dinner, drink, go home, shower, work at the bar all night, and then take speed so I could do it all over again," he recounts. "Everyone working in that world was like that, addicted to alcohol and drugs."

Everything changed in 1983, however, when Mark happened to cross paths with Rosa, a 65-year-old Italian woman. "She practiced the Erhard Sensitivity Training, or EST, which transforms the way people experience life, such that the very process of living fixes the things a person is struggling with," he explains. "She had garnered a small following, and when she met me, she confronted me for the first time in my life and said, 'On a scale from 1 to 10 as far as functioning human beings are concerned, you are a negative two. You're a mess, and you need help.'"

Mark signed up for her workshop, and when he saw it was work he wanted to embrace, he moved into her farmhouse with the group. Together, they focused on changing the world to improve quality of life—a goal that would become a cornerstone of Mark's character. As a community, they sifted through their memories from childhood to better understand themselves, and as a community, they exercised the demons that weighed them down. "It really set the foundation for me to know what integrity was, what God might be, and what relationships are all about," he remembers. "We committed to be drug- and alcohol-free, and we held each other accountable. There were bad things about it, but ultimately, it saved my life."

Through the five years that followed, Mark never spoke to his family. The group moved to San Diego, and then to Colorado, where he got married. He was thrown out several times through that period for drinking, and when his marriage ended after several years, he was thrown out for the last time. "I had no money and no place to go, but I was good at starting over," he says. "I'd get a P.O. box and a job as a waiter, and then Rosa would magically know where I was and call me up, and I'd go back to the group. But not this time."

Mark drove to Seattle, but opportunities weren't presenting themselves. So he drove to Portland, but found another dead end. Destitute, he called his brother, who convinced Mark to come join him in DC. The day of his arrival marks the first day of 28-years-and-still-counting sobriety, and he got a job at the Four Seasons Hotel as a waiter. The following January, he enrolled in college classes at Northern Virginia Community College, and the following year, he moved out on his own. A few years later, he got married.

Through his six years at the Four Seasons, and with the support of mentor and hotel VP Stan Bromley, Mark was the first employee permitted to transition from the restaurant into a professional position when he applied to become an accounts receivable clerk. "I had never seen a fax machine, and I didn't know what a copier was," he laughs. "I just wanted to get out of the restaurant business and do something different. At age 34, it was my first white collar job."

The following year, Mark landed a job as the Assistant Night Manager at the hotel—a gig he largely enjoyed, except for the stress of having to figure out within 120 seconds of having a fire alarm pulled whether there was actually a fire. "We had celebrities, royalty, and foreign dignitaries staying at the hotel, so they only wanted to evacuate if absolutely necessary," he recalls. "It was up to me to make that call, which was incredibly nerve-racking."

Mark quickly realized that the long hours and challenging schedule put him on a fast track to a career of limited earning potential, so he decided to leave the hotel business in 1998 to take his first sales job. "I took a career test and it said I should either be a writer, a lawyer, or a sales guy," he says. "It wasn't going to be either of the first two, so I decided to try sales. But when I went in to interview for a copy sales position and shadowed a sales rep while he knocked on doors, the manager told me I was a nice young man, but I'd fail miserably in sales. Later on, when I made my first million, I went back to kindly let him know he was wrong about that."

Mark landed a position selling computer training—a grueling challenge that led most hires to quit before the end of the first month. Each sales person had to make sixty phone calls a day, and at first, Mark found it miserable. The company did offer free classes, however, and he soon discovered that people were much more receptive to buying additional training when they came in for those sessions. With that, he shifted his approach to the phone call quotas, instead focusing on the free classes. Within two months, he was the top sales guy at the company. "Most importantly, I realized that when I had the opportunity to develop relationships with people, they trusted me and wanted to buy from me," he says. "That became the cornerstone of my success from then on."

The following year, Mark went to a technology show in DC, where a company was selling a SmartBoard that translated handwritten notes onto a computer. "It was the coolest thing I had ever seen in my life, so I walked up and told them I wanted a job selling it," he recounts. There, he also sold the first projector with a digital camera, and orchestrated several sales to the Marine Corps that marked the two biggest sales Toshiba had that year in the entire world. He was promoted to VP of Sales, and his salary doubled annually over the next several years.

Then, in 1999, Mark was offered a job at Data General by a friend that promised ample training opportunities to transform his raw talent into a seasoned professional sales executive. Shortly after he took the job, the company was bought by EMC, who promptly fired everyone but Mark. "I was their top sales guy in the Mid-Atlantic because I was the only one left," he laughs. "In 2000, I decided to talk my way into a job at their biggest competitor, Network Appliance (NetApp), even though I had no business getting that job."

Now at the fastest-growing startup in Silicon Valley history, Mark was terrified, but he embraced the challenge. That first year, he was named runner up to Rookie of the Year, and he quickly made President's Club. He finished his bachelor's degree in 2002 after transferring to

George Mason University and then to National Louis University, a phenomenal experience taught by committed business professors. By that time, Mark and his wife had two young sons, and his career was soaring. "By that point, the company was my identity, along with the money, the cars, and the status," he says. "The momentum was taking care of itself. On the treadmill, I was just enjoying success and not really questioning things."

In 2007, feeling burnt out and ready for a change, Mark took a job at VMWare, a software startup where he realized that his real talent was more in hardware. "Software sales don't allow for relationship building," he explains. "You can't be looking in the rearview mirror thinking about customer service when you have to focus on the next deal. So in 2007, I switched back to hardware with a data storage company that, again, was acquired by EMC."

Then, in 2009, Mark faced the darkest trial of his life when he separated from his wife and entered a downward spiral. Sick, depressed, and suicidal, he watched decades of work and progress erode to nothing. "I thought I was going to die," he says. "I wanted to die. My only reason to live was my two little kids. So I resolved to accomplish three things before I died. First, I wanted to make a million dollars to leave to my sons. Second, I wanted to donate $60,000 to charity to help atone for the mistakes I had made in life. And third, I wanted to run the Marine Corps marathon, even though I couldn't run at all at that point."

Mark still vividly remembers sitting outside his doctor's office, when Stan Middleman, an ultramarathon runner, came on the radio and claimed he could train anyone to run because humans are bipedal and meant to do it. Intrigued, Mark began running and then called up Stan to ask him to be his coach. Under Stan's guidance, Mark spent eight months training for the Marine Corps marathon, drinking the green drinks Stan swore by. Then, on race day, Mark cramped up at mile 15 and felt he couldn't go on anymore. "My ex-wife, who I'm still very close with, and kids met me around that mile marker, and when they heard I couldn't go on, they pulled out sustenance: an ice cold Mountain Dew, some dark chocolate, and a bag of Cheezits," Mark laughs. "Stan would have killed me if he saw me eating that stuff, but I couldn't disappoint my kids! And it gave me the fuel I needed to finish the marathon a full hour faster than expected."

That year, Mark did earn the million dollars, and donated $60,000 to charity. And in the end, he didn't die after all. "Instead, I found out that when you are maniacally focused on just a few important goals, and when your why is as strong as leaving a legacy for your kids, you can accomplish even the most impossible things," he affirms. With his new lease on life, as he continued his sales career, he did his own deep work to understand himself, through and through. In the process, he signed up for retreat in Hawaii with a renowned teacher, Allen Cohen. "I was surprised when he called me up and told me I should do his coaching program instead of the retreat," Mark says. "He told me that 'Spirit' told him that, so he offered me my money back if I didn't like it. I didn't even know what coaching was, but he convinced me to give it a shot."

By the third week of the course, Mark was furious with Allen, but he didn't know why. It soon dawned on him that coaching was the thing he had been looking for his whole life, and exactly what he was meant to do. "My ex-wife and I had always known it; we just didn't know the word for it," he says. "I didn't know how I was going to pull off making the career switch, but I knew I needed to be an executive coach."

Mark began practicing coaching, putting in the 10,000 hours it takes to truly master a craft. He worked on stillness, presence, and the ability to monitor the physiological clues of his clients. He learned how to be bold, deliberately setting people off to uncover long-hidden blocks. "My goal is to open people up like a can opener, and you have to be prepared for whatever comes out," he says. "I have watched some of the world's top coaches do that deep work with their clients, and they've helped me do my own deep work."

All through his career, every time he went to a new startup, Mark's customers were eager to support him. And true to form, when he launched his coaching practice, his first six clients were former customers who didn't know what coaching was all about, but believed in him so much that they jumped right in. "In sales, I never succeeded by being cutthroat competitive," he says. "I succeeded because I cared about my customers more than anything else and took care of their needs. I think people have been able to recognize that, and they trust me because of it. I've always been focused on helping people get where they wanted to go. That's what being a coach is all about."

Today, as a leader, Mark is sometimes referred to as the reluctant shaman, a bridge between two worlds meant to change people's lives. "I've almost died many times, yet I've always sprung back, ready to start over," he says. "So I'm embracing my purpose and figuring it out as I go." Part of that purpose is to give back, and Mark donates five percent of his fees to charity, primarily split between veterans organizations and a wolf sanctuary that brings inner city kids to see the animals and learn valuable life skills in the process. A man of iron integrity, he has always kept his obligations and his promises, even when he didn't have to. And he has managed to turn any disadvantage in life into fuel for his unyielding work ethic. "Humility beats self-importance any day," he affirms. "I always felt a little less than, so I always worked twice as hard. It's one of the reasons I've been successful."

In advising young people entering the working world today, Mark urges us to be authentic and vulnerable, because only in this state of honesty can people truly connect to your mission and purpose. "You can lead through fear, but that's false power," he observes. "True power is in being able to move people, and that requires authenticity and vulnerability. That's where true strength is. When you're vulnerable, you're invulnerable."

Beyond that, he underscores the importance of finding your ground. "Figure out who you are and what your foundation is before you go out into the world," he says. "Deep work begins with finding your core and your center—the foundation from which all else flows. Whether it's business, relationships, family, or just love of life, that's where it all starts. Everything else is superfluous. You can improve things in life, but you can't transform things until you do the real deep work and get down to the core."

BERNHARDT
WEALTH MANAGEMENT

James L. Speros

All on the Line

"As long as I'm the Governor, you'll never play in Memorial Stadium," said William Donald Schaeffer, respectfully yet firmly. Most people would have left it at that. But Jim Speros, a recipient of a Canadian Football League (CFL) expansion franchise, never left things unfinished.

The CFL was expanding by six teams, all to be located in the United States, for the first time in its 120-year history. At the same time, in the fall of 1993, the NFL was expanding their league by 2 franchise teams, with four cities as finalists: Baltimore, St. Louis, Charlotte, and Jacksonville.

Jim had his heart set on giving Baltimore the ball and building a CFL franchise in Charm City, but had to be patient and wait for the two NFL franchises to be announced first. Ultimately, in late October of 1993, Charlotte and Jacksonville each received an NFL expansion team. Baltimore was out, and the city was devastated, but the path was cleared for Jim and the CFL team to restore hope. He put up a $100,000 non-refundable investment with the CFL, and on December 1, 1993, the Board of Governors of the CFL awarded him a franchise, contingent on a successful lease at Memorial Stadium with the City of Baltimore.

Schaeffer, then the Governor of Maryland and a longtime powerhouse in Maryland politics, saw no realistic path forward for Jim, and told him so in no uncertain terms. Rather than see the city marred by a failed venture of that magnitude, he threw his weight behind opposing the idea, so Jim instead pitched his idea to Mayor Kurt Schmoke and five of the most powerful businessmen in the city. They gave him the green light, and on February 17, 1994—Jim's 35th birthday—the Mayor executed a lease to play at Memorial Stadium on 33rd Street, where the Baltimore Colts and the Baltimore Orioles made history. "Once that happened, things started to fall in place and gears were set in motion," Jim remembers today. "Everything I had was on the line, and I had to make it work."

Jim had to rely on ticket sales to pay off the $4 million bond he had been granted, and most people said there was no way in hell he could do it. But in just over two months' time, he sold a whopping 22,000 season tickets, raking in over $6 million.

Responding to the city's cry for the team they lost in 1984, Jim named it the Baltimore CFL Colts. And when he realized the Stadium needed to be completely renovated before the start of the season, he rolled up his sleeves. "The Mayor leased it to me for one dollar a year in exchange for a ten percent amusement tax on ticket sales," Jim recounts. "But it was completely dilapidated. The Baltimore Orioles had left two years earlier, and the stadium had been left unattended. There were rodents in the locker rooms, broken down elevators, an inoperable scoreboard and lights, damaged seats, and an unusable field. It needed $5 million worth of work just to be safe."

Through a laundry list of techniques including several trade deals and a grant from the State of Maryland's Sunshine Fund for $2 million, Jim managed to put together $7 million. By the end of June, he had brought in a new field, electronic scoreboard, computers, and office furniture; renovated the locker rooms, press boxes and offices; and painted all of the stadium seats. By the time he was done, the stadium was completely transformed.

Then, as Jim and the team prepared to kick off the football in late June of 1994, hours before the first preseason game, the NFL was granted a legal injunction barring the CFL franchise from any use of the word "Colts". "We had to spray paint the field, cross the word out on our programs, memorabilia and shirts, and throw away a ton of merchandise," Jim recounts. "We plowed through roadblock after roadblock. All I wanted to do was put a team on the field. But the NFL wanted to fight me on the name that truly belonged to the City of Baltimore."

Despite these setbacks, the team later known as the Baltimore Stallions made it out on that field for the first game of the season, greeted by the thunderous roar of a record crowd of more than 42,000 Baltimoreans—a scene forever memorialized on the front cover of *Sports Illustrated* in July of 1994. They finished the season with the most wins ever by a professional sports expansion team, going on to become the first and only American CFL expansion team to ever make it to the Grey Cup championship. The following year, the Stallions became the first and only American team in the League's 120-year history to actually win the Grey Cup. Jim stills wears his CFL ring today—a testament not only to the team he built with his own two hands, but to the strength of will that allowed him to do it in the first place

Jim's high-powered career has been vast and varied, taking him to unimaginable heights in sports, real estate, technology, and the restaurant industry. And as different as these ventures have been, his success always comes down to the same set of vitals. "Something was built in me early in life," he says. "I've always had this relentless will to go out there, accomplish my goals, and be the best that I can be, come hell or high water. I've carved my own path and pursued those chances, even when everyone around me said it wasn't possible. For me, success has been about putting it all on line, and then putting my all into making it work."

Jim came to be the founder, Chairman, and CEO of Velocity Restaurant and Hospitality Group, LLC, a marketing, technology and customer service company providing services and infrastructure support for restaurants, after his success landed him in a social circle of dynamic go-getters who had done very well in their own professions. After he joined several other investors in a series of failed baseball and golf ventures, he opted to shift his focus back to his roots. "Restaurants are in my blood," he affirms, hearkening to his youth spent working in his family's restaurant. "I know how to build, develop, hire, operate, and run them, with a bonus structure that incentivizes employees to do their best every day. I know this better than anything else. Herein lies my passion."

With that, in 2007, Jim decided to open a restaurant in Falls Church, Virginia, called Velocity Five Sports Restaurant and Bar. His vision was to create the Morton's of sports bars, with white tablecloths, nice booths, and multiple TVs. "With time, I scaled that back as I realized that people don't come to sports bars to eat steak—they come to get burgers, wings, and a cold beer to watch the game," he laughs. "Still, the restaurant was well received and very successful right out of the gate, and began hosting live sports shows with ESPN, Comcast, and The Fan radio program."

Within that first year, Jim was approached to buy a second restaurant in Sterling, Virginia by the name of Fox Chase Tavern, and a third called King Street Blues in Arlington, Virginia. He seized the opportunities, turning the businesses around to great success and prompting him to launch a restaurant organization. He then began considering his next move. "In the restaurant business, if you're not growing, you're shrinking," he says. "You have to keep growing to reduce your vendor costs and overall operational expenses, so I decided to look into franchising."

Velocity Five was the most promising candidate, but with its multiple moving pieces of dining, bar, and nightlife business, it proved difficult to replicate. Instead, in 2012, Jim set up a system with his vendor, U.S. Foods, to build a prototype for Velocity Wings, a hybrid version of the restaurant that cut out the dancing, DJ, and live sports shows for a simpler sports restaurant feel that focused on food, family, and fun. He would offer free-range, never frozen chicken wings, certified Angus beef hamburgers, and a variety of fresh salads at a competitive price. The first prototype went live in Purcellville in 2013, and was then successfully replicated in South Riding, Bristow, Manassas, and Lovettsville, Virginia.

The model worked so well that it soon attracted the attention of a private investment group wanting to join Jim in launching several additional units, and there are currently plans to develop ten more Velocity Wing locations in the Northern Virginia marketplace. "I still have the Velocity Five's and they're doing fine, but my focus brand and model now is Velocity Wings," he says.

By the end of 2017, Jim will have racked up five Velocity Wings locations and two Velocity Five locations. He has also created a new concept called Social House, an American Kitchen and Tap that recently opened its doors to a welcoming South Riding, Virginia community. "We filled a void that was missing in the South Riding community," Jim says. "We offer a menu that features steaks, seafood, street tacos, craft beer, and local Virginia wines, as well as a large selection of bourbons. The new restaurant in South Riding is an 'edgy' concept, but we maintain our values that made Velocity Wings and Velocity Five successful. You need to take care of your customers and have continued training for your employees, or you'll be out of business."

Through the Velocity Group, Jim has the opportunity to put all his abilities and experience to work. He finds the right sites and demographics, opting for shopping centers that do over $30 million in revenue, and buying up potentially competing real estate when he c.an. Today, he overlooks development and serves as his own general contractor. "My fingerprints are on everything I touch," he says. Negotiating vendor contracts is particularly important since he made the decision to only offer fresh products including the real money maker, chicken wings. "Building long term relationships with vendors like Pilgrims Food System, which has a main chicken manufacturing plant in Broadway, Virginia, is critical," he points out. "You've got to be able to get the best product year-round. The restaurant business is very competitive. If you can turn a 14- 16 percent profit, you are doing very well".

Jim's restaurant acumen stems from the earliest days of his childhood, when he grew up the second of seven brothers and sisters in a boisterous, entrepreneurial Greek family. His grandfather immigrated to America with only a nickel to his name, using grit and hard work to build a legacy of six restaurants, including a famous restaurant in Chevy Chase called the Silver Fox. People thought he was crazy when he later sold everything he had and bought a 150-acre farm in remote Potomac, Maryland, called Normandy Farms Restaurant, in 1952. But he had a vision.

Jim's grandfather converted the farmhouse into a 500-seat restaurant with a large kitchen, private banquet room and seven fireplaces, ultimately developing the capacity to do up to 3,000 dinners a night on holidays such as Easter, Thanksgiving, and Mother's Day. Notable regulars such as legendary D.C. attorney and former owner of the Washington Redskins and Baltimore Orioles Edward Bennet Williams, as well as sports legends like Vince Lombardi, George Allen, Larry Brown, Vince Promuto and other Redskins, and a family favorite and friend, Frank "Hondo" Howard of the Washington Senators, would frequent their restaurant. Jim's father, who inherited that same work ethic and drive, joined the business and made sure all the kids came to pitch in. "When I was eight, I thought it was fun to go wash dishes," Jim recalls. "We were all excited to be involved, and I loved being around the restaurant, with the fringe benefits of meeting and getting autographs from famous athletes and other people as they'd come through."

As Jim got older, however, he recognized that restaurant work was grueling and labor-intensive—challenges his parents and grandparents always embraced. "When the kitchen got backed up, my father would take his sports coat off, roll up his sleeves, and go cook," Jim remembers. "Being in a family business, you can't be scared to get your hands dirty. My father didn't want any of us following in his footsteps unless we wanted to. He wanted to make sure we had other options."

All through Jim's childhood, the Speros home was filled with family and friends, with big weekend gatherings and holiday celebrations. Family dinner were an undebatable staple of growing up, marking an important time each evening for everyone to convene and communicate. Sports, as well, were a defining factor, and Jim's father got all the kids involved in athletics early. In Little League, Jim first excelled as a catcher and later became an all-star player. He later picked up basketball, but due to his size, he didn't start playing football until sixth grade.

While loving, supportive, and diligently attending every sports game, the Speros parents were strict and regimented, ruling the household with an iron fist. The children were required to work for any unessential material item they wanted, but when it came to getting a good education, no expense was spared. The boys were sent to a Catholic military high school called St. John's College, while the girls went to Holy Cross and Holy Child. Jim had had his heart set on going to the public high school nearby, and disliked that his father forced him to attend a school where he had to wear a military uniform, get a haircut, go to drill and mass, and endure a twenty-mile commute from his house. "I thought my life was over," he recalls. "I couldn't believe my dad was making me do it."

The school's junior ROTC program was rigorous, but Jim soon found that he enjoyed meeting new friends from all over the region, and by the time he finished his freshman year, he had settled in. The school also had extremely competitive athletes, and by his sophomore year, Jim landed a coveted spot on the varsity football team. "St. John's really built my character and shaped by development," Jim says. "It got me very regimented and organized, and was the bridge that landed me a scholarship to play college football."

The University of Maryland was ranked third in the country in 1976, and Jim set his sights on going there, where his father had played. It was local and familiar to Jim, but two of St. John's graduates had recently dropped out of Maryland's program due to transfers and injury, and the coaches showed little interest in Jim when he visited. But while he was overlooked by Maryland, Clemson University came calling. "I didn't know much about the school, other than that it was 500 miles away in South Carolina and was in the Atlantic Coast Conference," he recalls. "But they saw something in me that other schools didn't. I decided to go where I was wanted. I took that experience and turned it into motivation. I was determined to prove that Maryland was wrong for overlooking me."

Thus, Jim graduated high school a strong, young athlete, confident in where he had come from, where he was going, and who he was. This foundation proved critical when he arrived at Clemson, where he knew no one and was in for a brutal freshman year. His roommate, a tough teammate who had attended Fork Union Military Academy and lived in South Carolina, quit after just one week. "Everyone's all-state when they get there, but you quickly realize that you're just a piece of meat and the low man on the totem pole as a freshman," Jim says. "The alarm went off each morning at 6:00 AM. We'd have three practices a day and come home black and blue to do it all over again the next day. There were definitely days I looked in the mirror and wondered what I was doing there, but I resolved to dig in and work through it. You pull together as a team, and in the end, it makes you better."

Each day, Jim would find another reason to keep trying. And once he finally had his freshman year under his belt, things took a turn for the better. "That summer, I stayed in Clemson and worked out in the weight room, determined to improve," he says. "I wanted to show Charlie Pell and Danny Ford, the head coaches that recruited me, that they had made the right decision in bringing this guy in from Maryland. My sophomore year, I finally got on the field on Special Teams and was recognized by my peers when I was voted Team Captain for the ACC Championship game against Maryland in none other than College Park. I remember the Terrapins sent all their seniors out on the field for the opening coin toss, but because I was the only player from Maryland on the Clemson team, I was sent out to represent our team alone—a huge honor. When they flipped the coin, I made the winning call, and Clemson went on to win 28 to 24. To this day, that coin is still a prize possession of mine that symbolized how I carved my own path. I never gave up. I was fortunate to be a member of four Bowl teams, including being on the 1981 National Championship Team where we defeated Nebraska in the Orange Bowl."

Football was Jim's whole life through those years, but thanks to his parents' watchful eye, he was careful to never let his grades slip, finishing Clemson with a business degree. "I chose business because my family had always been in business, so it was the major that made the most sense to me at the time," he says. "But I wasn't ready to go sit in an office. It just wasn't in my DNA. I wanted to stick with football, my first love."

Jim received offers to be a free agent at several CFL camps, and had a tryout with the Montreal Alouettes, but it didn't pan out. He then got an offer from Clemson's head coach, Danny Ford, to stay on as a graduate assistant coach in the Strength and Conditioning Department. "The university only hired two grad assistants per year," Jim says. "It was a big honor to receive that offer."

Jim figured he was set for a while, but a year into that engagement, he got an offer he couldn't refuse from Dan Riley, one of the best strength and conditioning coaches in the county, working under the Washington Redskin's coach Joe Gibbs. Jim had gotten to know Dan during his visits at Penn State through his brother Pete, an offensive guard and captain of the 1982 Penn State National Championship team. When Dan transitioned to the Washington Redskins, he needed to bring on an assistant Strength and Conditioning coach to help out. The position offered the opportunity to work with Bobby Beathard and Charlie Casserly in the off-season in the Scouting Department, and gave Jim a new perspective on the opportunities in professional sports. "I took the job and never looked back," he says. "It was one of the best decisions I've ever made."

That first year, the Redskins made it to the Super Bowl, landing Jim a bonus and a Super Bowl ring. Miraculously, the same thing happened the following year. "I couldn't have imagined a better life than what I was doing," he recounts. "We were like a family, training together and going out together. I loved every minute of it. I was also shocked to see how hard it is to be an NFL coach. The players go home in the evenings, but the coaches stay until midnight, mapping out the x's and o's it takes to win."

The following year, Jim was offered a job with the Buffalo Bills as the Strength and Conditioning/Defensive Assistant Coach, overseeing the Strength and Conditioning program while working hand in hand with the best defensive minds. This included two of the NFL's best, Pete Carroll and Monte Kiffen. "I learned more from those two in those years than I learned in my entire football career," Jim affirms.

"I used to want to be a head coach and nothing else," he continues. "But after five years working in the NFL, I learned a lot about life in general and developed other interests. I came to see that I had other skills and faculties that could work well in other professions, and that I was drawn more to business than coaching. My goals started to change, and I opened up to pursuing other things. And frankly, I wasn't very patient back then. I was ready to make money. I wanted to test the water in the business world, and it was now or never."

With that, in 1987, Jim moved back to D.C. after being recruited by Cary Winston, the commercial real estate company where a family friend, Brendon McCarthy, worked as an executive. Brendon was a well-known decorated athlete from DeMatha, Boston College, and the Green Bay Packers, who made Jim an offer he couldn't refuse. "It was a big deal to take the leap from football to commercial real estate, which I knew nothing about," Jim says. "But I felt a connection with Brendon. I figured if he could be successful in this business, so could I."

At Cary Winston, Jim was assigned a commercial office building, where his best bet was trying to move people into new spaces. "I buckled down and approached real estate like I did football, where nothing is given and everything is earned," he recalls. "I leveraged my football connections and hometown relationships. A year later, I was named Rookie Real Estate Broker of the Year for the Washington Metro area."

The true windfall lay in his representation of Marriott, which connected him to the investors of the Champions restaurant chain. They wanted to open 200 restaurants within Marriott locations across the country, and they asked Jim to spearhead the effort as the company's president. They offered stock options and were publicly traded at that time, and though Jim had very little experience in the field, he accepted the challenge.

Jim began networking with agents and athletes, working deals and setting up publicity events as he helped grow the restaurant chain from 3 to 37 locations. Marriott decided to buy the franchise in 1993, and thanks to his generous options package, Jim experienced the financial success that enabled him to pursue and purchase the Canadian Football Team.

For a time, Jim was King of Baltimore, becoming the youngest owner of a professional sports team in North America. The city loved its Stallions, and while that enthusiasm was great for Jim's success, it also stoked the NFL's interest in reclaiming the stadium. They got their chance in 1996 when Art Modell decided to move the Cleveland Browns to Baltimore, ousting the Stallions. With the help of Congressman and Vice Presidential candidate Jack Kemp, who sat on the Stallions'

Board of Directors, along with the CFL's Commissioner Larry Smith, the two orchestrated the deal for the Stallions to leave Baltimore intact and transfer the franchise to Montreal, where Jim had to start from square one rebuilding its infrastructure, brand and notoriety. But the deal Jack Kemp and Larry Smith structured enabled CFL players with short term contracts to re-enter the NFL—a windfall for players wanting to play in the CFL and have the flexibility to re-enter the NFL.

Through Cookie Lazaurus, a well-known attorney in Montreal, Jim met Mitch Garber, the brilliant and well-connected man that Jim named his Executive VP. They were successful in building the team back out, but within two years, Jim decided to sell it. He agreed to stay on as Vice Chairman of the CFL for a short period of time, but a year late, he remembers waking up at the Intercontinental Hotel on an off-season March morning, with the snow and rain falling outside in negative two degree temperatures. He recalls the momentous challenges facing the team—beyond political and language barriers, he had lost his head coach and was forced to change venues, resulting in massive stadium expenses. He carne to the realization that this was not Baltimore, and he didn't have the same infrastructure to work with. At the same time, it was not the league he had signed up for, and they were no longer a U.S. team playing on U.S. soil. "I called my wife and told her it was my last year there," Jim recounts. "I never fought so hard in my life as I did to make that team successful. But it didn't bring the same joy and satisfaction to me anymore."

Even before he descended from the mountain that was his CFL football team, Jim had his sights set on the next cliff face—a customer relationship management (CRM) technology company called Sideware Systems that specialized in real-time "chat" technology. He had taken an interest in the company the year earlier because it had promised to make his business more efficient, streamlining ticket sales and marketing. The platform had proven highly successful, so Jim had recommended it to others in the League. Out of appreciation, the company put him on their Board and gave him stock options.

Upon leaving the CFL, Jim went full steam ahead with Sideware Systems, accepting a position as its President and CEO at the recommendation of a mentor and brilliant business mind, Grant Sutherland. "I knew very little about tech at the time, but I knew how to build teams," Jim says. At the helm of the company, he raised $50 million through a variety of investment vehicles, executed several partnerships and customer contracts, opened twelve offices in the U.S., developed strategic partnerships with IBM and Oracle, and facilitated the platform's implementation into government agencies and several Fortune 500 companies. Along with founder Owen Jones and Grant Sutherland, he helped take the company from a startup to a market cap of over $1.2 billion by the year 2000.

High highs sunk to low lows when the dotcom bubble burst later that year, but Jim and his team still managed to come out ahead when the company was sold. He then signed on as Vice Chairman and President of Braintech, a company that specialized in robotics. There, he landed deals with automotive giants like Ford, GM, and ABS, and went on to raise $15 million. "My partners and I came up with a great dynamic," he recounts. "Owen Jones would build the technology, I would market and sell it, and Grant would set up the company's financial infrastructure. We were much more than the sum of our part and did very well together."

After growing Braintech to 60 employees, the trio sold the company and shifted its focus to Chalk Media USA, an e-learning company. After raising several million dollars, Jim and his team—which now included a seasoned CFO in Stewart Walchli—built a software application for clients like the Navy and PricewaterhouseCoopers. It included an innovative live video feature, but their key component was their partnership with Research Motion Blackberry, in which they focused their software on the Blackberry devices as a secure learning tool.

When they sold Chalk in 2010 to RIM, Jim's partners wanted to shift their focus to cybersecurity, but Jim knew he was ready to return to the bread-and-butter basics that had made him happy and successful in the first place. "I got into the tech world because I was a business guy looking for ways to operate my business more efficiently," he recounts. "I wound up hitting it out of the park with all of these tech giants, but at the end of the day, I'm still just a regular business guy with my roots in restaurants, where everything really started. The rest is history."

Through it all, Jim has treasured the unfaltering support of Ellen, the stunning young woman who walked into the grand opening party of a restaurant one night back in when he was still working for the Redskins. "Before I even said a word to her, I turned to my buddy and told him I was going to marry her one day," Jim remembers. It took him five months to convince her to even go on a date with him, but once she agreed, the connection was undeniable.

The two married in June of 1984, and for the first year of their marriage lived in Buffalo, where Jim had a coaching position with the Buffalo Bills. "She's always been as beautiful on the inside as she is on the outside," he says. "She's incredibly genuine and intelligent, and has been a great mother to our three children. She's also been involved in all my business ventures—not just as a support system, but also as a sounding board and partner. She's been on quite a rollercoaster with me these past 33 years, but she's always been behind me, and I'm very grateful for the bond we have."

Jim also honors the bond he has with his parents. His mother, the staple of the family, always worked to bring out the best in each of her seven children, while his father has always been his biggest supporter. "He has this remarkable way of bringing me back to the middle of the road if I'm veering too far in one direction," Jim says. 'When I'm passionate about something, it completely consumes my life, but he helps to ground me. I try to be that same support system and grounding force to my three children now. My legacy isn't the Baltimore Stallions or the Washington Redskin or Clemson. It isn't the restaurants and business ventures I've pursued. It's my kids. Through the highs and lows, you never stop being a parent."

In advising young people entering the working world today, Jim encourages them to find something they love, because it means they'll never work a day in their lives. "I tell my kids to work hard and follow their dream, and it'll happen for them," Jim affirms. "Just be patient, which I was never good at. Take your time, because if you do it right, you won't have to take the time to unwind it later."

Beyond that, Jim underscores the truth that people make people. "My success has always come from associating myself with good people," he says. "I've tried to emulate and learn from them, and I've tried to support them by building strong teams. Whether in football or in business, my whole life has been about building and developing winning teams."

Ultimately, Jim's success has been about having a passion strong enough to endure the grind, and resolve loud enough to drown out the doubt. And it's been about commitment to the crusade, putting it all on the line so nothing's left on the table. Sometimes, this commitment looks like a new stadium full of elated fans, all there because you found a way to sell them a ticket. Sometimes it looks like a signed deal, a strong quarter, or a smile at the end of a long day. Sometimes, on those days when it's most important of all, it just looks like not walking away. "It's easy to quit," Jim says. "That's why, at its essence, success is all about finishing. So in those moments, just hold on, because the reward of succeeding and truly being a part of something—that reward lasts a lifetime."

Gerry Stephens

The Things That Go Right

With anguished eyes, Gerry Stephens traced the jagged lines of the monitor, willing them to stabilize. But the oxygen rate line continued to plummet, while the heart rate line continued to climb in a futile attempt to compensate. Then suddenly, both lines fell flat. He was shoved away from the bed as a curtain was hastily drawn so the medical team could focus on the woman whose heart had just stopped—Gerry's wife of 46 years.

Not even an hour earlier, Gerry and Georgene had been eating breakfast together like normal. They were heading to the airport for a trip in a few hours, so she'd gone back into the bedroom to pack. Suddenly, Gerry had heard a gasping sound and came running. The ambulance arrived a few minutes later, and no one could figure out that she was suffering from a massive pulmonary embolism. "I've never been or felt so helpless in my life," he recalls today. "When I heard everything go silent on the other side of that curtain, words couldn't describe the depth of desperation I experienced. But then a voice said they needed to get her up to the ICU. It took me a minute to realize what that meant—that she was still alive. I hadn't lost the love of my life after all."

Within hours, Gerry and Georgene's three grown children arrived with their families for strength and support as the healing process began. Their middle daughter took charge to make sure things ran smoothly, and she even stayed an extra week to help Gerry calm down. Now, a year later, Georgene is miraculously better than new, recently logging 21,000 steps at Universal Studios and 23,000 steps at Disney World in a single weekend.

"The doctor told us that most people who suffer from a massive pulmonary embolism don't make it to the hospital," Gerry says. "Of those that do, one percent survive the emergency room. Of those that do, one percent survive without substantial impairments. Now, I call her Wonder Woman. Every time I see my wedding ring, I remember the hundreds of things that went right that day in order to keep her with me. The fact that I was home at the time, the fact that we weren't on the way to the airport or in the plane yet, the fact that we got her to the hospital in time—it's incredible."

In life, there are so many things we can't control. But Gerry, a chemical engineer by training who has spent his career cultivating a mind for solving problems and an eye for delivering value in business, excels at perfecting the things we do have power over. Now a Chair for Vistage Worldwide, a global network of peer advisory boards that help business owners and executives deal with the issues they face day in and day out, he is committed to clearing the way so things can go right for his members when their businesses need it the most.

Today, Vistage has over 1,500 peer advisory boards with over 21,000 active members across 17 countries. The model is fundamentally locally-minded, with each advisory board composed of 12 to 16 CEOs convened on a monthly basis to discuss their issues. But in terms of network reach and vision, the organization is decidedly global. "In some ways, it's a group therapy session," Gerry says. "But overall, it's a business issue and opportunity working group whose sum is so much more than its parts."

When they agree to undertake the role of a Vistage Chair, former business owners and consultants are formally indoctrinated with the Vistage Way via several months of training. After completing the process, Gerry launched his first group in March of 2016 and plans to launch his second in mid-2017. "I decided to do this because I was a successful business management consultant offering effective solutions that often fell outside my clients' normal range of thinking," he explains. "But as a Chair, my role in the group has evolved to focus on channeling the perspectives and experiences of fifteen other CEOs, so that the CEO seeking advice can see around the corners and confidently make a quick decision. I like to think I'm a pretty darn good consultant, but there's something magical about a group of peers giving advice and holding each other accountable. That collective action is powerful."

According to Dunn & Bradstreet, Vistage members grow three times faster than their counterparts, in part because its process accelerates clarity, accountability, and good decision making. Gerry is one of only two Chairs in the DC area focused on bringing this competitive weapon to small businesses, the backbone of the U.S. economy, with special proficiency in companies between $5 million and $25 million in annual revenue. His median CEO employs around 25 people, and with fifteen CEOs in a group, his impact touches an average of 375 individuals. When the lives of their families are also taken into account, that web of impact quickly skyrockets to well over 1,000 lives dependent on the small business communities represented by one of his Vistage groups—an impressive legacy that will be replicated with each new group.

Gerry's various aspirations and roles in life as a physician, engineer, project manager, corporate executive, business consultant, and executive coach are connected by a constant thread. "I've wanted to solve problems and create value for people ever since I was a kid," he says. After he was born in Hornell, a small town on the southern tier of New York State, his family moved to Buffalo and then to Cleveland when Gerry was in third grade. Around that time, his parents divorced, thrusting Gerry into a leadership position at home as the eldest child with two younger sisters. His father left his job at American Airlines to launch an independent photography business doing work for the Salvation Army, where he would become a commissioned officer years later. Meanwhile, Gerry's mother took a job as a bookkeeper and worked unflaggingly to support herself and her children.

As a kid, Gerry and his friends participated in Cub Scouts and Boy Scouts, enjoying the problem-solving challenges of camping, and he eventually became a counselor at a YMCA summer camp. Never particularly good at sports, he made a basket for the other team during his first basketball game and decided it wasn't for him. Instead, he joined the high school marching band in eighth grade playing the trumpet, though he'd sometimes accidentally march in the wrong direction. "My band director was fantastic and had a big impact on me because he thought I was pretty good, so he'd push me to get better and better," Gerry remembers. He later picked up flugelhorn in concert band and played bass guitar in a local Beetles-era rock band.

When Gerry was twelve, he made his first dollar working a paper route and later got a job as a photographic technician for his father making 25 cents an hour. His family was far from affluent, and he began buying his own clothes with his earnings. "Money was always tight, and I think that contributed to my work ethic as a kid," he says. "As I got older, I became a full-blown workaholic like my mother."

Academically, Gerry was a definite underachiever until his freshman year of high school, when he buckled down and ultimately finished twelfth in his class of several hundred students. Thanks to his stronger academic performance, he was permitted to put together independent study projects for course credit and opted to visit a hospital since he planned to become a doctor. "I liked that they helped people and made a good living, so it seemed like a good career path for me," he remembers.

The tour took months to plan and set up, and as the doctor was showing Gerry around on the big day, he got a twinkle in his eye. "Can I show you my new blood analyzer?" he asked. After Gerry enthusiastically consented, the doctor took him into the lab, pulled out a capillary tube, and pricked his finger. "I saw the blood go about an eighth of an inch up into the tube, and the next thing I knew, I was waking up on one of the stainless-steel tables," he laughs. "That was a defining moment."

By that point, Gerry had secured a full scholarship to a pre-medical school in Annapolis, but he knew he needed to reconsider. Fortunately, he was good in math and chemistry, so his guidance counselor sent him to visit a nearby chemical engineering college to gauge his interest. It felt right, so he adjusted his path. "My father was really upset with me for opting out of pre-med, but I decided to go to the University of Akron on an ROTC scholarship instead," he says.

Gerry had met Georgene in high school after accidentally knocking her over as their paths were crossing by the bathrooms, and he took her to his senior prom. When he started at Akron, she started college sixty miles away in Cleveland, where she taught school to cover her education expenses. "I had this neat, fast little car I'd use to zip over there through our first two years of separation," he recounts. "In our third year of college, we got married and moved into an apartment near my campus, so she'd take the car to Cleveland to finish her teaching obligations."

Gerry had put away his dream of becoming a physician, but had never completely closed the door on that possibility, and after three years in the Air Force, he was one of two officers selected to be in the first class of a brand new uniformed services medical school opening up in Bethesda. It was an incredible opportunity, and his path seemed to be shifting back to a career as a physician, but then-President Jimmy Carter delayed the opening of the school by one year. The delay eliminated his class's opportunity for attendance, so he rededicated himself to chemical engineering once again.

Upon graduating from college, Gerry went on active duty with the Air Force as a reserve officer and wrote a letter to the Air Force Secretary requesting an R&D assignment. He was classified as an aerospace engineer and sent to the service's aero propulsion laboratory, where he had formative early experiences in leadership managing a propulsion research facility over the next six years. There, he proposed a military construction plan to Congress for $50 million to transform the facility from reciprocating engine technology to turbine and ramjet engine technology. His hard work landed him a nomination for the Proxmire Golden Fleece Award, a tongue-in-cheek recognition accusing the program of wasting taxpayer dollars. But Gerry fought to convey its true importance, ultimately securing funding and managing the implementation himself.

In time, Gerry was reclassified as a chemical weapons officer and opted to leave military service. He was hired as a civilian to work at the same aero propulsion lab, where he stayed for another year. He then decided he wanted to work for an oil company, so he took a job at Ashland Chemical, an oil company subsidiary. "I figured I was set for life, but I came to find that they didn't have any of their own oil reserves," he said. "Still, it turned out to be a great position, where I spent almost five years working for their research center."

As part of that job, Gerry had cut off relations with a vendor because their products—microprocessor-based industrial controllers—didn't perform as advertised. One of the vendor's VPs called him up for an explanation, and the man ended up hiring Gerry to fix the problem as their Manager of Application Engineering. There, Gerry worked to advance their computer hardware so it could successfully run automation strategies incorporating math models of industrial processes.

Then, four years into that position, he made a bet with his boss that the Cleveland Browns would win the game that week. "Georgene is a diehard Browns fan, and I bet big on them, but they lost," Gerry recounts.

It wasn't a sum of money he had lost, but instead his next two years of freedom. "My boss thought I was too narrowly focused on the technical aspects of the field, so he said that if I lost the bet, I had to go back to school to get my MBA on his dime," Gerry says. "That was a major turning point for me. Up to that point, I math-modeled chemical processes and used those models to optimize economic performance. But with my MBA, I started to math-model business processes and use those models to optimize business performance. The MBA program equipped me with a whole new vocabulary that demystified business and allowed me to better convey my point of view to others, which was huge."

After completing the MBA program, Gerry began managing business units, starting with field service. A few years later, his boss left to take a job at Comcast, and Gerry decided to form a management consulting practice. The next 25 years were spent consulting with CEOs and business owners to improve shareholder value through optimization of business processes. Sometimes this meant joining the client's executive team to guide implementation of his recommendations, but he always returned to his consulting practice to seek out new challenges. As a result, Gerry has held a variety of VP positions in engineering, manufacturing, customer services, finance, marketing and business development.

In 1992, Gerry took a consulting engagement in California to help a privately-held scientific technology company. Its development arm was broken, failing to meet the commitments it had made to large customers like ExxonMobil to add new features to its software. Gerry ultimately accepted a VP position with them and set to work improving and formalizing their development processes, equipping the company with the tools it needed to make good on its promises while positioning the company for an IPO.

Gerry then took a consulting engagement in Philadelphia helping a friend make his company more profitable—a role that turned into Gerry's first position as a CFO. "The last CFO had mismanaged compliance with loan covenants, and I had to take the CEO down to the bank to convince them the company was worth more to them alive than dead," Gerry recounts. "It worked, so long as I agreed to be the one to manage the cash flow on a daily basis. So I learned all those skills, which was a natural transition thanks to my familiarity with numbers and processes."

With that, Gerry's career progression shifted from technology and related services, to broader business issues and leadership development. In 2001, he accepted a VP position at Technology Management Company, a government contractor focused on U.S. nuclear and chemical threat reduction in the former Soviet Union. When he learned that its President was trying to sell the company, he put together a buying group and financed the purchase with an ESOP. As a founding board member of the newly-purchased entity, and then as COO and later CFO, he shifted the company focus to biological threat reduction in Central Asia and Africa, and helped to grow the business from $7 million to $37 million over his ten years there, by far the longest stint he's spent with any one entity.

During that time, Gerry had the opportunity to create a subsidiary of Technology Management Company to provide anti-piracy security for ships operating around the Horn of Africa. Through his work as President of Daedalus Specialized Services LLC, he hired retired Navy Seals, Army Rangers, and Special Forces operatives—driven, impressive individuals that carried out the mission of providing technology-based, less-than-lethal security to defend vessels against bad actors with automatic weapons.

Overall, Gerry's experiences with Technology Management Company were exciting and engaging, but by 2011, sequestration and budget fights in Congress left the fates of many government contractors in question. He decided to sell his interest to his partners and set his sights on retiring into a life of teaching and consulting, but when he met a friend for lunch to discuss the idea, Gerry was instead convinced to help his friend launch a software development company. After three years as CFO for that venture, he was truly burned out and ready for something new.

At that point, Gerry had accrued almost 25 years of business management consulting spent guiding various company executive teams. He happened to run into a few colleagues at an event who told him about Vistage, and his interest was piqued. "I had never heard of Vistage, but the concept really resonated with me, so I decided to pursue it," he says. "After such a wide breadth of experience in business, there's very little that surprises me, and Vistage seemed like a great way to leverage my analytical, process-oriented, problem-solving mind for a greater benefit. After several months of thought and several more months of training, I earned my wings as a Vistage Chair, and I was ready."

Through it all, Gerry's career has been marked by great mentors who helped give him an edge. He benefited from the example set by his father, who provided a template for agility and success by pursuing a wide range of careers and turning any failure into a learning experience. He was also more successful for having picked up his mother's arduous work ethic. But by far, Georgene has been the perfect partner and key ingredient to his success. "We have three great kids that she raised into wonderful adults despite my long work days and wanderlust," he says. "I've done some great things, but I couldn't have done anything without her."

Today, Gerry serves on the advisory board of the Salvation Army of Central Maryland—a way of honoring his father. As a leader, he focuses on collaboration as a way to bring everyone to the table and engage them in creating value. "I've worked with all different kinds of people, from skilled labor to PhDs," he says. "The best thing you can do is facilitate collaboration by asking what they think. The people I work with usually know much more than I do about a particular area, so I've learned how to draw out that expertise and apply it to whatever we're doing. I feel most successful when I work as part of a team that solves a momentous problem."

In advising young people entering the working world today, Gerry echoes his father by reminding us that if you can imagine it, you can do it. "Your only limits are your stamina and your imagination," he says. "It took me a long time to figure out that, of all my competencies, I most loved solving problems. But once I figured it out, my stamina and creativity were really set free to serve others. Now, I'm so grateful I get to work each day to analyze problems and opportunities, smooth out the wrinkles, and make sure things go right for the CEOs in my group. We can't control everything, but through our dialogue and discoveries, we've learned how to work miracles together."

Kimberly H. Stewart

Believe in Yourself

During Kimberly Stewart's childhood, her parents believed she and her siblings could accomplish anything they put their mind to. Anytime she or her siblings approached their father and mother with an idea, no matter how far-fetched, they supported them. "They always believed in us and gave us the freedom to pursue it," she recounts today. "We would come up with a concept and they'd say, okay, what's your plan? Then it was up to us to figure out how to accomplish it. If we tried one way and failed, they encouraged us to find another way. It taught me how to believe in myself and figure out how to accomplish whatever I set my mind to do."

Years later, while working for American Management Systems, Kim was the Deputy Program Manager for a major Information Technology (IT) project. Over the next few months, as they neared the Go Live Day, it became apparent the system was not ready for end-to-end production. The Project Manager (PM) took a leave of absence, and the Go Live was a failure.

Thanks to the strong foundation of resiliency and industriousness set in her by her parents, Kim set to work strategizing solutions and forging a path forward. "In the immediate aftermath, we assembled a team and worked round the clock to rebuild the system," she recounts. "Once we got it up and running, we worked to improve it. It was not a position I wanted to have, but I resolved to get through it by taking each problem and laying it out on the table, giving my recommendation and then acting on the client's direction."

Little by little, things started to improve, and in the end, the strategy worked. "I still have great working relationships with the senior leadership from that client because they know they can trust me to tell it like it is, and to do everything in my power to get the job done," she says. "It was one of the most trying challenges I've ever gone through, but also the best learning experience I've ever had, and it absolutely defines how I work with clients today." Now the Founder and President of Stepping Stone Consulting, an IT Program Management firm that partners with the federal government to implement IT services and infrastructure solutions, Kim has built her career through the power of possibility—the kind of power unleashed when you're given the tools to succeed and then let loose to go figure it out.

Kim launched Stepping Stone in June of 2010 as a "stepping stone" to program management success in the federal IT space. "We support the government's IT program management offices," she clarifies. "We work directly with the program offices of these agencies, helping the government acquire, implement, and manage the products, services, and software." Now a small team of two employees that brings on contractors as needed, the company was focused entirely on the Department of Defense until it recently won a Department of Transportation contract, and plans to continue to grow.

This core business of Stepping Stone allows Kim to continue her lifelong dedication to the success of others through her focus on the growth and prosperity of her clients and employees. This aligns with a budding branch of the company, a coaching service for PMs in small and mid-sized businesses. "Smaller companies often don't have a senior PM that can act as a mentor, so they bring me on to provide that expertise and guidance," she says. "Whether I'm advising on an issue, guiding on certain deliverables, providing templates, or supporting staff during a meeting, I'm a safety net for executives because they know I'll always come to them before it's too late. I have a confidential relationship with the PMs I coach, but if there ever comes a point that the company or project is at risk, I'm the executives' backstop and get the appropriate people involved to avoid catastrophe."

Kim's love of mentoring and coaching junior PMs is a reflection of her broader focus on promoting the success of others—a passion she first connected with as a five-year-old girl while vacationing in Cape Cod. That summer, the kids in the area decided to clean up an abandoned boathouse on the water so they could use it to host a surprise dinner party for their parents. "Some of the parents helped with little chores, like getting the electricity working again," she says. "But we swept it, decorated it, and brought in all the food. I'll never forget how proud I was when our parents came for that meal, and I fell in love with the feeling of doing things for other people."

Born in the Columbia Hospital for Women in Washington, DC, Kim grew up in Chevy Chase, Maryland, as the third of four children, in the home where her parents still live. The back of the house juts up against the Kenwood Golf and Country Club, and Kim remembers cherry blossom seasons when she joined her older brother and sister in collecting tennis balls hit over the fence and abandoned in the woods. They sold them, three balls for a dollar, at a lemonade and cookie stand they set up for tourists—a lucrative venture undertaken mostly on their own. "Our mother would buy the first packet of lemonade mix and tell us we were responsible for everything else."

Through her childhood, Kim's mother stayed home with the children and worked part-time for the Campaign Committee of Texas

Congressman Jack Brooks. Her father was a partner at his own law firm in D.C. The children were never allowed to miss school, so when the exception was made for her father arguing before the Supreme Court she was very excited. "We were excited to finally miss a day of school, only to realize it was the Easter Monday, a school holiday," Kim laughs. "Education was our job, and a big priority for my parents."

During her early academic years, Kim worked with a speech therapist and recalls anxiety about reading aloud or speaking up in class. For her fourth-grade year, she transferred to Maret School, where her older sister attended. There, she began to flourish in math and gradually became more comfortable academically. The summer after her sixth-grade year, however, she noticed that the community around her identified her as "Angie's little sister." She was upset at first, but fortunately, things began to change when her sister invited her to come be part of the backstage crew for the school's middle and high school plays. "No other seventh graders got to do that," Kim recounts. "I loved the work and meeting the upper classmen, and I started standing out on my own."

A year later, the drama teachers created a new student drama position for her as a student producer of the middle school play. The following summer, she started working as a counselor at Maret's summer camp. Empowered by the sense of creating her own identity, she found she was drawn to leadership and decided to run for president of her ninth-grade class. "I intuitively knew the groups to reach out to and the support I needed to win," she reflects. "It was another step in defining who I was and finding that I was much more comfortable leading than following. I was always one to take initiative, never sitting back and just waiting for things to happen."

Through high school, Kim was often at school from 8:00 AM to 9:00 or even 10:00 at night, her time joyfully dedicated to class, sports, and drama rehearsals. She became president of the drama group, directing and producing plays. She played JV and Varsity softball and soccer, and also fell in love with Physics. Well-rounded and a master of time management, she stood on her own with her own identity.

When it came time to consider colleges, her mother encouraged her to apply to attend Wellesley College, the women's college in Wellesley, Massachusetts, where her mother grew up. "When I went in to interview, we had a great conversation," Kim recalls. "The interviewer said that every school was going to want me, given my grades, athletics, and community engagement. She asked if I would come if I was accepted. Without skipping a beat, I answered honestly, 'No.' When the interviewer asked me why, I said that if I was going to compete with men in the real world, I wanted to compete with them in the classroom."

Kim effectively threw the interview and was waitlisted at Wellesley, ultimately accepting a place at Hamilton College in Clinton, New York. She remembers her high school graduation day with tremendous love and gratitude, particularly for her father, who handed her her diploma. "He was President of the Board of Trustees at the time, so he handed out all of the diplomas, including mine," Kim recounts. "I was probably the third or fourth person in Maret's history to receive their diploma from a parent. For me, it symbolized that my parents had given me the foundation and guidance to be successful, and now I was on my way. I treasure that memory very much."

At Hamilton, Kim planned to major in Physics but was discouraged when she kept failing tests in Physics 101. Her professor confirmed that her conceptual understanding made her one of the better students in the class, but her answers weren't the exact answer as his, and he didn't give partial credit. Frustrated, she switched to a government major with a minor in economics. "Leadership was what I was really interested in, and I felt that leading a country was the ultimate test of leadership," she explains.

Upon graduating Hamilton in 1992, Kim spent several months working on various political campaigns and then interviewed at the University of Maryland University College for the role of Assistant

Director of Annual Giving, during the interview, she was asked why she wanted to wake up each morning and take money away from people. Without missing a beat, she spoke from the heart. "I told them I didn't want to do that," she recounts. "I said, I want to give people the opportunity to support a cause they're passionate about. If they don't want to support it, I don't want their money. Looking back, that's what's driven me through my entire career—that desire to provide opportunity and to make individuals or organizations successful. It's the same goal I work toward now through the framework of program management."

Kim landed the job, setting the tone of her professional career with the mission-focused mindset of the nonprofit world. There, she raised money and served as the campus representative on a University-wide committee to evaluate a new alumni and development software system. That experience marked her initial foray into the IT world—a path furthered when she left in 1995 to accept a similar position at the Chesapeake Bay Foundation. She implemented and ran their new development software system as well, and grew even more intrigued by the power of data and IT to manage and transfer information quickly and efficiently. "I worked with consultants that were implementing software and teaching people to incorporate it into their processes to do their jobs better," she says. "That experience helped clarify for me why I wanted my MBA."

Kim knew she wanted to one day have her own consulting business, and when she applied to business school, she decided to write her business plan for the admissions essay. She married her husband, Gary, obtained a position at American Management Systems (AMS), and completed her degree in 1999.

AMS, known for producing high-caliber consultants that share an iron bond of strong values and unyielding work ethic, was a hugely transformative experience for Kim. She started her tenure working on Army projects, but when she returned to work after giving birth to her son, Patrick, she found herself thrown into the fray of the a severely challenging system implementation for the Federal Agency—a critical learning experience that taught her how to navigate a crisis from a place of strength. "It really drove home the reality that bad news doesn't get better over time, so it's most important to be upfront and honest," she recalls. "If there's a problem, don't hold onto it—get other people involved and figure out together how to come up with the solution. It was the best lesson I could have learned so early in my career—one I return to all the time. It has never failed me."

In 2004, while preparing for the birth of her daughter, Ashley, AMS was bought by CACI and CGI. She took a position with Preferred Systems Solutions (PSS), a small business focused on professional and technical services contracts, where she quickly rose to the rank of VP and wore many hats. "I fine-tuned my business acumen, developing my experience in proposal work, budget management, and building business," she says. "It was perfect training ground for preparing to start my own company."

By 2007, Kim felt ready to take her entrepreneurial leap, but as she prepared PSS plans and budgets for the following year, she realized she was responsible for a significant portion of the company's revenue. "I knew I had to tell the CEO my plans to resign in February." Prepared to leave two months ahead of schedule if requested, she ended up being able to stay on until her ideal departure date in February. When the leadership then had to let go of another VP a couple of weeks before her last day, she was asked to stay longer, so she negotiated an ownership stake in the company. Finally, in 2010, she stepped out, stepped up, and started Stepping Stone Consulting.

Today, Kim focuses primarily on supporting her team members in their pursuit of success. Sometimes this requires guidance and mentoring, which might warrant a chat over her highlighted and heavily-notated copy of Stephen Covey's *The 7 Habits of Highly Effective People*. Other times it requires doing nothing, which can be the hardest challenge of all for Kim. "If something's not getting done, my tendency is to jump in and do it," she says. "But I've learned that sometimes I need to just sit back and give others the space to step up on their own terms."

She also measures her success through the success she helps create for others, like a longstanding Army client who was recognized as a Top 100 CIO by *CIO.com Magazine*. "I helped set up a program management office in his shop, which really moved the needle for him."

None of this would have been possible without the love and support of her husband, Gary. A defense consultant as well, he has maintained a stable career that has given Kim the leeway to take bigger risks. "Gary goes into work early because he knows I often have to work late," Kim says. "I get the kids to school, and he makes sure he's there by the time they get home. He's always believed in my vision for my career path, and been the core that has helped me do everything I want to do. I'm very grateful for what we've built together."

Now, as they raise their two children, Kim strives to provide Patrick and Ashley with the same boundless sense of possibility and capability that her parents gave her. To them, and to young people entering the working world, she underscores the importance of authenticity and honesty. "Be true to yourself," she stresses. "If it doesn't feel right, take the time to think about what you're doing and why you're doing it. Look deep inside and make sure it resonates with your values, passion, and identity."

Beyond that, Kim invokes the positivity of her parents as a foundational key to success, shaping the character and vision that brought her here today. "Thanks to them, I'm always looking at the positive side," she affirms. "Things happen for a reason. You might not know what it is right now, but you will eventually. So, if tough times come, just focus on how you'll come out stronger. Set out your goals, figure out how to get there, and believe in yourself, because you are the only real limit you have."

Dawn Sweeney

The Homerun Hitter

More than 400 baskets of strawberries. That's how much produce Dawn Sweeney collected from her family's 40-acre farm the summer she was twelve, a mad sprint to earn as much spending money as possible in advance of a family trip to Nova Scotia, where her grandfather was from. "We grew all kinds of vegetables that we sold at our roadside stand, but strawberries were my thing," she remembers. "I made five cents a basket. Nickel by nickel, I was able to save $18, plus enough to buy a little, patent leather, orange purse to carry it in."

When the family crossed the border, Dawn was delighted by the magic of the international monetary system. Her $18 transformed into nearly $22. But she soon discovered a different kind of magic—one that wouldn't fade with time. As they traveled around, visiting her grandfather's twelve brothers and sisters for the first time, she saw that many of them were living in impoverished conditions. Over the course of the two-week trip, she left every cent of her earnings hidden in various places around the homes of those relatives in need. In her quiet act of philanthropy, Dawn discovered joy.

"When my father realized what I was doing, he cried," she says. "It was one of only two or three times I saw him cry in my whole life. He knew how hard I'd worked for that money, but we knew our relatives needed it far more than we did. It was a defining moment because it was so clear to me what I needed to do, and because it made me so happy to do it. It wasn't about recognition or presentation. I just wanted to help."

Dawn hit homeruns like that all through her formative years, but didn't think of them as such until decades later. Then, in 1997, she attended a particularly impactful staff meeting where her CEO went around the table clarifying everyone's roles. "When he got to me, I was surprised when he said he was counting on me to hit a homerun every single time I stepped up to the plate," she recounts. "I'd always wanted to be successful and deliver, but his words completely reoriented me."

The impact of his words were, in part, his belief in her—a confidence demonstrated by his ability to envision greatness for her, even before she saw it for herself. It also came from her own willingness to give everything she had. "I started putting power behind everything I did in a different way because the goal was no longer just 'not striking out,'" she says.

Now President and CEO of the National Restaurant Association (NRA), the largest national advocacy and business services support organization for the U.S. restaurant industry, Dawn's career has spanned four industries and myriad roles. But in each case, guided by her lifelong commitment to make a difference, she's always swung for the fences. "If your intention is to hit a homerun every time, everywhere you go, in everything you do, no matter who you're with, you'll do much better than you would otherwise," she affirms. "It's changed my entire life, professionally and personally."

Launched in Missouri in 1919 to tackle local restauranteur concerns about the price of eggs, the NRA today is a trade association representing an $800 billion industry that employs 14.7 million people—10 percent of the nation's workforce. From the smallest individual shops to the largest chains, it has partnership relationships with 50 state associations, and represents those organizations and members at the federal level. It also has a $10 million foundation dedicated to providing scholarships to underserved populations, and keeps an eye toward the international stage. "Our association is focused on promoting, protecting, advancing, and advocating for the restaurant industry domestically, so most of our work is in the U.S. market, but we also do a lot of global work with our counterparts in other countries," Dawn says. "Trends in other parts of the world often make their way here, so that global exchange is important."

When Dawn joined the NRA in the fall of 2007, it was a $50 million organization with 400,000 restaurant members. It has since grown to $120 million in revenues and represents 650,000 of the million restaurants in the U.S. today. It clocks in at one of the twenty largest trade associations in the country and has an impressive board of almost 100 visionaries representing the diverse breadth of the sector. With many different business models in the industry, each one comes with his or her own policy considerations, and the NRA strives to tackle the issues that tie the whole industry together.

With a staff of 325 people spread across offices in Washington, D.C., Chicago, Orlando, Lansing, and Rhode Island, the NRA's advocacy work is supplemented by funds earned from a large annual trade show, training and certification programs on food safety, a health-insurance plan product created specifically for restaurant employees, and several other business subsidiaries. "I'm grateful that my work in trade associations has always been so business-oriented," Dawn remarks. "I love doing business in a mission-oriented organization, but the most rewarding part of the work is the people that make up the industry.

They are incredibly creative, hardworking, persistent, kind, community-oriented people, and I love them. They're why I decided to come to the NRA in the first place."

Dawn spent her childhood years surrounded by people of just that caliber. Growing up in Westbrook, a community-oriented paper mill town near Portland, Maine, she was raised in the 200-year-old farmhouse where her father was born. Her mother was one of twelve, with lots of relatives living nearby throughout Dawn's childhood. Thanks to their remarkable work ethics, her parents were solidly middle class. Her beloved father, a reserved and dependable accountant at a local dairy company, would come home to work on the farm each night. He also served as a city councilman and mayor of the town. "He absolutely taught me what unconditional love was," Dawn says. "That was a huge blessing."

Her mother, very outgoing and personable, was more achievement-oriented. She also was a role model as a pillar of responsibility and self-sacrificing care for others. "I watched her do so much for so many people, always," Dawn recounts. "Her sister had a stroke when I was 10, and she devoted her life to taking care of her. She was always stepping in and stepping up."

On the farm, the family grew corn, peas, strawberries, potatoes, and other vegetables, and raised cattle for meat. "When my brother and I discovered what was going on with the cattle, we started a campaign with paper airplanes to stop selling the animals for meat," she laughs. "He also had oxen, which he used for ox-pulling competitions at fairs. We had one of the first old-fashioned movie cameras, and based on the footage filmed, it seemed that he much preferred filming the oxen pulls to filming us kids."

Dawn's brother worked the farm chores, while she took responsibility for picking the vegetables and running a roadside stand. Her grandfather, the hardworking driving force behind the whole venture, insisted each vegetable had to be "merchandised," and inspected. If they weren't just right, they weren't sold. Under this banner of excellence, Dawn would answer the phone, take the orders, and calculate the payments. "I honestly did not know what a weekend was until I went to college," she avows. "I had no concept of what it was to take a day off. We never took vacation and I was paid only when I picked the strawberry baskets. Everything else was just us pitching in to help the family."

When she wasn't working, Dawn read voraciously. She made her own library, forcing her parents to check out books and pay a fine if they forgot to return them on time. Dawn and her brother attended public school, where she worked incredibly hard and got excellent grades. She was never much of an athlete, but she still remembers vividly an intramural basketball game in which she saw one of her own teammates trip another teammate, just so she could steal the ball and make the basket herself.

"We ended up making a comeback to win that game against one of our biggest rivals, but I walked off the court with a profound feeling that we had lost," Dawn recalls. "I was so troubled by what I had seen. It was the moment I decided I only wanted to be on teams with people I could trust and respect. Now that I'm in a position of leadership, I'm privileged to have the opportunity to choose who's on my team, and I make a point to surround myself with people I trust and respect. Now, if I ever see teammates tripping each other intentionally in the workplace, I call it out because I believe that's one of the worst, most destructive things you can do."

Socially, Dawn was never cliquey and made a point to get along with everyone. Devoted to marching band in high school, she remembers the incredible feeling of taking a bus all the way to Florida with her team to compete in the national championships. "We were from this little town, and no one thought we had it in us, but we rallied and won!" she remembers.

No one in Dawn's extended family had ever gone to college, and when it came time to consider schools, her parents didn't know how to guide her in getting the right experiences or navigating the application process. Still, her family's help was invaluable in other ways. "My parents always insisted that I'd go to college one day," she says. "They saved for years to pay for it, with my father plowing snow in the winter or buying small houses to rent out. Even with all their ventures combined, my parents never made much, but they were incredible savers. They also gave me the most important thing of all—an unyielding work ethic."

Part of that meant working 25 hours a week at the local grocery store while in high school, starting as a bagger and working her way up to office manager for the evening shift. She also applied her work ethic academically, signing up for the honors track and excelling in every class except physics. Despite taking the most rigorous course load available, she realized she was far behind her peers when she enrolled at Colby College. Many of the other students had attended private schools, so she kicked it into high gear to meet the goals she set for herself.

Each semester, Dawn remembers going to the admissions office to sign up for classes, where the students had two lines to stand in—one for those whose tuition was already paid, and another for those whose tuition was outstanding. "Every single semester, I stood in the first line because I knew my father had paid it," she recalls. "That was such a gift. Many of my friends were far better off than we were financially, but still had to stand in the other line." My parents prioritized education. By the last year, Dawn was a resident assistant in her dorm. Her room and board was free, and she arranged to cover the rest of her tuition herself to take the burden off her parents.

In college, Dawn got involved in humanitarian organizations like Oxfam. She graduated in 1981 with a major in government and moved to Washington, D.C., where she had spent one of her junior year semesters. She landed a job at the International Dairy Foods Association, the trade association for the dairy processing industry, and spent several years saving money for law school while working as an education coordinator, a lobbyist, and then in public affairs. Then, her boss offered to send her to business school if she promised to stay on for four years after completing her degree. She agreed and spent the next four years working full-time during the day while taking classes at night at George Washington University.

As soon as she completed her MBA, Dawn took on a project that turned into the "milk moustache" advertising campaign—a tremendous opportunity. Also around that time, she attended a Leap Day party and met Tim, the man who became her husband. He helped her make the decision to pursue new professional experiences after 13 wonderful years at IDFA. She left in 1994 to become the head of marketing and business development for the National Rural Electric Cooperative Association. There, she pulled off a remarkable feat and raised nearly $50 million in less than a year allowing the organization to build a national brand. Then in 1999, she was recruited to join AARP. There, she revitalized the organization's brand and expanded and diversified its membership. Over the next ten years, she succeeded in reinventing the brand, growing its reach from 30 million to 42 million members.

Through that time, Dawn and Tim had their son, Kevin, who was born happy and healthy in 1998. Their second child, Allison, came three years later. Born with Down syndrome and a hole in her heart, she was not so lucky. She had open-heart surgery when she was 9 months old, and at 13 months, complications from a different procedure grew gravely serious. "That was a major defining moment in our lives," Dawn remembers. "Nothing else even comes close. She died in my arms and I had to make the decision to turn off life support. The nurse told me that my choice was the true definition of love—to love someone so much that I could put away my need for her to live and acknowledge her need to go. As hard as it was, I was able to do that."

After Allison had gone, Dawn and Tim sat in the hospital room for five precious hours with their daughter. They then braved the unspeakably painful challenge of navigating "Life After," coping with their own grief while helping 4-year-old Kevin through his. And, while a staggeringly high number of marriages fail after the loss of a child, Dawn and Tim vowed to come through stronger than ever. The following May, on Mother's Day, they drove to West Virginia together with their son and bought 20 acres of land, where they built a cabin over the next 18 months. It was a labor of love in honor of their daughter, and a beautiful, restorative place that contributed to their healing and closeness as a family. "Tim is my rock and confidant in every way, both in business and in life," she says. "He's authentically clear on what's right and wrong, and is a perfectly calm, solid balance to my driven, intense demeanor." Allison's death also inspired Dawn to get involved with Save the Children, a global humanitarian organization where she currently serves as Vice Chair of the Board. And among other philanthropic work, Dawn and Tim endow the Sweeney Family Foundation, granting special scholarships to kids with disabilities.

When Dawn worked at AARP, she loved the organization and was on the shortlist to become its future CEO. But then she received a call from a recruiter for the NRA. She told them she wasn't interested, but they convinced her to meet with them so they could get a sense of the skills they should be looking for. "It wasn't technically an interview, so I was very comfortable with the conversation," she says. "Unbeknownst to me, they had been interviewing people for many months—impressive candidates like Members of Congress and former cabinet secretaries—and were looking for a hospitality gene in addition to many other qualities."

After learning more about the potential impact she could have working to represent the second-largest private-sector employer in America, touching everything from nutrition standards to education, she ultimately went all in and accepted the position. Because she had never worked in a restaurant growing up, she spent several days each month of that first year filling various positions in the industry. From hostess, to bartender, to prep cook, to dishwasher, to drive-through attendant, she learned the issues from the inside out. "I never worked so hard in my life," she says.

Now, as the NRA's first-ever woman CEO and its longest-serving in 98 years of operation, Dawn advises young people entering the working world today to develop their own authentic style. "Figure out who you are and where your guardrails are," she says. "What's important to you? What will you let slip? What will you never allow to happen? This is your compass. Then do the best you can to make your life decisions based on those guiding principles."

That philosophy has been instrumental in landing her on *Washingtonian Magazine*'s list of the 10 most powerful people in Washington and on a nationwide list of the 15 most powerful people in food, as well as the great honor of being named the Association TRENDS Association Executive of the Year. Each recognition, and every other homerun she's hit along the way, stems back to her patient, unwavering commitment to the Japanese principle of *kaizen*, or continuous improvement. As a leader, Dawn embraces it in every element of her life, striving to do things a little bit better each day. "If you can do that, you'll wake up in three years and be a lot better," she says. "In life, we can't always be *the* best, but we can be *our* best. Ultimately, that's the most important homerun of all."

BERNHARDT
WEALTH MANAGEMENT

Randy Taussig

Embracing Your Genius

Growing up, Randy Taussig saw things differently. He wasn't effortlessly good at school like his older brother, and had to work hard to achieve academic results. "For the longest time, I didn't feel smart enough," he remembers now. "I always felt like I had to prove myself. Society tends to define 'genius' pretty narrowly—that particular brand of book-smart intelligence that shifts paradigms. But as I got older and came to know myself better, I saw that there was more to it. I came to realize that most everyone has genius."

It took Randy a long time to accept that he had a particular kind of genius all his own, and even longer to embrace it. He tried to fit into the normal structure of companies, but he always felt suffocated, unable to pursue his natural inclination to invent and create. With time, he realized that those inclinations were entrepreneurship, and that his unique point of view could add significant value. "Everyone has a genius about them in some way," he says. "Everyone has their own ideas, perspective, skills, and talents, uniquely combined to create an unparalleled gift. I think everyone needs an opportunity to understand what they're good at. Then once they embrace their genius, everyone has the responsibility to create the space to fly with it."

While this advice is meant metaphorically, Randy has a literal passion for flying inspired by his great grandfather, Noah W. Taussig, a stamp collector who got President Woodrow Wilson to sign the first envelope to ever be officially mailed by plane. Now the founder and CEO of BlueCore Leadership, an Entrepreneurial Operating System (EOS) implementation company dedicated to equipping entrepreneurs with the leadership and management tools they need to succeed, Randy sometimes tells the story of the day his plane almost went down. Hurrying to evade forecasted thunderstorms, he missed a simple step on his checklist of procedures. He forgot to secure the cockpit, allowing cloud condensation to whip in mid-flight. He had to make an emergency landing, and in the end, the forecasted thunderstorms never even materialized.

Even if they've never flown a plane before, entrepreneurs find the story deeply relatable. Each one has had that fly-by-the-seat-of-your-pants experience where things suddenly go very wrong. But each knows they're undeniably drawn to the risk and reward of the cockpit. "Entrepreneurship is freedom," Randy affirms. "There's a cost to that freedom, but I'll take it any day. Let me make my own destiny. Let me succeed or fail. Let me create."

Every ride is smoother with procedures, checklists, and a wiser understanding of weather patterns, and for entrepreneurs, BlueCore Leadership is all those things. Randy launched the company in 2012 after reading Gino Wickman's *Traction*, a method and philosophy for better business success through utilization of the EOS tools. Comprised of six key components, the process begins with the leadership team. "They need to be crystal clear about their vision so they can back it with solid execution and create a healthy, functioning organization," Randy explains. "A lot happens that can throw a business off track, so EOS helps founders and leadership teams stay very true to their vision and execute it in the most effective manner."

Making hard decisions is a vital skill in leadership, so EOS includes a mechanism to facilitate the decision-making that is critical to moving an organization forward. Another key component of EOS revolves around a method for solving problems called IDS, or Identify-Discuss-Solve. "Everyone has issues, and the sooner we identify them, the sooner we can get through them," says Randy. "It's essential that we get to the truth of a situation, even if there's resistance. My best moments are the breakthroughs that come when I decide to 'go there' and take a risk, initiating that hard discussion."

BlueCore Leadership typically works with leadership teams of organizations that fall between $2 and $50 million in revenue, though EOS can be implemented to improve businesses of any size. Its process is typically a two-year journey, and though the details of business problems are typically unique to each organization, the EOS framework is built to address all manner of headwinds. "For example," Randy says, "family businesses often struggle with legacy, expectations, and an inability to be direct and honest with members of the family. 50/50 partners sometimes don't see eye to eye. Husband/wife companies have their own unique dynamics. EOS allows us to understand those dynamics and adjust the flow of a business so entrepreneurs can reach their highest potential."

Internally, Randy has always felt connected to the energy of his entrepreneurial roots, which run deep to the time of his great-great grandfather. In the 1800s, the man started two bakeries in DC that served the Union Army, and Abraham Lincoln himself is quoted as saying, "There's something about their molasses pies!" Those businesses grew into a publically-traded company, Ingredient Technology Corporation (ITC), the multi-million-dollar molasses and sugar refinery business where Randy's grandfather, a dealmaker and people person, served as President. "I think I got some of my entrepreneurial tendencies from watching my grandfather," Randy says. "But even though I never met my great-great grandfather, I do believe there's a piece of his legacy living in me."

Randy was born in Littleton, Colorado, and moved to the small New Jersey town of Mountainside at the age of five. He liked school and sports, playing Little League and obsessing over the Yankees. He also remembers the time he and his brother set their sights on buying a Boonie Bike that they could ride down the hill in their backyard. To raise the money, they sold lightbulbs door-to-door, washed cars, and did yardwork. "Turning that bike on was like starting a lawnmower," he laughs. "It could probably only do 30 miles an hour, but it felt like we were going a hundred! It was so much fun."

Randy's father was a PhD chemist at Mobil Chemical Company, now ExxonMobil. He was often working, and Randy's mother—a stay-at-home mom—was the more dominant figure in the household. "She's from the Bronx, and I picked up from her an element of street smarts," he reflects. "She was always very savvy and able to cut through any "BS." My father is more the classic intellect with a brilliant technical mind, and while I didn't inherit that kind of genius, I got his positivity, kindness, and ability to connect with people."

Randy should have learned that good things can come from surprise curve balls when he made the junior high baseball team, even after a pop fly ball hit him right between the eyes on the last day of tryouts and sent him to the hospital for stitches. But he was devastated when, poised to enter his eighth grade year, he got the news that his father was put in charge of a new acquisition in Taiwan. "I had lots of close friends and was just getting into girls," he says. "Life was good, and then our parents sat us down and broke the news. It felt like someone had just put a knife through my heart. My brother and I weren't even sure where Taiwan was. It was the first time in my life where I realized that things can hit you out of left field, and you have no control over them."

On foreign soil for the first time, Randy distinctly remembers the complicated feelings of guilt he felt living in a nice home while local Taiwanese subsisted in shacks just across the street. It was his first experience with what was then a Third World Country, and that first day, the shock of encountering poverty made him cry. The cost of labor was so low that the family could afford a driver, a cook, and a maid, and he never got over the uncomfortable feeling of such blatantly inequality. "It was a completely different reality, and seeing it made me grow up a lot," he says.

But even in its hardship, living in Taiwan was a deeply positive experience. Randy played soccer, joined the swim team, and attended the Taipei American School. "I remember being very worried that we'd be behind in our studies when we got back to the United States," he says. "As it turns out, we were actually ahead." His father had four weeks of leave each summer, and instead of going home to visit America, the family traveled to Europe, Fiji, and Australia. "I made great friends, experienced whole new cultures, and learned that traveling is a way to open your mind and your heart. I learned about myself and about what it means to be an American in the world. And above all, it taught me that life can throw you curves—sometimes really big ones—and even if you're terrified at first, it just might turn out to be the best thing that ever happens to you."

Of all he encountered, among the most life-changing aspects of his time abroad was the set of Rogers drums, complete with Zildjian cymbals, that he was able to buy for half of what they cost in the US. Randy and a few friends formed a band called Persuasion, sparking his lifelong passion for drumming. They would play at the teen club in town, and Randy will never forget the night they opened for a popular act in a concert hall of 5,000 people. "It was the most exciting thing I've ever done," he exclaims. "Playing drums had been a way of expressing myself with pure, raw energy and emotion. To this day, I have so much gratitude for my parents for letting us practice our hearts out in our basement. That was really an act of love and tolerance on their part. I also remember how our family dog would sit by my side even through those thunderous practice sessions. In this way, drums came to symbolize not only freedom of expression, but also the love and support of my family."

After three years in Taiwan, the family returned to Mountainside for Randy's senior year of high school in 1976. Interested in testing the entrepreneurial waters, he and a Persuasion bandmate, Dave Powell, formed a legal partnership and started a pool service company, purchasing products from a regional wholesaler and selling them for a 200 percent markup. They did pool openings, closings, rental equipment, and other odd service offerings, figuring things out on the fly over their next two years of operation. "We did actually turn a profit, but I'll never forget sitting in our office in Dave's basement, trying to deal with a customer that wouldn't pay us," Randy recounts. "I couldn't believe something like that could happen. It resulted in our first write off."

College planning wasn't a focus in Randy's family, and upon graduating, he found himself at a lax institution where students were more interested in skiing than studying. "I began to realize, wow, maybe I actually want more than I think I want," he recounts. "I saw that I hadn't done enough to take responsibility for where my life was going, so I transferred to the University of Delaware." At the advice of the guidance counselor, he signed up for economics, accounting, statistics, computer science, and engineers' calculus—an incredibly difficult course load that almost killed him. "I found a happy medium the following semester," he says. "But the defining moment of that experience was the choice to take responsibility and the importance of taking charge. I was right to transfer, but wrong to take the guidance counselor's advice without questioning it. I didn't even know until halfway through the calculus course that it was for engineers, when I was a business major!"

After graduating with a Bachelor of Science in Business Administration with a concentration in Finance, Randy got his first job at ITC, the large publically-traded company that had evolved from his great-great grandfather's bakeries. "Because I had the Taussig name, I really had to prove myself," he recalls. "But it was really incredible to be there during a period where they were growing through the rapid acquisition of small, privately-owned food ingredient companies. It was my first exposure to the world of small businesses and acquisition."

While working at ITC, Randy took night classes at Rider University to complete his MBA. He then took a position at one of ITC's newly-acquired companies, a manufacturing business, to run their marketing. When ITC sold that division to a German company, Randy decided to stick with the jettisoned division, marking his departure from the family business. He spent the next twelve years working his way up at Sued Chemie Performance Packaging, maneuvering his way through several high-stakes nail-biters and ultimately running marketing and sales for an international division.

When Randy was ready for his next challenge, he landed at Packexpo.com, a startup in the packaging industry at the end of the dotcom boom. As the VP of Business Development, he focused on landing large clients to raise their valuation—a star-crossed mission, given the timing of the ensuing bust. In 2002, he founded Taumark Systems to provide marketing services to small businesses. "That company was profitable but challenging because every project was different," he says. "I decided it wasn't a good model. When I got called for a VP of Sales & Marketing job in 2008, I decided to take it."

While Randy enjoyed the work, he couldn't shake the feeling that he was adjusting his skills to fit a conventional job mold. Then, in 2011, a client-turned-EOS implementer gave him a copy of *Traction*. "As it did with so many people, the book really resonated with me," he says. "I loved the simplicity of it and truly felt it was a game changing roadmap for small entrepreneurial businesses."

The following year, Randy decided to confront his fears and start his own business—one that would plunge him back into an entrepreneurial life while helping others with theirs. There were hard times, but at the end of the day, his excitement for the work—coupled with a core belief in himself—kept him moving forward. "Too often, entrepreneurs are stifled or lost when they find out how hard it is to run a business," he says. "But if you can give them tools and encouragement, surround them with good people, and say 'keep the dream alive,' you empower them to embrace their genius and bring their vision to life. I know that for me, I'm at my best when I'm driven by opportunity and excited about what's possible. That's the experience I work to create for others."

Perhaps inspired by his passion for flying, Randy's entrepreneurial journey has been a wild one, and the ride has been accompanied by his beautiful daughter and by his partner of sixteen years, Mary. "While she's a healthy skeptic when she needs to be to help me stay grounded, Mary has been absolutely supportive along the way," he says. "We want the best for each other, and though she spent her career in Federal and County government, she's always been very interested in entrepreneurship. In fact she ran a county program to prevent child abuse, which had a lot of entrepreneurial elements to it. We're a good balance."

Today, Randy remains a dedicated student of the EOS process, attending quarterly collaborative exchanges in Detroit and always looking for ways to explore its nuances. An inclusive, collaborative leader, he strives to engage others so the overall process benefits from the strengths of all involved. He's innately compelled to fix whatever problem he encounters, but he also has the wisdom to recognize that not all problems need fixing. In his work with clients, he's a teacher and coach, pushing entrepreneurs to be their best. "I love working with clients that have ideas sparked by necessity, or excitement, or their own genius," he says. "They take risks, and they fall. They've taken falls that some people would feel were the end of the world. But they get back up, take responsibility, and embrace the power of their own genius to persevere."

In advising young people entering the working world today, Randy cautions against the kind of victim mentality that leads people to believe they aren't in control of their own lives. "From Day One, take complete responsibility for your path and realize that you're always the one in the driver's seat, no matter where the road leads or how rough it gets," he says. "Take the time to understand and embrace your own intelligence. Guard against complacency, because you could miss an important opportunity. Take charge of your destiny and embrace adversity, because there's probably something really great if you can make it to the other side. And never forget—you're a genius."

BERNHARDT
WEALTH MANAGEMENT

Paul Thieberger

Where the Buck Stops

Every year, you can be sure it will rain on the day Paul Thieberger and his wife, Pamela, host the annual ServiceSource picnic at their home in Northern Virginia. But nothing dampens the fun and enthusiasm of the guests—around a hundred families of individuals with disabilities—who come to take a break from the daily grind and celebrate life and togetherness. "I've known a lot of these folks since we were kids, and we love ServiceSource in its mission to provide the disabilities community with everything from jobs and housing to friendship and community," Paul says. "I can't tell you what a difference it makes for them to get to go to work, spend time with friends, and live a meaningful life."

The ServiceSource Family and Friends Picnic is labor of love and a grand do-it-yourself effort that brings the whole community together. Paul puts up his own tents and tables, while a friend gets a discount on chair rentals. Some friends help flip burgers, others man the face painting station, and many others help out wherever they are needed. Most years, there are as many friends as there are participants, and Paul couldn't do it without them. "Over the years, it's taken on a life of its own," he says. "I'm so proud of my family and friends, and the way they come together each year to make it happen. Even our young Granddaughters, Lacie and Keira, help out in a big way."

Paul's parents helped launch ServiceSource in the 1970s in an effort to build support and community for people like Paul's two sisters, who were both born with Down Syndrome. "Back then, one of the very few options for help was an institution, and those were terrifying places," he says. "You wanted better for your family members, so my parents joined with other families and helped build better."

The Thiebergers used to host big gatherings for the group down on their farm near Charlottesville, sometimes with hot air balloon rides. But as Paul's parents' generation aged, the social events ceased. That's why Paul and Pam started going to meetings and decided to take on the annual picnic themselves.

Today, as a Chairman of the organization's operating board, Paul also tries to visit and support its branches across the country, attending numerous ServiceSource events in Colorado, Delaware, Florida, and elsewhere. "They've done so much for my sisters and my family," he says. "I love to see the incredible things our members are doing to serve and support people with disabilities."

Paul is also the President of K&B Plumbing and Heating, founded in 1972 by Bill Minnick as part of consortium comprised of an HVAC, plumbing, electrical, and general contracting company. While the electrical and general contracting divisions eventually closed up shop, the HVAC (BILMIN Company) and plumbing division persevered. Paul came onboard in 1984 after answering an ad in the *Washington Post*, when the company had only one other employee and somewhat strained relationships with vendors. "Had I known how bad it was at the time,

I probably wouldn't have taken the job," he laughs. "But thankfully I stuck it out."

On paper, K&B Plumbing could be doing even better if Paul prioritized the company's bottom line. But his top priorities are the people that work for him and the families they support. "I could have been more selfish over the years and made quite a bit more money, but we've always had people depending on us for paychecks," he remarks. "I also thought about going off to start my own company before Bill left, but loyalty really bound me to the legacy he started. I was also able to build up good will and valuable relationships to go along with the infrastructure we already had in place, All these factors became the inertia that kept me at K&B Plumbing."

Today, K&B Plumbing specializes in commercial work and remodeling. Their project sizes range from $1,000 to over $2 million, and they've worked in almost every office building in the DC metropolitan area through their partnerships with general contractors. And just as he enjoys leadership at ServiceSource, Paul is truly in his element as a leader in the construction industry. "I love being a business owner," he says. "You have more possibilities than if you worked for somebody else. You have freedom and agency. With that comes responsibility, stress, and constant work, but there's something very rewarding and compelling about knowing that at the end of the day, the buck stops with you."

Paul's deep perseverance and resilience perhaps stems from his father, born in Vienna, Austria, where his family—of a quarter-Jewish ancestry—owned a prosperous lumber yard. Adolf Hitler's influence was on the rise, and when Paul's father came home one day at the age of thirteen wearing a Nazi brown-shirt uniform, his mother saw the writing on the wall. She sent him on a Quaker Boat to England, where he lived on his own for several years. Finally, at the age of sixteen, he immigrated to America with his mother, passing through Ellis Island and settling in Scranton, Pennsylvania. Two years later, in 1943, he joined the Army and was sent to assist with the Nuremberg Trials as a

German interpreter. He then attended Pennsylvania State University on the GI Bill, later working for the Federal Aviation Administration and the Department of Defense. His final job was as an international logistics negotiator in the Middle East, where he was held hostage in Jordan by Yasser Arafat of the Palestinian Liberation Organization. "For my father, a hand shake was as good as an iron-clad contract," Paul says. "He was a true model for honesty, perseverance, and service to others."

Paul's mother came to DC during World War II as part of the "lipstick brigade"—a wave of women drawn in to work government jobs in support of the war effort. She was working for the Navy when she met Paul's father, and after Paul was born, she stayed at home to care for the children. "She was always very grounded," Paul remembers. "I watched her take care of my sisters for years and refuse to listen to the doctors who said she and my father should put them in an institution. My father, as well, worked so hard and was extremely selfless, always showing such dedication to us kids. My parents taught me that family was everything, and that you don't shun your family just because there's a problem."

A native Washingtonian born in 1958, Paul grew up in Suitland, Maryland, until kindergarten and then moved to Alexandria near Mount Vernon. "The whole neighborhood was full of kids," he remembers. "We'd leave home on Saturday morning as soon as we finished breakfast and didn't come back till dark, spending our days playing in the woods or swimming in the river." The most defining aspect of his childhood, however, was his sisters. At a young age, Paul was more than a brother—he was a patient caregiver, a strong defender, and a calm in the storm when situations grew stressful and chaotic. "Having them in my life made me a more tolerant, caring person," he affirms. "Things people found unusual and shied away from, were just completely normal to me. I understood that there are folks out there that need my help, and from an early age, I was determined to give that help."

Paul's father was Scout Master for his Cub Scout and Boy Scout troops, and Paul remembers observing his deft negotiating and leadership skills in managing the strong personalities of the other fathers in the group. "When there was a disagreement, he would speak firmly to these other guys, some of whom were pretty high-ranking in the military," Paul says. "He would say, 'General, I respect everything you've done in life, but you all put me in charge of this troop, so this is how we're going to do it.' The experiences were designed for us boys to hone our leadership skills too and see how it felt to be in charge, and the dads really let us do our thing and lead the younger kids. They let us go to flourish or fall on our faces, offering guidance along the way." In many ways, the experience would parallel the "freedom to fly or fall" environment he experienced when he first came to K&B Plumbing.

Growing up, Paul volunteered often at the Special Olympics with his sisters, and he always seemed to have a part time job somewhere. He shoveled driveways, had a paper route, and later worked at restaurants. He also volunteered from a very young age at Fairfax County's summer special education recreation program—a great experience that helped shape his future—and worked for four summers at Camp Tapawingo, a residential camp in Manassas, Virginia. "Given the restrictions and regulations around disability care today, I wouldn't be able to have the same opportunities if I was growing up now," he says. "But I'm so glad I had those experience when I did. They taught me to take charge of things and to be a leader in times of crisis, like when an individual in my care stuck their hand through a window and bled profusely. I learned that you don't think twice, and you don't let the stress get to you. You just step up and do what needs to be done. I also learned to never underestimate what teenagers are capable of."

Paul played baseball and soccer through high school, enjoyed his coursework to an extent, and belonged to the United Methodist Youth Fellowship. He was more social than academic, with friendships that spanned groups and social circles. Every summer through high school, he worked in special education somehow, and he always imagined he'd go to college and pursue a career in the field.

When he graduated from high school in 1976, Paul drove cross-country with a friend in a Volkswagen Beetle, visiting friends at 20 or 30 different colleges to get a better idea of where he might want to pursue his own education. "We had a lot of free meals and free nights on dorm room floors, and we ended the journey on a rooftop in San Francisco overlooking the Bay and Alcatraz," he remembers. "And despite all the campuses I saw, I most enjoyed the week we spent on a friend's ranch in Idaho putting in fence posts to pick up a few extra dollars. I decided blue collar was more my style."

By the time he returned to the DC area that fall, Paul knew he didn't want to go to college. His father wasn't happy about the decision, but he never judged his son or tried to push him in a different direction. With that, Paul took a part-time job connecting returning Vietnam War veterans with classes in the building trades, enjoying it so much that he decided to walk up the street one day to a nearby construction site and ask for a job. "It was a residential subdivision where they were building houses," he says. "Someone told me that if I wanted a job on a construction site, I had be standing there before they started in the morning. If someone was late or didn't show, they might put me in. So that's what I did. The plumbers hired me, and that was it."

While working for one of the biggest construction companies in the area, Paul entered into a plumbing apprenticeship program and began driving twice a week from Springfield to Greenbelt to take night classes toward his Master Plumber license, which he completed in 1982. He later got additional licenses for DC, Delaware, Richmond, and two jurisdictions in Maryland—each an important stepping stone along the path to owning his own company. "Today, I take as much continuing education I can," he says. "I also make a point to offer those opportunities to my employees, whether it's apprentice programs or English as a Second Language classes."

After several years, Paul went to work for a one-man plumbing operation owned by two non-plumbers who knew nothing about the construction business. It was a college education in hard knocks, and Paul gained invaluable experience with contracts and other aspects of the work. After several years of working 80-hour weeks, he decided he was ready for a change, making the switch to K&B Plumbing.

When Paul first joined the company, it was focused only on commercial work. And almost from day one, the buck stopped with him. "It was a highly entrepreneurial setting where you could go like hell, as long as you could make payroll," he says. "Once you understood the importance of cash flow, there was a lot of leeway."

In a short time, Bill let Paul run the plumbing company as its General Manager, while Dave Kerrigan took responsibility at K&B's quasi- partner company, Bilmin HVAC. "Bill was very good to us," Paul affirms. When he retired in 2000, Paul and Dave bought the two companies, which remain tied together today through shared staff and offices.

The Great Recession marked ten years of trying economic conditions for K&B Plumbing, but fortunately they were able sustain operations, thanks in no small part to help from Dave Kerrigan and the fact that Paul was able to put some of his own money back into the company. When their bank froze their credit line, BB&T bank saw value in the company and extended a much larger line of credit. "Our banker used to drop by our office to sign papers and chat," Paul recalls. "Things don't work like that anymore, unfortunately. Those were sleepless nights, for sure. Some people told me to walk away, but I just couldn't go through with something like that."

Today, as a leader, Paul believes in delegating but following up, and trusting but verifying. He gives others the space and freedom to excel in their own way, and continually strives to be a better communicator. "I assume people are on the same wavelength, but that's rarely the case," he acknowledges.

Just as it was when he was young, family remains the defining factor in Paul's life, with his world revolving first and foremost around the woman he met years ago as just a pretty voice on the other end of the phone line. Pamela used to work as the answering service for the emergency line at Paul's first construction company job, and when he would get a beep on his pager, he'd call in to her. "She had a nice voice, so eventually I asked her out," he laughs. "After some begging, she finally said okay, and the rest is history." Pam became a special ed teacher, doing the work Paul had once thought would be the centerpiece of his own professional career. She later retired to help care for Paul's mother and two disabled sisters, a full-time job in itself. "My wife is an angel," he says. "She's always been so supportive, even when I worked long, crazy hours when our three kids were young."

One of Paul's sons now works alongside him at K&B Plumbing. His other son is in sales, while his daughter followed in Pam's footsteps with a profession in special ed. Paul is on the board of Rising Hope Mission Church and the Lorton Community Action Center, both in southern Fairfax County, where Pam also volunteers.

In advising young people entering the working world today, Paul underscores the importance of hard work and tenacity. "Turn your hat around, pull your pants up, and go to work every day," he says with a smile. "If you work forty hours a week and do what your boss asks without complaining, chances are, you'll do pretty well in life. If you have to work a few hours beyond that, don't go looking for overtime. There will be things you don't like about it, but that's just how it is. Go to work every single day with no excuses, and you'll be just fine."

Beyond that, Paul's work has been defined by a leadership style that compels him to accept responsibility and ownership of challenges, even when he doesn't have to. From his refusal to turn his back on his employees, to his commitment to ensure the legacy of ServiceSource, his quiet fortitude echoes the adjectives enshrined in his father's old Boy Scout Handbook: trustworthy, loyal, helpful, courteous, kind, obedient, cheerful, thrifty, brave, clean, reverent. "My father lived all those things," he affirms. "I try to live them, and I watched my own kids embrace them when I was their Scout Leader."

With these qualities, Paul is steady and reliable—a source of strength for the employees that look to him for their livelihoods, and the ServiceSource community that knows he will always speak out for them. They know he will be the one to stand before policymakers and politicians at advocacy hearings to tell the ServiceSource story, and he will be the one to make sure the annual picnic happens again and again. He's where the buck stops.

To Paul, it's all worth it when he glances at the hand-carved plank of wood from a young cub scout—a gift "for being a grate leader." It's worth it when he sees the happiness and success of his family. And it's worth it when he reads the notes of gratitude from the people counting on him, like the letter from Hailey that reads, "To: The Thieberger Family. Thank you for having me at your beautiful farm and residence. I had so much fun at the picnic. See you again next year!"

BERNHARDT
WEALTH MANAGEMENT

Jenni Utz

The Compass Within

When Jenni Utz was sixteen years old, she took control of her own destiny and made a choice that would change her life forever. During her Christmas break from school, she decided to go stay with her father, the man who had been largely cut out of her life since her parents' divorce three years earlier.

Growing up, Jenni always thought she had a perfect family. Hers was the home where her friends most loved to congregate. She was thirteen when the tone took a dramatic shift. Fighting broke out, and when things fell apart completely, she and her brother and sister were forbidden from seeing their father except on very rare occasions.

Jenni, however, had never been one to relinquish her agency and independence to others. In time, she decided she wanted to get to know her father in earnest and on her own terms. When their Christmas break together came to an end, she decided she wanted to stay permanently.

If she hadn't followed her own heart and judgment, she may never have gotten to know the person who became one of the greatest, most positive influences on her life.

As time passed, Jenni and her father grew closer and closer. At high school basketball and football games, she preferred his company over that of her friends. She loved hanging out with him on the weekends. He was a Maryland State Trooper, and six months into their time living together, she decided to take a snapshot of him standing by his police car. A couple days later, on a Friday, Jenni left for a church retreat in remote West Virginia, while her father left for work.

That day, he pulled over a speeding vehicle on the beltway. As he was standing outside the car waiting for the person's license and registration, a drunk driver passing by swerved and sideswiped the car. Jenni's father was pulled under the vehicle, and as it spun back out and sped away, he was left all but dead in the middle of the highway.

One bystander followed the drunk driver, who had no idea he had just mowed down a dedicated community leader and shattered countless lives in the process. Another person pulled Jenni's father off the road while the ambulance came. He was rushed to the hospital in critical condition to undergo a series of surgeries in a dramatic race to save his life.

It wasn't until the next day, when Jenni received a call on the camp's main phone line from her grandmother, that she was filled in on the severity of the situation. The state police helicopter almost came to get her, but her mother told them not to, so there was no way for her to get home until the bus came on Sunday. "I remember just sitting in the bunkroom crying," Jenni says today. "I had no idea what was going on or if he was going to be okay. Nothing could have prepared me for the experience of walking into his hospital room the next day."

When Jenni saw her father, he was unrecognizable—swollen, completely black, hard to the touch, and unconscious. For the next two weeks, as he fought his way back to life in the shock trauma ward of the hospital, Jenni moved in with the family of her pastor. A state trooper picked her up each day to take her to the hospital, allowing her to stay as long as she needed. "I was so exhausted," she recalls. "I wanted to be polite and conversational for those rides, but the greatest gift was when I could just put my seat back and sleep."

Beyond his work as a dedicated state trooper, Jenni's father had been a long-time volunteer at the Westminster Fire Department, where he served as the fire chief. They were the ones who transported him from shock trauma back home, where a hospital bed had been set up in their living room. "When people talk about the brotherhood in the state police and the fire department, they truly mean it, for better or for worse," Jenni says. "They truly took care of him."

But it was sixteen-year-old Jenni that served as her father's primary caretaker through the next eight months of intensive therapy and grueling recovery. "My father had always been so strong, so invincible," she reflects. "Seeing him in a hospital bed, with no ability to do anything for himself, was incredibly difficult. It was an experience that helped me grow up fast, and also reinforced my resolve to trust my instincts and follow my sense of what's right for me and my family."

Those instincts came into play again shortly after she graduated from college five years later, when her father and sister happened to be taking a course to earn their real estate licenses. "I figured, why not join them in the adventure and make it a team effort?" she says. Her father found that he loved the sales aspect of the work, while Jenni was drawn to operations and the business side of residential real estate. In 2009, with her father's help and support, UTZ Properties was founded. She has spent the last eight years serving as founder and President, leading the company to success according to the internal compass that has never steered her wrong.

While that compass has led her to undertake some bold and daring entrepreneurial journeys through life, all have taken place within the lines of Westminster County, Maryland, where she's lived since she was born. "In Westminster, everyone knows an Utz," she says proudly, alluding to her grandmother and grandfather's service as Chief Judge on the County's Orphans Court, as well as her father's current stint as Mayor. Growing up the middle of three children, she remembers that she and her sister gave up on dolls early on, when her brother ripped all the heads off their Barbies. Instead, they spent long days playing outside, running around with walkie talkies and building forts with friends.

Growing up, Jenni remembers how her mother was a good listener who was always there for her children and made sure they were taken care of. Her father, a visionary who was always posing and pursuing forward-thinking ideas, often worked multiple jobs. They lived close to their grandparents and would often visit to swim and play with cousins. Jenni also had a large circle of friends she knew through regular church attendance, where she learned the kind of moral and ethical standards that last a lifetime.

Jenni was an honor roll student at school, but she was always testing the limits. Anytime she was told she couldn't do something, she asked why until she got an answer that made sense to her. If she wasn't convinced, she did things her own way. If she didn't see the value of certain classes at school, she didn't see the point of fully investing herself. Even in those moments, her parents rarely scolded her. "They knew it had to be me to decide to fix it on my own," she says. "They rarely interfered and let me do as I saw best, which created a sense of independence, responsibility, and good judgment, now defining aspects of my personality."

Jenni was a tomboy from an early age, and sports played a pivotal role in the development of her character and leadership. She played football, soccer, and basketball with the neighborhood kids, holding her own with the boys and often beating them. She began playing softball at age eight and joined the traveling team at age ten, which meant up to ten games in a single weekend. On that team, she formed a core group of five girls—short stop, third baseman, first baseman, outfielder, and Jenni as pitcher—that played together all through her formative years. "We were incredibly close and had a blast together," she says.

To help their daughter master skill and precision, Jenni's parents set up a five-gallon bucket in the backyard and let Jenni practice pitching dozens upon dozens of eggs. If she didn't make the pitch into the gallon, which was smaller than her strike zone in softball, she wouldn't strike the batter out. She practiced pitching balls through the rungs of a ladder, mastering arc. She had one coach who was a particularly good influence, and who also coached her travel basketball team. "I remember laying on the court floor side by side, practicing shooting motions with our hands, making sure our gestures were sending the ball in the right direction," she says. "He was always coming up with new ways to help us hone our craft. We made it into the world series, and we went undefeated in some years. I loved it; sports were my life."

Thanks to this rigorous commitment, Jenni became an all-star pitcher, embracing her role as the leader of the team—always cognizant of every player on the field, and always directing the team to victory. When she entered high school her athleticism and leadership translated well into field hockey, which she picked up her freshman year of high school. By her sophomore year, she had made varsity—a testament to her commitment to throwing 100 percent into any task she picks up.

This steady rise in sports was brought to an abrupt halt with her father's tragic accident. After eight months of recovery, he was able to return to work in a desk job, but things never truly went back to normal. School was the last thing on Jenni's mind at that point, and though she still got good grades, she was able to retain information only long enough to get through her tests. With the weight of the world on her shoulders, it was hard to concentrate and learn, and even harder to relate to the teenagers around her who were living normal lives with normal issues. "I was no longer interested in boyfriend drama and the typical things high schoolers are concerned about," she recalls. Though she often missed school to care for her father, she managed to graduate a year early, eager to leave the trauma of her high school years behind and move on with her life.

Jenni started college at McDaniel College, where her mother worked, with goals of becoming a physician's assistant. She enrolled in tough biology classes that prompted her to give up field hockey, but soon decided to switch to a dual degree in business and economics. She also joined a sorority when she moved on campus for her junior year. "I made great friends who I'm still very close with today," she says. "Those years were a time for me to recuperate after my father's accident."

Things got tough in her senior year, when her mother decided not to sign the paperwork that would allow Jenni to get free tuition under the employment agreement she had with the college. Jenni had to struggle to pull together student loans, but she made it to graduation. She continued the process of growing up after college, and still remembers vividly the time an erroneous charge popped up on her first credit card. "I didn't know what to do, so my dad told me to put on my big girl panties, call them up, and stand my ground," she laughs. "As funny and trivial as it sounds, that was a turning point for me. From then on, I was really empowered in my vision of how things were going to be. If things weren't right, I was going to make them right."

Jenni made her foray into the professional world in a job with a telemarketing mortgage company, which first sparked her interest in real estate. She obtained her residential real estate license, and though she loved the sector, she found she was less than impressed by the leadership style and company cultures of the various businesses she encountered. "My dad and I would work as a team under a given company, and would assemble our own team of realtors under us," she recounts. "He would be out selling, while I would run everything. We set up our own systems within our team and made sure they matched the company's policies and procedures, which only worked as long as the company itself followed them. Surprisingly, they didn't always do that."

Jenni particularly remembers an instance when she approached the owner of a company to ask why he hadn't followed his own rules. He told her that he had changed the rules, but never told anyone. In fact, the revised guidelines were sitting at home on his printer at the time of the conversation. "In my opinion, that was no way to run a company," she says. "If you expect people to follow your policies and procedures, of course you need to let them know what those rules are! I decided to get my broker's license so I could start my own company, where I could set my own tone for how to do things."

With that, Jenni launched UTZ Properties as UTZ Real Estate in 2009, which happened to land her entrepreneurial efforts square in the aftermath of the housing market crash. Fortunately, she and her father had always marketed and branded themselves as Team Utz Real Estate—professionals committed to excellence. They maintained this brand as they transitioned out on their own, keeping the same logo and color scheme to help with brand recognition and consistency. "All we knew at that point was how to work hard, and that we could no longer put out a listing and expect it to sell in a day," she recounts. "We had to hustle."

Jenni threw herself into the challenge, mastering the systems, procedures, marketing, and advertising pieces needed for success while her father built a team of realtors. They sold very well those first couple years, but noted an influx of calls looking for rental assistance. They kept turning them away until a lightbulb went off and they decided to tailor their offerings to market demand, launching UTZ Property Management in 2011 to supplement the work they were doing through UTZ Real Estate. They brought on additional staff for the new division and purchased a small property management company to increase their portfolio, venturing into homeowner's association (HOA) and condominium management.

Through that time, Jenni continued to pursue her own education and skills mastery, pursuing classes and designations to advance her expertise. "I'm a firm believer that, if you don't know what you're doing, you can't do justice to whatever task sits before you," she says. "It's important to me to do things justice. Whatever I commit to, I give it a hundred percent and always strive to do my absolute best. And I couldn't have done it without late-night discussions with my father, who has always been my sounding board and biggest supporter. No matter what happens, he's always been my constant, telling me I can achieve and succeed at anything I put my mind to."

Jenni responded to market demand again when she struggled to find reliable maintenance services staff to serve their property management company. She launched UTZ Handyman and Remodeling in 2011 as well, and today, that division does just as much business as the other two divisions. Demand for remodeling work has been especially high, and UTZ now employs four full-time employees that accommodate a steady stream of home remodeling work. "Each of our divisions has blossomed into their own strong companies, with fourteen employees total," Jenni says. "We've had strong growth of 20 to 35 percent every year since we launched, and we don't plan on changing that track record of success any time soon."

Along with overseeing the smooth functioning of those divisions, Jenni now focuses her time on growth prospects, with an eye to acquisitions in Maryland, Southern Pennsylvania, and Northern Virginia. As a leader, she is oriented around a sense of gratitude for the trustworthy, reliable, committed team that enable Utz's success every day. "You can't be a leader without having great people underneath you," she affirms. "I'm grateful for them, for my father's unwavering belief in me, and for the opportunity in general." Her leadership and vision have landed her recognition as a National Association of Realtors 30 Under 30, *Baltimore Business Journal's* 40 Under 40, National Association of Professional Women's Woman of the Year, and Maryland Chamber of Commerce Small Business of the Year.

These days, Jenni's internal compass has led her through an amicable divorce with the father of her son and daughter—a friend she has known since the age of sixteen. She now lives in a beautiful home on fourteen acres of land, where she treasures the life she has with her partner and children. "I love that I can come home at the end of a busy day and just clear my head," she says. "Instead of traffic and neighbors, we have chickens, dogs, cats, and solitude. That's my work life balance. I'm a big family person, and I love hosting dinners to get everyone together."

In advising young people entering the working world today, Jenni warns against the dangers of an entitlement attitude. "You don't deserve anything unless you earn it," she says. "Just as importantly, if you have a vision, don't' give up on it. There was a time I was making $9,000 a year, living on ramen noodles and peanut butter sandwiches because I knew what my end result was going to be, and I was going to do everything I needed to do to get there. Achieving success doesn't happen overnight, but if you're willing to work hard and overcome obstacles, staying true to your own compass and your own path, you'll get there."

BERNHARDT
WEALTH MANAGEMENT

Charles Vollmer

Reinventing the Future

In the fall of 1977, Charles Vollmer appeared to have it all—a highly decorated fighter pilot, awarded six Distinguished Flying Crosses and eleven Air Medals during his 175 combat missions in the Vietnam War, and married to his high school sweetheart, a beautiful and loving woman. Other men on the base looked up to him, and the General considered him one of the best. But all was not well. "I was just hollow," Chuck says today. "Something was missing. I was recognized but not fulfilled."

One night that fall, walking alone and depressed down a dank street in Yokota, Japan, Chuck looked up and challenged God. "If you're up there, prove you exist," he muttered indignantly. The next day, he reported for duty as usual, but something was very different. The General, typically friendly and on Chuck's side, had bad news. Rather than heading for a cockpit position, Chuck was told to go to the command post.

"Command post duty was a demotion," Chuck explains. "I was outraged. How could this be? It was a job that anyone could do—a job beneath me." With that, despite being something of a star on the base, Chuck was sent to cool his heels for a year in a highly-secured basement facility.

Down in the command post, Chuck encountered a seasoned Master Sergeant who sat quietly reading a Bible. "You actually believe that crap?" Chuck scoffed. "That got me a harrumph," he recalls. "He thought I was a jerk, and he wasn't wrong." Day after day, the 12-hour shift passed in silence. Finally, bored out of his mind, Chuck accepted his own copy of a Bible as a gift from the sergeant's wife, and began to read it.

Two months went by with Chuck challenging virtually every passage of Scripture that pricked his heart. Then one night in his apartment, Chuck was jolted awake at two in the morning by an apparition. "Christ appeared to me," he says, of that transformative moment. "He told me I had been granted two months of instruction, answered questions, and a few minor miracles. Now, it was time to choose or reject Him." Chagrined, Chuck asked this divine interloper, "If I accept Your offer, do I have to become a Holy Roller?"—a roll that he was reticent to take. To his surprise, Jesus chuckled and said, "I want you just as you are."

From that moment on, as the fighter pilot who become one of His squadron's black sheep, Chuck developed a deep but unconventional relationship with God. "I tend to be an anti-establishment kind of guy, and I'm not very religious," he explains. "But I tried to understand Jesus and what made him tick. Why was the Firstborn of creation born in the flesh in a lowly barn? Why did he choose a path of suffering, sacrifice and servitude? Why did he hang out with the marginalized? And, why did He speak truth to power in such a way that led to ridicule and His execution? Through these and many other questions, I slowly yielded to His way and allowed Him to orchestrate a future that He designed specifically for me."

Over the ensuing years, Chuck pursued a deepening and often turbulent relationship with his Mentor, maintaining an authenticity that others often sacrifice for religious conformity. He still carries that same Bible, dog-eared and falling apart. And, by grounding himself in his faith, Chuck's life took on a new purpose. "The world's rewards are prestige, passion, power and wealth, which are adornments to the outside of the cup but never filling," he says. "In the four decades since that night in Japan, I've learned that God's rewards are love, joy, peace, patience, kindness, goodness, gentleness, faithfulness and self-control—all things that didn't come naturally to me—and if I allowed His transformation, I could make an impact by tending to the needs of others."

Though Chuck had, in a sense, found his way home, his path was anything but straight. Over the decades, his professional path took him from fighter pilot; to test pilot; to aerospace engineer, designer and marketer; to corporate executive; to international consultant; to serial entrepreneur; to author, as well as a half-dozen side trips to miscellaneous misadventures. Eventually, after thirteen different careers, he set his sights on his ultimate legacy: mass-producing small businesses and millions of new jobs at the base of America's socio-economic pyramid. That's the mission—as crucial as it is ambitious—of Jobenomics, the concept Chuck has dedicated his personal and professional legacy to realizing. "Essentially, Jobenomics is a platform with a research library on the economic, community, business, and workforce development challenges facing America," Chuck explains. "While we support big business and government job creation, Jobenomics' top priority is serving the small and self-employed business community that employs 80 percent of all Americans and produced almost 80 percent of all new jobs this decade. We can help startup businesses succeed and restore the American Dream by focusing on the demographics most in need, and with the highest potential—women, minorities, new workforce entrants, veterans and the financially-distressed who want a job or to start a business."

Jobenomics started as a book project in 2007. At the time, Chuck was an advisor to the McCain presidential campaign team. Charged with identifying national security concerns, he drafted a report about the unstable and unsustainable nature of America's economic model. His thesis stated that the poor economic security would prove to be an important national security issue, but the campaign ignored him. "They threw it all in the trash," Chuck recalls. "Disheartened and dejected, I was ready to switch sides and vote for Obama!"

Concerned by the research he had done, Chuck took his findings to Wall Street and began to lecture about sustainable economies and labor force growth. Over the next two years, he researched and wrote what would become the first of many Jobenomics books, reports, articles and blogs that attracted the attention of tens of millions of people. "Before I wrote the first book, I unwittingly predicted many of the structural flaws that precipitated the Great Recession, including the exorbitant use of exotic financial instruments, called derivatives, which played a pivotal role in the sub-prime mortgage crisis," Chuck remembers. "I didn't know the mortgage crisis was going to happen, but I knew the environment, and I see the same risk factors persisting today. Due to sclerotic GDP growth, the dearth of business startups and the hollowing out of the American middle class, the U.S. economy is not sustainable with more citizens departing the labor force than entering. In addition, the U.S. labor force is transitioning from a standard full-time workforce to a contingent workforce replete with part-time, task-oriented, and automated (smart machines and algorithms) workers. Today, contingent workers represent 40 percent of the U.S. workforce and will soon be the dominant form of labor due to rapidly advancing digital and network technologies, adverse and arcane business and job creation practices, and the ethnological or cultural differences of next generation workers. Moreover, our welfare system is becoming an increasingly attractive alternative to workfare in 21st Century America."

Driven by his vision of a stable, safe economy, Chuck continued to produce research and recommendations for highly-scalable business and job creation. He met with over a thousand government, business, and community leaders, incorporating their very best ideas into the Jobenomics body of work. Today, the Jobenomics platform consists of nine books, all authored by Chuck and regularly updated to feature the most current economic and labor force issues, trends, and solutions. It also features special reports on cutting edge issues like international competition, the emerging digital economy, and numerous articles on how the Trump Administration can effectively realize their bold economic vision of 4 percent GDP growth and 25 million new jobs over the next decade.

Over the last decade, over 20 million people have been reached by Jobenomics, and the platform has garnished widespread support for its economic, community, business, and workforce development programs. The Jobenomics.com website receives an average of 30,000 page views each month, with the majority of viewers spending a half hour or more online, not including the amount of time spent reviewing volumes of downloaded material. Jobenomics is advancing four national initiatives, including Energy Technology Revolution, Network Technology Revolution, Urban Mining, and Urban Agriculture. These initiatives aim to assist with modernization of the national economy at a time when too many experts are looking to the past for employment solutions. "You hear a lot of optimistic rhetoric about trying to revitalize manufacturing jobs that will likely be automated or outsourced to the contingent workforce," Chuck points out. "By contrast, Jobenomics has its eyes on the future. Its four focus initiatives have the potential to create tens of millions of new jobs as the digital economy continues to grow, and as our energy and agricultural ecosystems transform."

To date, over a dozen local leaders have launched Jobenomics programs in their own communities to empower women, minorities, youth, veterans, and other disadvantaged populations with tremendous untapped potential. Urban Renewal Jobenomics initiatives are now being considered in impoverished communities in New York City, Baltimore, Phoenix, Charlotte, and Erie. Chuck and his team are also working with national organizations to implement Jobenomics Community-Based Business Generators, which are designed to mass-produce startup businesses and provide skills-based training and certification programs. For instance, its strategic partnership with The Hope Collection will allow Jobenomics to offer over 9,000 online technical training and certification programs. eCyclingUSA, a company where Chuck serves as CEO, is working to recycle waste from used electronics and appliances to generate a revenue streams to pay for skills-based training and microbusiness loans. And his partnership with ACTS Freedom Farms is intended to foster 25,000 veteran-owned micro-farms to create over 100,000 new jobs in the next five years. "The idea is to create jobs within months and careers within a year," Chuck explains. "And we do all this with our sights set on building the sustainable, resilient economy of tomorrow, partnering with organizations like EmeraldPlanet to disseminate best green business practices and deploying green technologies."

Through Jobenomics, Chuck's vision boldly goes where few have gone before—the product of a defiantly independent and contrarian mindset that developed at an early age. He was born on a U.S. air base in Germany, where his father—also a pilot who flew in the Berlin Airlift—was stationed with the post-WWII occupation forces. Five years later, the family moved to Falls Church, Virginia, and relocated again to Lincoln, Nebraska. Chuck was ten when his father passed away of a brain tumor. His mother took the loss extremely hard. "She wasn't ready to be a widow with three kids, with the oldest (me) being particularly hard to handle," Chuck says. "The last words that my father said to me were, 'You are now the man of the house.'"

After Chuck's father died, his mother moved the family to be closer to her relatives in Lewisburg, Pennsylvania. The family struggled to adjust to their new normal. As an adolescent, Chuck knew he needed to become financially independent as soon as possible, so he got a job as a checkout boy at Weis Markets, the local grocery store. The supermarket helped him get a scholarship to Bucknell University, the local college, and Chuck dreamed of one day becoming a manager at one of their local grocery stores. Then fate intervened.

One summer day in 1964, Chuck was bored, hanging out with friends from high school, when a recruitment ad for the military played over the radio. Service Academy try-outs were being held in Harrisburg, a mere 60 miles away, and it was a paid weekend. "I said to my friends, let's go volunteer for this," Chuck remembers. "We'll drink some beer in Harrisburg and have a good time, and it gives us a reason to get out of town." The trip was intended more as a lark than anything, but at the last minute, Chuck's friends bailed. He decided to go on his own, and because he didn't have any distractions, he focused on the battery of tests before him.

Day one was academic testing, and day two was athletics. At the end of the weekend, the attendees were asked to declare. Of all the boys there, he was the only one who didn't have a clue what was going on. "I raised my hand and asked, declare what?" he recalls. "The Sergeant says, 'Well you've got the Army, Navy, Air Force, and Coast Guard.' He talked about Annapolis and West Point. I'd never even heard of them! I knew about the Air Force because of my dad, so that's what I picked. Then they told me I needed to pick a sponsor to get admitted." Chuck again raised his hand and asked, "What is a 'sponsor?" The now exasperated Sergeant replied, "A Congressman, Senator, the Vice President, or the President. Son, why don't you select them all and maybe you'll get lucky?" With that, he shook his head and left.

Months later, in April of 1965, Chuck got a call from his Congressman. He and his mother went to meet him, but were told that Chuck hadn't been accepted. The Congressman brusquely congratulated him, told him to try again next year, and abruptly ushered the Vollmers out of the room. Two months later, unexpectedly, Chuck received a certified letter, this time from President Lyndon Johnson. Much to his surprise, it was a Presidential appointment only weeks before he was expected to report for duty.

By that time, Chuck was dating Trish, his high school sweetheart and future wife. They had met as square dancing partners in sixth grade, but had only recently begun dating. He called Trish and told her he was going to Colorado, to the Air Force Academy. "I hadn't even seen a picture of the Academy," he remembers. "I knew it was Colorado, but I didn't know where. I just got on the airplane! There wasn't any internet then, so I couldn't just Google it. I was thrilled—not because I wanted to be in the military, but because I was curious, excited for an adventure and for relief of the burden of being a failed man-of-the-house."

Chuck, independent-minded, rebellious, and entrepreneurial, never had a true military mindset. After his first year, he thought about quitting. But Trish moved out to Colorado that summer, giving him renewed stamina to knuckle down and see it through. He never made the Dean's List, but he found a more natural fit for his temperament and skills after the academy, when he entered pilot training and found he had a natural knack for flying. What he lacked in subservience, he more than made up for in talent, graduating first in his class. "It was two-thirds flying and one-third academic," he remembers. "I was in the bottom third of my class in academics because I never studied, but I still graduated first."

At the end of flight school training, it was time to fill out what was called a "Dream Sheet" and pick an airplane of his choice due to his class standing. "Trish wanted me to be a 9-to-5 flight training instructor in a place like Phoenix, Arizona," he says. "She thought we could have a nice little life there, so I put that first. Then I put the F-105 Thunderchief second, and the F-4 Phantom as my third choice, both of which were fighter aircraft used in high-threat areas in Vietnam. Seeing a look of consternation on my face, one of my flight school buddies said, 'I know what you're thinking. Don't do it!' He knew that a quiet life wouldn't suit me. So I scratched out Trish's choice of assignments, and I was on my way to South East Asia at the height of the anti-Vietnam War movement."

Shortly thereafter, Chuck began training in the Thunderchief in Wichita, Kansas, but his class was cancelled since most of the F105s in Vietnam had been lost in combat. The Air Force notified him that he was being transferred to bombers. Chuck said no and threatened to relinquish his pilot's wings if they reneged on their fighter pilot promise. The Air Force countered with serious disciplinary action but recanted after higher headquarters decided they needed more Vietnam volunteers, not less, and sent him to an F-4 crash-course pipelined straight to Vietnam.

Six months later, stationed at Korat AFB in Thailand, Chuck was suiting up for his first combat mission. But his squadron commander informed him he'd be riding along in the backseat. Again, Chuck said no and was immediately grounded for insubordination. He had volunteered during a time that few did, trained hard, and insisted on flying in as the pilot in command, the position for which he trained. After two weeks and an unrepentant pilot, the squadron commander gave in. "He said, 'I'll tell you what, I'll let you sit in the front. If you don't screw up, and if you earn their respect, you can stay. But if you screw up, you have to sit in the back.'" Chuck agreed. Had his commander known that he had never flown in overcast conditions and didn't know how to use the aircraft's air-to-air missiles due his crash course in Arizona, he would have changed his mind. Notwithstanding, Chuck adopted a fake-it-till-you-make-it policy and soon distinguished himself as a competent combat pilot, completing 175 combat missions over some of the most highly-defended areas on the planet like Hanoi, which had more anti-aircraft guns than all of Germany in WWII.

After Vietnam, Chuck was sent to be an F-4 instructor in Phoenix, which pleased Trish, who had moved to Bangkok to be near him for most of his tour. After four years in sunny Phoenix, Chuck and Trish moved to a headquarters staff position in Japan and his eventual conversation with God.

After leaving Japan and the Air Force, Chuck considered two vastly different job offers. One was flying 727s for United Airlines, while the other was working as a test pilot at McDonnel Douglas. Drawn to adventure, he decided against piloting commercial jetliners. Over the course of six years at McDonnel Douglas, he transitioned into engineering and ended up on the initial design teams of the F-15E and stealth fighter aircraft. Chuck then managed the marketing team for the F-15E, ultimately helping the company close a $32 billion deal with the U.S. Air Force.

Shortly thereafter, General Dynamics, a competing firm, recruited Chuck. He was hired as the Head of Operations Analysis with eleven divisions under him, and charged with Strategic Planning for the entire firm, which was then the largest aerospace corporation in the world. He then founded and headed up the Defense Initiatives Organization (DIO) at General Dynamics, which focused on emerging advanced technology programs.

Then, in 1991, when Chuck was at the top of his game, General Dynamics was sold. The company restructured, and Chuck's advanced technology organization was shuttered. Soon thereafter, Booz Allen, a leading Washington consulting firm, offered Chuck a partner position. In this capacity, he organized a massive industry consortium that was an integral part of history's largest program to privatize 70 percent of former Soviet Union industries. He also formed and led the Community Learning and Information Network program, a forerunner to today's online educational network. Using this experience, he decided to strike out on his own and start his own consulting business.

With that, in 1996, Chuck founded VII Inc., a strategic planning, systems engineering, and investment capital firm serving major government agencies and corporations, both domestically and internationally.

Over the decade that followed, he developed his expertise in many directions as a serial entrepreneur. In 1999, he was retained by the U.S. Central Command to be an "Arab coach," helping to build coalitions in the war on terrorism. Initially reluctant because of his past work with Israel, Chuck ended up accepting the job, immersing himself in counter-terrorism work while learning more about Arab culture and the Middle East. "In addition to conducting dozens of military coalition-building conferences, I started trying to understand their religious and cultural views by studying the Koran and Hadith," he says. "I began to give lectures on Islam in the U.S. to the pleasant surprise of my Arab clients that included Generals, Ministers, Crown Princes and Kings. When 9/11 hit, I was one of the few people in Washington who knew anything about Islam in the Arab world."

It was his lifelong commitment to defense and national security that ultimately put him on the road to Jobenomics. When Washington didn't listen, Chuck spread his message as a sort of "Jobenomics Johnny Appleseed" that grew into a national grassroots movement. Deeply committed to the mission, he has not taken a paycheck in over ten years, and prefers to lead by silent example rather than by authoritative instruction. "If you like what I write, just download it from Jobenomics.com and use it," he says. "I don't like to tell people what to do any more than I like being told what to do."

In advising young people entering the working world today, Chuck reflects on the value of dead-ends. "Looking back, the biggest lessons learned were the things that didn't work out," he says. "I could have shot for a four-star general or CEO position, but as it turns out, hitting road blocks in my careers was the best thing that could have happened to me. It kept me striving, and striving got me here, to what my real ministry and mission was meant to be: helping to bring hope to distressed people and beleaguered communities."

In many ways, he's a triple oxymoron—a combat-hardened fighter pilot, serial entrepreneur, and dedicated Christ follower. Only by drawing on these competing internal traits was he able to conceive of a solution powerful enough to make a difference. And only by straying from the beaten path to follow an ever-changing internal compass was he able to see the needs of others and respond.

Mark Watson

Building Integrity

At age 19, Mark Watson had already been through three major moves, adapting to wildly different geographic locations and cultures. But this fourth and final uprooting, from The Netherlands to Northern Virginia, proved the most difficult of all. "European culture is very community-based, but in Virginia, it was harder to tap into that," he remembers today. "I had already graduated from high school, so I didn't have that entry point to meeting people. I felt completely alone and depressed. I was searching for something, though I didn't know what it was."

Mark was enrolled at Northern Virginia Community College at the time with an interest in international business, and a friend mentioned he was going to a job interview based on a vague advertisement suggesting the ability to make $20,000 in a month. Intrigued, Mark tagged along and found himself interviewing at American Building

Contractors (ABC), a national insurance restoration company working in exterior home improvements like roofing, siding, and gutters. "A bad hailstorm had just hit, and they told us the job would be highly intense, requiring complete dedication," Mark recalls. "Saul, the guy who interviewed us, had this infectious energy and passion for the work. I made the decision that day to drop out of school and take the job."

Mark and his friend were hired as part of a group of ten other workers to canvas for leads and do inspections in territories affected by the storm. By the end of the week, they were the only two left on the team. But Mark was used to outworking the people around him, and he had a clear picture in his head of where he was going. "At first, I drove around in my parents' van carrying a 24-foot extension ladder inside the vehicle with me," he laughs. "I had this vision of being successful, and after seven months, I had made enough money to buy a truck, which meant I could attach the ladder on top. The harder I worked, the more I made, and the more successful I was. The money was good, but more importantly, the job plugged me back into a community through my network of coworkers. It gave me a sense of purpose, success, and confidence again, and it allowed me the freedom to be entrepreneurial. That was a big turning point for me."

Now the cofounder and partner of Exterior Medics Inc., a residential and commercial exterior home improvement and roofing contractor serving the Greater Washington area, Mark is still driven by that strong sense of purpose and service to community, dedicated to building integrity from the ground up in all aspects of life. He and his partner, Joe LeVecchi, had shared a passion for entrepreneurship and the dream of one day starting their own business since they first began working together in 2000. They decided to seriously begin working on a business plan in 2007, and in April of 2008, they made that dream a reality.

There's no shortage of home replacement contractors in the DC metropolitan area, but Exterior Medics sets itself apart through its dedication to going above and beyond. "Exterior Medics was created amidst the greatest economic recession since the Great Depression, but we were committed to making it work," Mark says. "We saw that, too often, companies just send someone out to do home improvement work based on their perception of what the customer needs. They don't know your story, your why, your family, or your plans. We wanted to take a more consultative, collaborative, personal approach to home improvements."

Exterior Medics gets the majority of its work directly from homeowners, and 60 percent of their residential leads come from either a prior customer or a referral—a testament to their long term and enduring relationships. They also work with builders looking to contract out with exceptional partners, and are known for their refusal to cut corners. Recognizing the dramatic innovations taking place in the materials and manufacturing sectors, Mark takes his cues from leading engineers and cutting-edge science when it comes to installing roofing, siding, and windows. "We will never work on a builder's grade level, just meeting minimum requirements," he says. "When we do work, it's meant to last. If you do it right and take the time to figure out how it all fits into the client's story, then you can truly build something of integrity for your clients."

Committed to the highest standards and best quality home improvements, Mark is also driven by the impact Exterior Medics has on the community, beginning with their thirty employees and array of subcontractors. The company's work is only as good as its exceptional team, all brought on for their strong character, drive, and motivation. "I believe in hiring for character and training for skill," Mark says. "I look for people of integrity who are hungry to do more and want a better opportunity. Some are from this great nation, and some immigrated here in the hopes of achieving the American Dream. Some join us as laborers and work their way up to leadership roles, growing and blossoming along with the company. Our company creates opportunities for people who might not otherwise have them, and that's very meaningful to us."

Mark, himself, is one of those people who ultimately came to the U.S. looking for opportunity—though he didn't realize it at the time. He was born in Bedford, England, in 1980, where the majority of his family still resides. His father was a blue-collar roofer who also did gutters and window fittings, while his mother worked odd office and cleaning jobs to help make ends meet. His younger sister, Samantha, was born when he was two. He was very close with his cousins, Iain and Martin, and loved running around the neighborhood riding bikes and playing football (soccer). He did well when he applied himself in school, but he enjoyed socializing with friends and could have focused a bit more on coursework.

When Mark was eight, his maternal grandfather passed away, and a few months later, his parents decided to divorce. It was a tough time for the family, but a turning point that afforded Mark an important world perspective. Divorce is never a happy thing, but it brought life-defining opportunity," he says. "At that time, except for a vacation to New York, I had never been on a plane or out of the country. All of that was about to change."

Mark remembers his mother as a true mainstay for him and his sister, doing whatever it took to support them. They moved to a new town, and their extended family stepped up to help. "I remember going to the post office to collect welfare," he says. "We never went without." Several years after the divorce, Mark's mother met his stepfather, Mark, who was serving in the U.S. Air Force and stationed in England at the time. "I still remember when they told Samantha and I that he was being reassigned to Hawaii," Mark says. "We asked if that meant they were getting married, and they asked us what we thought about that. I was completely naïve at the time about what it would mean to leave, I just thought moving to Hawaii sounded like fun."

The two married in 1991, and in January of 1992, the new family moved to Hawaii, where Mark started sixth grade. When it finally sunk in that they were leaving England and everything he had ever known, things got very tough, but Mark worked through it. "It was a brand-new culture, and through my experience of both diversity and adversity, I began learning a lot more about the world. Opening up to the world taught me a lot about people, and about myself, as I learned how to fit in and connect."

Mark tried baseball for the first time, and though he didn't take to it, he picked up basketball and loved it. Seven months later, as soon as they had begun settling in, that education continued when the family moved to Mississippi. There, he made a concerted effort to lose his British accent and fit in. He cut grass on the weekends to make spending money, and he played basketball on a team for the first time. Two and a half years later, when he was fourteen, they moved again—this time to The Netherlands for five years. "We left the summer before I started high school, which I'm very grateful for, because the schools in Mississippi were not good," he recalls. "I had friends who were up to bad things, and there were a lot of bad influences around."

The Netherlands was yet another dramatically different experience, where he made close friends of all different nationalities. He traveled to Germany, Belgium, France, Switzerland, and elsewhere, expanding his global perspective even further. Through school, he worked as a teacher's assistant in a kindergarten class, and he decided he wanted to become an elementary-level teacher. "When they're that young, kids just absorb everything, and I remember watching these kids transform before my eyes," he recounts. "It had such a positive impact on them, which was very rewarding."

At age sixteen, he got his first job on base at the bowling alley, and transitioned around to different positions at the pizza shop, the taco shop, the hot dog stand, and the Baskin Robbins. Even at that age, he had his own ideas and didn't like taking orders from people. "I took a lot of pride in my positions," he laughs. "I wanted to make the best pizza, or the best cheeseburger. I had a strong sense of responsibility and accountability, and was often trusted to teach others and close up shop at the end of the night. I wanted to do my best, and I outworked most of my colleagues and supervisors."

Mark grew up idolizing his biological father, and didn't give his stepfather much credit. But looking back now, he recognizes the big decision his stepfather made to take on and provide for a ready-made family. His own children from previous relationships, Alex and Amy, would visit on occasion, but he also focused much of his parenting energy on Mark and Samantha. He was always supportive when I had a basketball game, soccer game, or track meet," Mark recalls. "He ran the house kind of like the military, with hard lines and a clear sense of authority. I didn't appreciate those things as a kid, but they definitely kept me out of trouble and taught me to do the right thing. I have a lot of love and respect for him."

Mark was captain of his soccer team during his senior year, which he remembers as an important leadership experience. College was not a priority in Mark's family, and he was never pushed in that direction. When he graduated in 1998, he stayed on as a coach for the high school varsity soccer team, landing them a spot in the European Championships. He also got a job at a German butcher shop, where he observed the pride and work ethic of a job well done. "My parents always taught me to truly value and respect money, and I became very self-sustaining when I turned sixteen. They provided food and shelter, but everything else I wanted was on my dime."

When Mark came to the U.S. at the age of nineteen, he got a job as a laborer on a construction site building a school. He didn't fit in with anyone he was meeting, and he made up his mind that he wasn't going to be happy. "I had decided that I hated it here, and that was that," he recalls. "I really had my blinders on, and all I wanted was to get back to Europe."

All that changed, however, when he took the job at ABC. He spent the next five years of his life focused on building integrity through his sales work, realizing his passion for the business, the opportunity, and the identity it gave him. He enjoyed considerable success at an early age but also went out with friends multiple nights a week, having a little too much fun and picking up the tab for everyone at the end of the evening. On one of those nights, at age 22, he went to dive bar called TJ Reynolds. He met a girl named Mandy who was home visiting from college. "She was poised, smart, with it, and beautiful," he remembers. "I could see that she really had it together and wasn't like the other girls I knew. I knew that if I wasn't driven and doing the right things, I wouldn't win a girl like her."

From that moment on, Mandy became a key influence in his life, inspiring him to take things to the next level. "She was the first person I met that gave me something to work for," he says. "Building my success wasn't just for me anymore—it was also going to be for her, so we could build something together. She's been my foundation and balance ever since, and we now have three amazing daughters—Cara, Evelyn, and Lila. They're a big part of my why."

In 2005, shortly before Mark and Mandy got married, he was driving one day when he heard a familiar voice over the radio. The local sports show, Sports Junkies, had just switched to a new station, and the man on the line could hardly contain his excitement. "I'm so happy to hear you guys back on the radio!" came the voice. "I was so excited that I jumped in my truck without tying down my ladder, and when I started driving, it flew off!"

When Mark realized it was Joe LeVecchi, a colleague who had left ABC several years earlier, he called up his old friend. Joe invited Mark to a party at his house that weekend, where Mark was convinced to come work for Shiner Roofing, where Joe was employed. He and Joe quickly became the top producers on a team of eight salespeople, driven by his passion for relationship building after a lifetime of transitions from one radically-different place to another. They had deep admiration for their boss, Kevin, who set a culture of high ethical and moral standards. But they also had a strong entrepreneurial drive and ideas of their own, and decided to put together their own business plan.

When Mark and Joe decided to strike out on their own, they didn't bring along anyone from their past employer, and they weren't deterred by the state of the economy. "It was just the two of us and a truck, out selling these jobs, and in a way we felt that that put us at an advantage," he explains. "We were getting back to our roots of knocking on doors, putting out flyers, and doing whatever it took to bring in those jobs."

From April to December of that first year, Exterior Medics did an impressive $1 million in business. That number climbed to $2.3 million in their second year, and $4.3 million in their fourth. By 2016, their revenues had reached $10.5 million. "We're proud that we've maintained our margin along the way, running a profitable business and acquiring new talent that makes us better for our clients," Mark reports. In 2014, they had the great honor of receiving *Remodeling Magazine*'s Big50 Award, a recognition of their vision and workplace culture. They've also won a number of other awards and recognitions typically reserved for larger design/build firms, and in 2016 were listed the 178th top remodeling company in the country.

Today, Mark credits his success to the perspective he gained not through formal classroom education, but through lessons learned out in the world. His father still lives in England with Mark's stepmother and three sisters—a window into another life he could have had, if he'd stayed. "I'm grateful to have learned strength from my father, kindness and compassion from my mother, and courage of conviction from my stepfather," he says. "The adventure and success I've achieved today is thanks to where I came from."

As a leader, Mark is an educator committed to walking people through the nuances of a process or task. He is deeply invested in the success of his employees, and never forgets the family he comes home to each night. "Mandy and I actually wear matching bracelets, which remind me always of the bond we share and our life together," he says.

"On those hard days, it's a reminder of what I'm working for. Thinking of that love brings me a lot of joy."

In advising young people entering the working world today, Mark encourages them to find their passion and run with it. Beyond that, he is living proof that our greatest tests can cultivate in us our greatest attributes, and the very qualities that go on to make us most successful. "The big moves I made through my formative years were tough at the time, but they taught me how to meet people, how to fit in, how to listen, and how to appreciate more," he recounts. "That's what commission-based sales is all about, and it is absolutely why I persevered and rose to the top. It didn't matter that I didn't have a college degree; what mattered was my ability to connect and show others how we could build integrity together."

BERNHARDT
WEALTH MANAGEMENT

Jeffrey Weinstock

On the Right Track

After nearly ten years of practicing law, Jeff Weinstock, now the President of the DC staffing firm R & W Group, found himself at a professional crossroads. Life as an attorney was taking its toll physically and emotionally, and he couldn't shake the feeling that he wasn't on the right track. The hours were long, the work was arduous, and while he liked what he did, he found he didn't love it. He disliked spending so much time away from his wonderful wife, Carolyn, and their two young children, especially given his commitment to always put family first. He believed there must be a way to combine his talent for helping people access opportunities, his knowledge of the law, his background in college recruiting, and the connections he'd built throughout his career. There must be a way to create a new opportunity that would allow him to capitalize on those skills and spend more time with family.

Within a year, Jeff found the genesis of those skill sets in an opportunity presented by the Kelly Law Registry, a staffing firm that connects qualified candidates with jobs in the legal services industry. Early on during his time at Kelly, one particular placement cemented his conviction that he was on the right track and had found the perfect career path. "A young woman named Jill walked into the office," he recalls. "The receptionist called me and said, 'I think you're going to want to meet with her.'"

Once Jill sat down with Jeff, she immediately began crying and explained that she had found herself in a desperate financial situation. The small law firm where she worked as an attorney was declaring bankruptcy, and Jill had bills to pay. Although she was an attorney, she was willing to take a paralegal position or anything else that was available since she needed work quickly.

Jeff immediately had something in mind, but he knew it would take some politicking. Kelly was staffing a project for the DC office of a large national firm, and the team needed six attorneys and six paralegals. The attorney spots were filled, but there was still room for one more paralegal. The only issue was the policy of the paralegal manager, Marlene; she never hired attorneys for paralegal work. Undeterred, Jeff called Marlene and worked to sell her on Jill.

"I said, 'I know your policy, but I just have this gut feeling. I think you'll really like her.'" Jeff said. "And Marlene said, 'You know what Jeff, because I know you and you are asking, I'll talk to her. No promises, but I'll talk to her.' At 4:00 PM I got a call from Marlene, who told me they were going to give it a shot. Jill was to start the following Monday as a temporary paralegal."

The paralegal job alone would have been a happy ending to the story, but Marlene called back with more good news the following week. The attorneys loved Jill so much that they had decided to create an additional contract attorney slot on the case, and by the next week, her pay rate was increased as she moved into a temp attorney slot.

Six months later, the project was beginning to wind down, and people were being released. In fact, everyone except for Jill had been released, and Marlene called Jeff to inform him that for the first time ever, the partners chose to retain a temp attorney as a full-time employee. Jill had gone from a temp paralegal to a full-time attorney with a solid firm in mere months—an incredibly rewarding achievement for all involved, and an affirmation that she had found the right track for her.

"Jill called me and wanted to come by," remembers Jeff. "She walked into my office with a big box of chocolates and said, 'I can't thank you enough. I was so depressed when I walked in here last time, but you calmed me down. You don't realize how much you've changed my life.' I still get chills thinking about that. And luckily, that's happened several times since then, for me and for others on my team. It was one of the first times where it really dawned on me that I had been given an incredible opportunity to really help people through my work."

In the years that followed, Jill's story met its elegant coda when she became a full partner at the firm. From temporary paralegal to partner—that's the journey Jeff wants to take qualified candidates on now as the CEO and President of R & W Group, the staffing and placement business he founded in 2009. Today, R & W Group places candidates in legal, administrative, accounting & finance, and IT jobs, in positions both temporary and permanent. R & W Group's team of eight recruiters boast various specialties, with about half of the placements going to law firms. Another large portion of their placements go to other businesses, and the small remainder land at non-profits. Clients range from start-ups to Fortune 50 businesses, including an international supermarket chain, large law firms, and the American Civil Liberties Union.

The success of R & W Group was truly built from the ground up. During his first year running the business, Jeff didn't draw a dime in salary. During his second year, he took only modest compensation. "We were actually profitable within 3 months," Jeff says. "All the money we brought in was put back into the company, though, whether that was buying laptops or starting to hire staff."

Drawing on his prior experience in staffing, Jeff was careful not to repeat management mistakes he had seen working for other agencies. Instead, he established early on the principle that R & W Group would go the extra mile for clients—a striking level of service compared to other staffing agencies that had a more blanket and rigid approach. "We have some clients that want invoices formatted a certain way," Jeff points out. "When I was at other companies, the answer would've been, 'No. This is how we format invoices, and we can't vary it just because one client wants us to.' But at R & W Group, we can. We're small enough and flexible enough that we can go out of the way to make accommodations for our clients."

Additionally, Jeff established several practices designed to optimize the matching process. R & W Group won't submit a resume for a position without explicit approval from the candidate—something other staffing companies often skip in order to get a jump on potential competition. At times, agencies even submit resumes of candidates they haven't spoken to or met with yet. "We want our clients to know that this candidate is interested in their specific position," Jeff explains. "We find that, in the long run, clients will typically say, 'Agency X has sent me this resume, but they know nothing about this candidate, and they don't have the candidate's authorization, so I'm not going to accept resumes from Agency X anymore.' We will never be that agency. Clients know we do things the way they would want us to. We meet with the candidate, make sure they are right for the position, and then get the candidate's authorization to be submitted."

The same sense of commitment to providing quality, specialized service extends to the candidates as well. "We tell our candidates we can't guarantee that we're going to find you a job, but we can guarantee that we're going to help you find a job," Jeff affirms. "I love being in a position where I can help people, like teaching someone how to strengthen their resume or giving interview advice. That kind of assistance doesn't take too much time and can help tremendously, so we make a point to provide those services whenever possible." Jeff also insists on careful accounting and has all candidates as W-2 employees rather than 1099s, a tax workaround sometimes used by other staffing firms.

Jeff's honesty and "can-do" attitude can be traced back through his history to two important influences: his parents. Growing up as the oldest of three on Long Island, some of his earliest memories are of being dropped off at his grandparents on Sundays so his father could study for his law school classes. After graduating, Jeff's father went on to become a tax attorney.

Although he was exposed to the legal profession early on, Jeff hardly found it appealing. "I remember going into my father's office and seeing these books that just looked incredibly boring and saying, 'I don't want to practice law,'" he laughs. "I didn't realize that was accounting, not law. My dad practiced on the accounting side of tax law."

Jeff's mother worked as a speech therapist who took great care to ensure that her children did not pick up her own New York accent. All four of Jeff's grandparents were immigrants from Europe, and both parents were first-generation Americans who demonstrated strong values and remarkable work ethic. "They taught me to never give up," Jeff reflects. "If something is important to you, keep trying. Both of my parents really pushed the importance of family and education. They taught me not to cut corners—a particularly important value when it came to business later on in life."

His parents' emphasis on hard work shaped his fundamental view of the world. For fun, he remembers playing with friends in an era before cell phones, when the only rule was to get home before dark. He played baseball and soccer, ran track, and played trumpet in the high school marching and jazz bands. In his senior year of high school, he began working at Burger King—a position that earned him some extra social stature with his classmates when the restaurant gave him a stack of coupons to share with friends at school.

Family was particularly important to the Weinstocks, and every Thanksgiving they would go to Philadelphia to visit with Jeff's aunt, uncle, and cousins. "Family was first and foremost, always," Jeff says, "That was something my parents felt very strongly about. Even if there's a little bit of distance, family's still family. Family's always first."

After high school, Jeff attended Vassar College in Poughkeepsie, New York, and remembers it as one of the best times of his life. He did well in nearly every class, and he became involved in campus politics. Along with eleven other students, Jeff helped create the multidisciplinary Cognitive Science program, now a popular major at the school. He also was elected Vice President of the senior class after showing a knack for leadership, delegating responsibilities and planning events on campus.

At Vassar, Jeff first discovered his passion for connecting candidates with opportunities. After conducting campus tours for several years, he was one of the few students selected to become a senior interviewer for the college. In this role, he met with prospective students to speak with them about their desire to attend Vassar, and help determine if the school might be the right fit. He enjoyed it so much that he wondered if he could somehow turn his work with the college into a career. Unfortunately, he quickly discovered that such Admissions jobs pay very little. However, having no family of his own yet to support, he decided to look for work in the field while he applied for law school.

The following year, Jeff took the LSAT, completed his applications, and worked as the Assistant Director of Admissions for Sarah Lawrence College, a small, liberal arts school like Vassar. He loved the work and was happy to travel across the country meeting with students at their high schools. He liked it so much, in fact, that after being accepted to Boston University School of Law, Jeff decided to defer admission and remain on the road, recruiting, for one more year.

After two years working at Sarah Lawrence, a school that doesn't issue grades to students, the hyper-competitive nature of law school seemed foreign and even damaging to some of his classmates. "I enrolled at the Boston University School of Law, and I can still remember going to pick up my grades at the Registrar after first semester and being disturbed by the scene there," he says. "Some of my classmates were literally crying as they walked out. I saw one woman who said, 'I really want to practice criminal law, but I got a C in criminal law, and now I can't!' I thought how crazy it was for her to say that, because one thing has nothing to do with the other. A grade shows how you did on one test. With that, I decided I wasn't going to obsess over grades and was instead going to keep things in perspective by focusing on the big picture of what we were learning." Jeff never picked up his grades from the Registrar throughout the rest of his law school career. His strategy of staying focused on the work served him well, and Jeff graduated with honors and as a member of the Law Review.

Just before graduation, in January of 1990, Jeff met Carolyn, the love of his life. She was studying for an MBA, and they both attended a holiday party thrown by a mutual friend. When he asked for her phone number, Carolyn said, "Look it up." Within three dates, he knew she was the one. On their third date, Valentine's Day, he showed up with a box of chocolates, only to find that she had a box of Godiva chocolates for him too. Without telling her, he kept the box. That summer, the couple moved to DC where Jeff had accepted his first job out of law school.

A mere eleven months after they met, in November, Jeff was ready to propose. He put the engagement ring in the empty chocolate box, took it back to a Godiva store, and asked the clerk to rewrap it. He gave it to her at a private dinner that evening, and after accepting the proposal, she began calling their many friends with the good news. "Looking back, she's really gotten me through every tough spot in my career, providing both solid business advice and crucial support," he says with gratitude. "I couldn't have done it without her."

After graduating from BU, Jeff worked at McKenna & Cuneo for five years, where he practiced government contracts litigation and maintained an exhausting travel schedule. "I travelled to Fort Worth every week for two and a half years," Jeff recalls. "I knew Fort Worth better than I knew DC. After we bought our first house, in Vienna, I remember coming back to Dulles Airport, handing my address to the taxi driver, and saying, 'Here's where I live; I have no idea how to get there.' In that moment, I realized there was something wrong with that picture."

In addition to the litigation work, Jeff had taken on pro bono cases in family law, the work he truly enjoyed. An opportunity arose for Jeff and another attorney to join a team at Sherman, Meehan, Curtin & Ain, as they staffed up for a prominent divorce case. He practiced family law with the firm for several more years before realizing he was truly burnt out. "I was working six days a week," he says. "It felt like I was always preparing for a hearing or going to trial, and just working in general. I felt good about what I was doing, but it just wasn't right. It wasn't enough."

Carolyn was supportive, encouraging Jeff to figure out what it was he truly loved. He knew he loved recruiting from his work at Sarah Lawrence, and now he had expertise and contacts in law. After some thought, he knew that recruiting for law firms was the obvious solution. In 1998, he began working at Kelly Law Registry, marking the start of his recruiting career. He was comfortable doing legal staffing, but continued to expand his recruiting network by pushing himself into new arenas. In 2007, he went on to join Sparks, a regional staffing group mostly known for administrative work. Jeff enjoyed working there, where he launched an IT staffing group within the company. Everything was going very well, so he was shocked to find himself, at the height of the recession, laid off. "I was totally surprised," Jeff recalls, "That was really tough. I was 45 at the time, and I didn't feel like I was done with the industry."

JEFFREY WEINSTOCK

Rather than look for a new job, Jeff decided to make a bet on himself and start R & W Group. With the severance pay from Sparks, and with the full support of Carolyn and his parents, Jeff founded the business that the *Legal Times* has since named the #3 recruiter in DC.

R & W Group has succeeded in large part because of Jeff's big picture approach to business and life, which is something he recommends to those starting their careers. For young people leaving school and entering the working world today, Jeff advises taking the long view. "This is just your first step," he says. "Your career is long, and you will likely have several major job changes along the way, so don't put too much pressure on yourself. Try to learn something from every job you take, making a point to understand both the positives and the negatives. Whatever you experience, use it in your next position, and the position after that, and the one after that. This is how you become better and better over time, with evolving skill sets and never a wasted experience."

For Jeff, caring about people and trying to help them in their next step has always been a top motivation. From interviewing high school students at Vassar, to running his own recruiting business, he's spent his career putting people on the path that's right for them. "When people ask me what I do, I say I help change people's lives," Jeff says. "I know how discouraging it is to feel like you're on the wrong track, and I know the sense of freedom and exhilaration that comes from finally finding the right one. Everyone deserves that chance to reach their true potential, and through R & W we're on track to help them get there."

BERNHARDT
WEALTH MANAGEMENT

Mary G.R. Whitley

Breaking Through

Those who work in our nation's capital are accustomed to meeting high performing executives who spend long careers honing their leadership and management skills in military service, civilian government service, or private sector executive positions. But much rarer is the executive that has successfully transitioned from one of these distinct careers to another. Why take the risk of leaving a successful career in the military to start over as a civilian in the Executive Branch? Or why leave an SES position in government service to start over as a business leader responsible for P&L?

Most would say such huge career changes are too difficult to manage, and fraught with risk. Navigating successfully through all three stovepipes in one working lifetime could be seen as nearly impossible, and it would be unthinkable to do so and then start a woman-owned, service disabled veteran-owned small business to top it all off.

While her chronicle of daring career risks may seem crazy on paper, Mary Whitley has routinely defied convention and built a reputation as a level-headed, successful leader as a military officer, an SES at GSA, and a Senior Vice President in the private sector. She also founded Whitley Strategic Consulting with the goal of using her unique insights and experience in military, government, and industry to assist CEOs and their leadership teams in evolving and growing their firms in the Federal contracting environment. Her story is one of charting her own unique career path and breaking through barriers to reach her goals, no matter how impossible the challenge might seem.

As a high school senior in the mid-1970's, Mary dreamed of going to college to study engineering. Coming of age in the context of the women's revolution, she had other spirited young women walking alongside her into the brave new world of traditionally male-dominated professions, but there were few female role models to follow. She could see her dream through the glass ceiling above her—now all she needed to do was break through.

Mary was the oldest of four children in a family of modest means, and while her parents could offer her room and board support if she worked, lived at home, and attended the local community college, she knew she'd have to make her own way if she wanted more. Despite her good grades, she struggled to piece together the scholarship funding she needed to make it a reality. "I had no connections, but given my college aptitude test scores, I had this strong feeling that I would figure out a way to make it work," she recalls today. That's when she received a postcard in the mail.

In an extremely controversial move, President Ford had signed legislation in 1975 requiring military academies to begin admitting women. In 1976, as Mary prepared to graduate high school, those academies began actively searching for qualified women to join their ranks. The postcard she received pointed to her strong standardized test scores and academic record and invited her to apply for a full scholarship to West Point. Without telling her parents, she signed the bottom of the card and mailed it back to launch the process that would forever change her life.

Mary didn't know anything about the military, but she knew the U.S. Military Academy at West Point had a first-class engineering school. She applied, passed a physical, and interviewed with a local West Pointer. She succeeded in securing the required appointment from a Member of Congress. When she was accepted, she knew it was an opportunity she had to take, and a glass ceiling she had to break. With that, she joined 119 other young women in West Point's first-ever co-ed class.

"It was a life-defining experience to have my father tell me he couldn't help me with college, and that I'd have to do it on my own," she reflects today. "It gave me the motivation to go after difficult goals and the drive to actually achieve them. It really solidified this attitude I've had my whole life, that I can take risks and go after goals that other people don't think I can achieve successfully."

The journey, however, had just begun. When she arrived to start classes that fall, it was the first time Mary had set foot on the campus. She thought the rigorous coursework would be her biggest concern. "Looking back, we women were all extremely naïve about how hard it would be," she says. "The Academy had spent years trying to bar women from their community, and from the very first day, we were told we shouldn't be there. The professors, administration, and older students all made their opposition very clear, and in time, even many of our own male classmates began to develop that same attitude."

Many of the individuals entrusted with their training were the very same people who dedicated themselves to getting rid of the new female plebes within the first eight weeks of Beast Barracks. Through marching, physical fitness, Army training, and tests of discipline, the boot camp phase is designed to break new cadets down and then build them back up. Instead, the young women faced unrelenting hostility that continued into the academic year, and many dropped out in the first year. "Those of us left were excited to get past our plebe year and be accepted onto the team," she remembers. "But that only happened for our male classmates. For us, the harassment continued. Most West Pointers didn't think women should be in engineering, let alone in the Army, but I decided to dig in my heels. I was going to make it to graduation, whatever it took."

Through those years, Mary remembers kindnesses made all the more special by the hardship. When the cadet companies were reorganized, and she was discouraged from socializing with her original company, the friends found ways to see each other and still share a close bond to this day. And Colonel Barney Forsythe, her assigned mentor, encouraged her along the way, promising that it would be better once she got into the Army. "Going through those hard experiences broke that glass ceiling for others, and I'm grateful that I could make that contribution to the careers of women who came after me," she says. "But it was not easy."

Now the founder and CEO of Whitley Strategic Consulting, an independent and experienced voice guiding Federal IT companies as they transition from small to mid-size businesses, Mary has dedicated her work to helping others break through whatever ceilings are barriers to their success. "Many businesses in that space have grown from small-business set-asides and have only vague plans for how they're going to transition into a mid-size company that has to compete with the big boys," she explains. "Some haven't thought beyond a year. Based upon my experience in leading both Federal acquisition and commercial operations, I'm able to counsel them through that process, helping them consider options and strategize five years down the road. This not only creates successful companies—it creates successful CEOs with the leadership, management skills, and vision to see their companies through to a new era."

Mary launched her company in 2007 with the intention of doing part-time strategic consulting at the intersection of government, military, and commercial federal IT. She had just left a full-time job to have a double hip replacement and planned to limit herself to only part-time work, but she soon ditched that idea to accept a full-time position with ICF International until June of 2016. She has now refocused on Whitley Strategic Consulting with the goal of helping companies grow smartly, smoothly, and sustainably. "Over the years, I've met so many companies with hockey stick trajectories that come to an abrupt halt when they reach the end of their small business set-aside period," she explains. "They have the right people, projects, and contracts, but they're unable to design and execute a strategy that enables them to continue a successful growth trajectory. That's where I can add value."

Mary's own trajectory didn't exactly follow the route she anticipated, but in breaking through barrier after barrier, she's charted a course that is all her own. Born in the suburbs of Detroit, Mary and her siblings all followed in the footsteps of their father, a mechanical engineer. He had met their mother while getting his degree at the University of Detroit on the GI Bill after serving in the Korean War, and the young couple was thrilled when he landed a coveted job at Ford. But things didn't go exactly as planned, and he was laid off while they were expecting their third child. He took a position with Whirlpool Appliances, prompting a move to the other side of the state. There, in a small town of 12,000 people called St. Joseph, Mary grew up.

Mary remembers having fun with the other children in the neighborhood, running around outside in the summers and playing cards or reading novels in the winters. Her family was Catholic, attending church regularly and volunteering often. Her mother was a successful substitute teacher and homemaker, while her father was deeply connected to the veteran community, instilling in her a strong love of country and service. He was also a sportsman who taught his children how to shoot early in life—a skill that helped her get into West Point later on. "My parents taught us the importance of working toward goals, whether they were schoolwork objectives or goals you set for your family or community," she recalls. "They were great examples for me."

Mary started babysitting at the age of thirteen and was a Girl Scout until she was sixteen. A tall, skinny girl, she could never find clothes that fit her, so she took to making her own. By the time she was in high school she made most of her own clothes, winning 4-H awards for her outfits and talent. She was friends with a great many classmates, defying social norms that suggested she had to choose a clique. She worked part time at fast food restaurants, was co-editor of the school newspaper, played the guitar, and ran track. "Title IX wasn't passed until 1974 and the school didn't allocate any money to girls' sports," she says. "Track was our only option, because it didn't cost anything."

Computers were just coming into workplaces as Mary entered high school, and she hoped to pursue college at Michigan State to study computer science. She always knew she wanted to have options in life, and that good grades were the key to opening doors. She was especially strong in math, science, and English, and when she took the SAT and ACT, she landed in the top one percent. "I took all two of the advanced courses available at my school," she laughs. "By the time I got to college I thought I was pretty competitive, both academically and athletically, but it turned out I was a big fish in a small pond, and that high schools on the East Coast were operating on an entirely different level."

At West Point, Mary encountered peers who had played softball, competed on diving teams, and run marathons. Despite the unique challenges of her situation, she focused on the institution's unparalleled curriculum in leadership, strategy, and engineering. In 1980, she became one of the first 62 women to graduate from West Point—an incredible achievement that took courage and tenacity. "It was the hardest thing I've ever had to do," she says. "But I definitely benefitted from the experience I had there."

Upon graduation from West Point, Mary became one of five woman officers at the 24th Infantry Division, at a 15,000-person post. There, serving as the 2nd Lieutenant Platoon Leader of 45 truck drivers at Fort Stewart, Georgia, she found she enjoyed the work. "I came from a family of people who built cars," she says. "I liked the trucks and the truck drivers, and 30 percent of my 45-person team were women. I had never before met women sergeants, and I was accepted as part of the team from Day 1. For the first time, nobody was questioning why I was there."

With that acceptance, Mary could finally be the person she wanted to be, honing her management skills—especially in working with non-commissioned officers who were adjusting to life after the Vietnam War. She volunteered to be the Battalion Motor Officer, so she was sent to school at Fort Knox to learn more about heavy duty vehicle recovery and maintenance. In that class, she met Lieutenant Roy Whitley, the man she would later marry in 1985.

Mary and Roy were reassigned to Germany, where she served in the 4th Transportation Command and 590th Trans Co overseeing long-haul trucks and a truck company of over 200 people. "It was the mid-80's, and we were preparing to defend Germany against the Eastern European invasion that never came," she says. "I learned a lot about leadership and management there at a very visceral level, but I wanted to navigate into IT. I decided to take night courses at Ramstein Air Force Base to get my master's degree from the University of Southern California." She completed the Systems Management degree with an IT focus in December of 1985 and applied to become a Logistics Automation IT Manager at the Pentagon.

During her four years in that capacity, Mary had two children and was assigned to both the Army and Joint Staffs. She then went to Fort Belvoir, where she worked as a Product Manager of tactical logistics automation during the First Gulf War. Then, after serving eleven years of active duty as an officer, she entered civilian life and took a GS-13 job at General Services Administration managing Federal IT acquisitions. "Although my military friends and mentors advised me not to resign my commission and move to GSA, that turned out to be another great job," she reflects. "I was hired and helped through military to civilian transition by Rick Davis and worked for the Federal Systems Integration and Management Center, which handles the most complex IT procurements for all of the federal government, with a particular focus on the Department of Defense."

Thanks to her ten years of previous management experience, Mary was promoted after only one year. The organization had one GS-15 woman who was running the software division, and when she decided to retire, Mary was selected for another promotion. "It was a meritocracy and a wonderful place to work, but all of the deputies to the division leaders were women, while all of the leaders of the division were men—except for me," she says. "I eventually became the deputy to my mentor, Charlie Self, the IT Solutions Assistant Commissioner at the next level up, when we were responsible for over $1 billion in federal procurement per year. Through my position there, I was able to mentor other talented men and women to be promoted to leadership positions."

Several years later, at the age of 42, Mary landed a Senior Executive Service position, breaking another glass ceiling a good six years before she could have attained an equivalent position of General Officer in the military. Responsible for CRM and Sales, she set to work creating an entirely new protocol for GSA based on industry principles, and installed the first industry standard CRM system in the Federal government. "We ended up training many government employees in customer relationship management and sales methodologies on that platform, and they really took to it," she recalls. "It helped get everyone on the same page in their thinking about obtaining and retaining customers."

Four years later, Mary decided she was ready to go to the private sector. With that, she wrapped up 27 impressive years in public service and took a VP job at Unisys Corporation, a Federal IT service provider. Again, she found herself in a male-dominated environment, but also found a great mentor. "I knew about contracts and IT services management, but had to learn pricing and how to manage the P&L," she remembers. "Drew Cramer's business mentorship was incredibly important to me as I managed an operational group of over 300 people in multiple locations across the nation and in Europe. I refer to it as my time in the salt mine—I was there when the doors opened in the morning and closed at night, trying to absorb everything I could."

After two years in that capacity, Mary transitioned to MAXIMUS, a professional services company specializing in implementing government health and human services programs that allowed her to pursue her interest in Health IT. "I felt that big changes and exciting innovations were going to be taking place in that space," she explains. She was charged with growing a small 8(a) company acquisition into a larger information security offering, but a few years later, the MAXIMUS CEO and leadership team determined that the Security Management Division did not fit well into their evolving strategic plan. Mary knew the Division had valuable customers and trained team members, so she worked to spin off that business unit through its sale to a West Coast biometric engineering firm. "It was a good transaction for both companies—and my first time leading an M&A," she says.

After launching WSC, Mary landed a Senior VP position at ICF working for her friend and mentor, Ellen Glover, who set her at the helm of a brand-new division created through the purchase of an 8(a) firm of aggregated HHS services. "The Division lacked a mission statement and a unifying strategy, so I worked with the team to formulate the Health Informatics Division Strategy, which combined IT, information science, and health program expertise to support HHS's missions," she says. The "health informatics" route proved hugely successful, growing the initial group from $28 million to $80 million in revenues. She was then asked to integrate and lead a new division which came to fruition during a 9-month project to create three business lines involving IT, programs, and research. Once that process was complete, she decided to strike out on her own under the Whitley banner to focus on her most lasting legacy.

Parallel and integrated with her professional success, Mary has been happily married since age 27, and is the mother of two adult children who have made successful careers for themselves in cybersecurity and health informatics. "I decided early on that I was going to be a working mother and wife, and I never wavered in that," she says. "When I entered the service, very few women in the military were also wives and mothers, so making that choice was a seminal moment for me. Roy has always been incredibly supportive—a self-made man, a loving father and husband, and a great leader. We've both found ways to have very full professional lives through being true partners to each other and a solid team, pulling off the balance between family and successful careers."

Now, as a leader, Mary's philosophy evolves around the belief that people and organizations evolve. Seeing change as an inevitability that can be channeled in a positive or negative manner, she embraces the power of mentoring as a force to enable positive evolution, as notable people did for her as she, herself, evolved. "All along the way, I've had mentors who have helped me, showing me how to make good decisions and be a strategic thinker," Mary recounts. "Through WSC, I want to be that mentor to other business leaders, and also to help accomplished women in the DC metropolitan area who desire to serve on boards. In fact, I've recently begun collecting resumes to do just that."

In advising young people entering the working world today, Mary underscores the importance of the first step. "After you've decided what you're ultimately aiming for, set your sights on that first job that will get your foot in the door so you can start learning," she says. "It might not be the career you want right away, but it's a place to start. Chart your own path, even if others like you haven't walked that way before. If you believe it's the road that will lead you to the right place, be courageous and tenacious and don't listen to the people who say you can't do it. Where there's change, there is opportunity, so break through and find out what comes next."

BERNHARDT
WEALTH MANAGEMENT

About the Author

Having grown up on a farm in Nebraska, Gordon Bernhardt left the Midwest in the early 1980s for Washington D.C. to work as an assistant in the U.S. House of Representatives. He left behind the rural lifestyle but he carried with him the values of hard work, a focus on what you can control, and service to others—values that continue to influence his life, today.

After completing a bachelor's degree in Commerce at the University of Virginia, Bernhardt began a successful career in finance at a leading accounting firm and two different brokerage companies. In 1994, in order to make the kind of difference in people's lives that he hoped to make, he established Bernhardt Wealth Management, an independent registered investment advisory firm built on the principle of fiduciary care: providing investment and wealth management guidance, service, and advice that places clients' interests and needs ahead of everything else. By adhering to this higher standard, he removed the conflicts of interest that were prevalent elsewhere. Rather than be restricted by a large company's cookie cutter methodology, he and his team are able to create customized plans that are far more appropriate for individual clients. Today, Bernhardt Wealth Management is recognized as one of the top fee-only wealth management firms in the Washington D.C. region.

In addition to being an entrepreneur and wealth manager, Bernhardt is the author of *Buen Camino: What a Hike through Spain Taught Me about Investing and Life*, a memoir about the 35-day, 618-mile pilgrimage he completed in Spain and the lessons he learned along the way. He also writes a weekly finance blog. Bernhardt writes the *Profiles in Success: Inspiration from Executive Leaders* book series, and hosts a podcast with the same name, to expand the influence of outstanding leaders while inspiring the next generation of executives.

Find out more about Gordon Bernhardt at
www.BernhardtWealth.com and www.ProfilesInSuccess.com.

Pvt. Jonathan Lee Gifford was the first U.S. soldier killed in Iraq. He was killed just two days into the war on March 23, 2003. Spc. David Emanual Hickman was killed by a roadside bomb in Iraq on November 14, 2011. *The Washington Post* on December 17, 2011, said Hickman "may have been the last" U.S. soldier killed in Iraq. After reading an article about Gifford and Hickman my sister, Gloria, was inspired to write the following poem.

From Gifford to Hickman
by Gloria J. Bernhardt

From Gifford to Hickman…and all those in between,
You fought bravely amid chaos and dangers unforeseen.
Twenty-one guns have sounded, the riderless horse walks on.
Fond memories are remaining. A nation's child is gone.

Sons and daughters; fathers, mothers—broken hearts intertwined.
Hugs and kisses; their successes—major milestones left behind.
Your selfless gift—a life laid down; for fellow soldier, family, land.
Duty called—call was answered—no greater love hath man.

"I'm getting taller. I lost a tooth. I got 100 on my test!
Miss your pancakes and your tickles, goodnight kisses were the best.
Who will answer all my questions now? I've important stuff to learn!
You said you had a big surprise on the day that you'd return."

"I talk to you at bedtime—after lights go out at night.
I told Jesus that I miss you…sure wish you could hug me tight.
When Grandpa says I look like you, Grandma starts to cry.
I'm mad that you're not coming home…I need to say goodbye!"

From Gifford, to Hickman, through every soldier who has served,
Liberty's fruits are savored and freedom is preserved.
We live freely due to soldiers, willing to support and defend
Our Constitution, our country—against enemies 'til the end.

Sons and daughters; fathers, mothers—broken hearts intertwined.
Hugs and kisses; their successes—major milestones left behind.
Your selfless gift—a life laid down; for fellow soldier, family, land.
Duty called—call was answered—no greater love hath man.

"I had a dream the night before…you smiled and walked on by.
When I awoke, I thought it odd…it seemed like a 'good-bye'.
I couldn't put my finger on the dark cloud that remained,
When the phone began to ring…I knew my life had changed."

"I questioned God, 'Why MY child? Why do I have to lose?'
I imagined His response would be 'If not your child, then whose?'
Your bright life flashed too briefly… seems He only takes the best.
I'm thankful for the time I had. For that I'm truly blessed."

From Gifford to Hickman and every warrior who has passed,
The price you've paid bought freedom, but will we make it last?
Your last breath drawn for citizens in this country and abroad
Are we worthy of such gifts is known only but to God.

Sons and daughters; fathers, mothers—broken hearts intertwined.
Hugs and kisses; their successes—major milestones left behind.
Your selfless gift—a life laid down; for fellow soldier, family, land.
Duty called—call was answered—no greater love hath man.

"My world stopped spinning…I couldn't breathe! Lord, how can I go on?
My days are all one midnight…but they say it's darkest 'fore the dawn.
I can hear you say, 'I'm proud of you! I know that this is hard.'
What do I do without you here? What dreams do I discard?"

"I miss your laugh. I miss your smell. I even miss our fights.
No more messes. No embraces. It's more 'real' late at night.
I saw you in a crowd today; but you vanished in the throng.
Wishful thinking changes nothing! I know my "rock" is gone."

FOR Gifford, FOR Hickman…FOR all the fallen in between,
You've trudged through shadowed valley and joined heroes' ranks unseen.
Upon freedom's altar, we sacrificed our daughters and our sons.
Empty boots stand at attention. The flag is folded. Your mission's done.

© 2012 Gloria J. Bernhardt. All Rights Reserved.
Reprinted by permission.

BERNHARDT
WEALTH MANAGEMENT